ELI

ELI

More Than Just a Kitten with Ambition to Go on a Mission

Written and Illustrated by
Sherralee Tinney

Copyright © 2019 by Sherralee Tinney.

ISBN-9781645507000

All rights reserved. No part of this book may be reproduced or transmitted in any form or by any means, electronic or mechanical, including photocopying, recording, or by any information storage and retrieval system, without permission in writing from the copyright owner.

The views expressed in this work are solely those of the author and do not necessarily reflect the views of the publisher, and the publisher hereby disclaims any responsibility for them.

Matchstick Literary
1-888-306-8885
orders@matchliterary.com

Contents

Acknowledgements xi
Dedication xiii

Chapter 1 1
Chapter 2 9
Chapter 3 20
Chapter 4 27
Chapter 5 34
Chapter 6 40
Chapter 7 47
Chapter 8 56
Chapter 9 66
Chapter 10 77
Chapter 11 81
Chapter 12 91
Chapter 13 100
Chapter 14 106
Chapter 15 117
Chapter 16 126
Chapter 17 136
Chapter 18 144
Chapter 19 151
Chapter 20 167
Chapter 21 182
Chapter 22 188

Chapter 23 192
Chapter 24 208
Chapter 25 215
Chapter 26 221
Chapter 27 235
Chapter 28 248
Chapter 29 264

Epilogue 277

About the Author 281

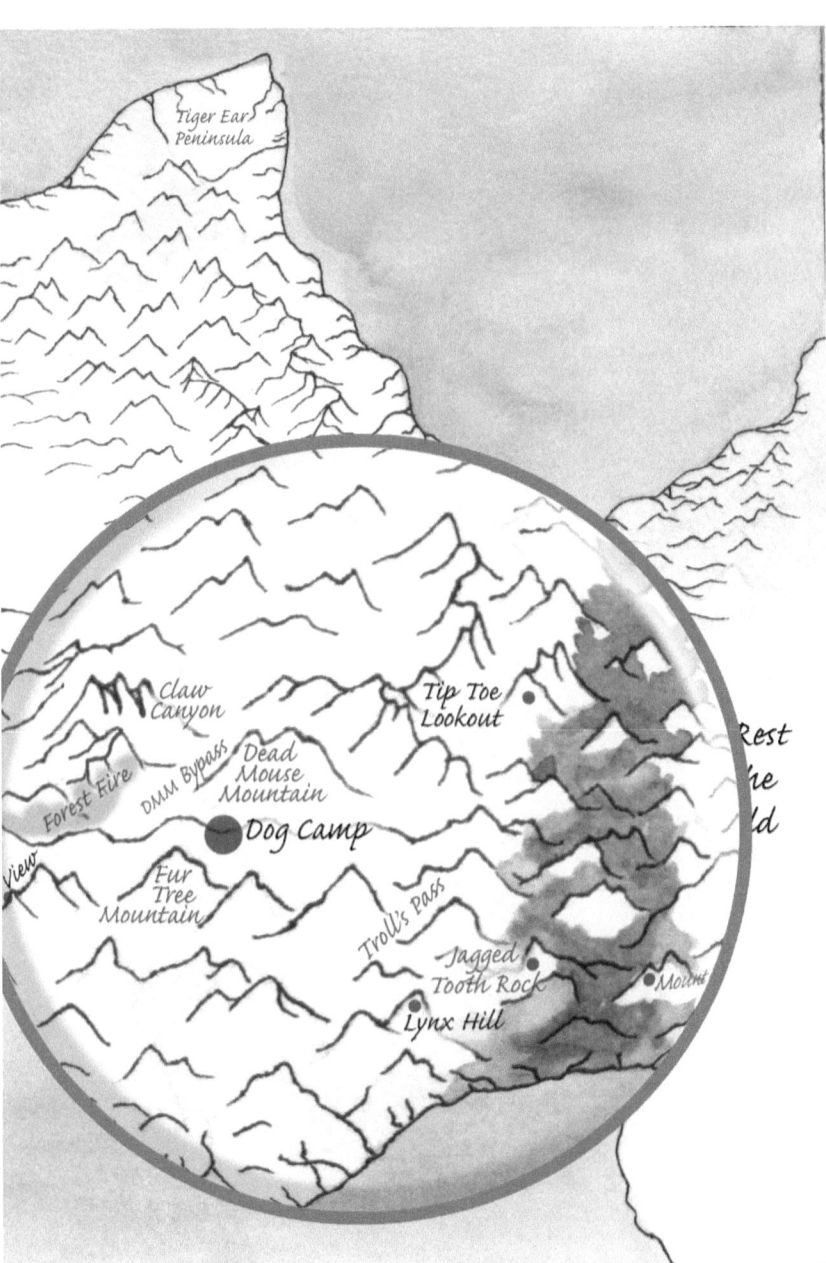

Acknowledgements

First and foremost to my husband Martin, without you this book would never have been completed. Thank you my dear for not only supporting me but for putting up with my antics as well.

To Lynne Hoeppner, saying thank you for all your hard work for editing this book doesn't seem enough. You are so appreciated, and I am truly grateful.

To Megan Dart, no matter how much time spans between our lives, you will always be an inspiration to me. Thank you so much for your initial assistance in writing this story. I am truly one of your forever fans.

To Crawford Killian, my creative writing instructor from way back in the days of college, you believed in me before I did. Thank you for your encouragement and direction. Without your *Communications Book, a workbook for writers* and your words of wisdom, "Don't worry about your grammar and spelling, that's what editors are for," I would never have dared do this. I'm just sorry it took me so long.

And to my friends and family, particularly Claire Callbeck, who provided input and was a sounding board when I needed it, thank you.

Dedication

To Launa, Logan Lee, Brooklynn, Jennae, Sierra, Morgan, and to all my young readers, may you be encouraged to stand up for everything good and just in this world.

And to my grandmother Reta Alldread who was the first person that tried to get this uncooperative girl to write. Your efforts were not in vain. I can still hear your voice telling me how "wonderfully fun" it is to make up stories. You were right grandma, until we meet again…XXOO

Chapter 1

Eli peered out of his dad's cubbyhole—one of many his dad had in the region. The air felt bitterly cold, like one million tiny needles all poking Eli's nose. Winter was blowing snow around and being very noisy about it—howling as he made his way through the trees. Winter was giving his last blustery storm before stepping down and allowing Spring to take his turn on the throne of Weather.

Eli felt chilled immediately and knew Chill was nearby. Chill and Winter were almost always together. Eli didn't know which one was worse. Chill could set in a cold that went straight to the bone and Winter seemed to hang around forever. Forever was much longer than Winter's allotted three-month reign. To keep warm, Eli fluffed-up his silky coat, which was still dense from Winter's reign, stepped out and trotted down the snowy narrow path.

There was no one around, but Eli expected that because Sun wasn't awake yet. "It's too cold, and it's getting old," grumbled Eli. The path was surrounded by Evergreens in one of thickest parts of the forest in Catland. Snow hung on the heavy branches like patches of white fur shed in the spring. Eli didn't like Winter—never had. Winter was always throwing temper tantrums and was the moodiest ruler of all four seasons.

Eli muttered, "Who is he mad at this time? He's gotta be out of line."

Winter couldn't hear him because of the blustery ruckus he was making. One had to watch what one said around Winter because he was very sensitive and would go off in a flurry. Or so Eli had been told. He had never met him himself.

Eli often wondered why Winter's parents, Father Time and Mother Nature, allowed him to behave like he did. But for now, Eli would have to do his best to ignore Winter. Eli was on a mission.

It was only two days ago when Eli had received his first mission. He had been at home with his mother, brother Elliot, and sister Samantha. Eli and his siblings had been play-fighting when their mother interrupted and sat them all down.

"Now, it has come to my attention," she said gravely, "and that's why not previously mentioned,
your father has returned,

but hush—he has been burned."
The kittens exclaimed, "Burned? Burned!
Are you kidding?
How could he be burned?
Please, Mom, tell us, what have you learned?"
She took a deep breath, the worry was undeniable in her eyes, saying, "He wishes to depart,
away on a mission, take heart.
He must be accompanied with care.
Oh my beautiful kittens,
not one do I want to spare!
He's now resting in bed.
For I have bandaged his head,
as for his burns, it cannot be said.
On all four of his paws,
he cannot use his claws.
So badly singed, perhaps permanently flawed."

His father might not be able to use his claws anymore? That was one of the worst things that could happen to a cat in Catland. Eli had heard enough. With that he ran to his father's bedroom crying,
"I must see him!
I have to see him!
This story is far too grim."
With a look of surprise, his mother replied:
"Eli come back here!
Your father must rest.
I want you to hear,
I know what's best."
But it was too late Eli was gone.

Eli slowly opened the door to his father's bedroom. His father lay on his back in the bed, all four of his paws bandaged and sticking straight up in the air. He was missing large patches of fur along his sides and on the underside of his tail. His beautiful fur coat was frizzy and singed all over. His head was bandaged, just as Eli's mother had said. Eli had never seen his father in such a horrendous condition.

Eli's father, Tom, was well respected in Catland. At

twenty-nine centimeters in height and all muscle, he was a majestic blue-point Siamese cat.

"He's a force to be reckoned with.
That's truth, not myth," Mr. Patches the old farmer next door had once told Eli.

Very quietly, Eli crept in to the room.
"Pa-pa, are you awake?"
He gasped, "You're missing fur!
Oh, what a state!"

His father smiled weakly and tried to get up.
"Eli, my son.
Since you are here,
you can be the one.
Help me up, we must go,
we must leave—time is low."

"Oh no, you don't! Let you go—I won't!" Eli jumped, startled.
His mother was right behind him and she was angry. "You'll stay in bed, or I'll lock you in the shed!"

Eli's mother turned toward him. She scowled at Eli. "And you young cat, I'll ground you to your mat!"

Eli hung his head. His father groaned,
"My darling wife your intentions are grand.
But please try to understand,
the nature of my mission,
is to save our land."

Eli's mother looked over at her husband. Her face softened and her big blue eyes filled with worry.

"My darling husband, you must heal.
Otherwise in this state, over you'll keel.
We'll fetch the doctor.
He'll know how to deal."

"There is no time for that. Eli, fetch my hat," he said.
Just then they heard a loud gasp as Eli's brother and sister entered the room. They both went running over to the bed.

Samantha asked, "Pa-pa, how did this happen?"
"What evil caught you nappin'?" asked Elliot cutting off his sister with an attempt at misplaced humour.

It was a well-known fact in Catland that if a cat was caught napping, all sorts of bad things could happen. Cats love to nap. That's why cats got good at sleeping with their eyes partly open. Not fully open though—too much light would get in and a cat couldn't sleep.

Their father flashed Elliot a look. "I wasn't nappin'. I was actually trappin'." Elliot could find something funny to say at the worst times but Tom didn't mind he thought it made Elliot endearing.

"My handsome husband, you cannot go.
You cannot walk, even in the snow," their mother said.

"Pa-pa, we can help you.
Tell us your mission
and what we can do," Eli said.

He looked at them all. What future was for them now? Was the safe haven of Catland on the verge of war? What terrible things were in store for his precious kittens? Was there any saving Catland? Perhaps . . . if they moved quickly. Besides, his body hurt. Every time he moved, it felt like his wounds were opening again. How could he complete his mission in this state? It was too soon now but it wouldn't be long before they would be old enough to join the Royal Monarch's defenses. His kittens weren't babies anymore. So, with a deep breath Tom decided to involve his family.

"You see, I was out on patrol
when I heard a rustling in the bushes.
I thought maybe it was Fuzzy the troll,
or perhaps Hiker the mole.

But then I saw it.
It was no friend.
And all my hair stood on end."

Tom closed his eyes. Just the thought of it made him want to run for cover.

Samantha whispered, "Was it evil—like a hog? Was it slime on a log?"

Their father was quiet, then slowly he shook his head and saying,
"Oh so much scarier than a hog,
and far worse than slime on a log."

Pausing he looking at each one of them, continuing he said,

"It has been over five hundred years since Catland has seen a dog."
    Everyone gasped!
"A dog! A dog?
Oh dread, we prefer a hog!"
    Wide eyed they looked at one another. Their mother closed her eyes, fearing the worst.
    Then Eli said,
"Just one dog?
He'll be like a frog.
I'll pounce,
and that dog won't bite an ounce.
I'll give him the hook!
He won't know where to look.
See! I've worked it up sharp.
That dog won't get out a bark."
    Eli smiling held up his paw to show everyone his special claw. He had been working on it for weeks. Now, the hours of sharpening all seemed worthwhile.
    "No, no, Eli," his father said.
"You mustn't even try.
It's not just one.
There's a pack,
and they'll put you on the run."
    Taking a deep breath and forcing his body to relax, their father continued, "I couldn't believe it—
a dog in the thicket?
I had to know why.
I couldn't just let him go by.
So I followed his tail,
but far enough back I wouldn't fail.
He led me right to his camp,
So many dogs I saw from a ramp."
    Their father paused again. Eli noticed his father's body tensed up. He looked afraid.
    He whispered, "There's something worse.
It's some kind of curse."
    "Worse than a dog,
on Catland sod?" asked Eli.

Eli

Tom glanced at Eli, a strange glaze came over his eyes, as if he was seeing it all over again.

Continuing he said, "As I stood on the ramp
overlooking the camp,
something caught my eye:
a creature so gruesome, so fierce,
I wanted to cry.

It was bound and chained
and it screeched where it laid.
It had wings on its back,
and its tail was frayed.

Compared to this beast,
the dogs, I now fear the least.

Seen nothing like it, I had.
This creature of theirs,
it's worse than bad.

Then all of a sudden, out of the blue,
it spotted me. I didn't dare move.
It wailed and it cried,
revealing my location.
I thought I would die.

With a burst of speed,
I decided to run.
The dogs spotted me,
and gave chase in fun.

I ran and I ran,
covering lots of land.
Soon the dogs were far behind.
Then there was a swoosh above,
and a shadow fell over the pine.

In the midst of the snow,
flames leapt up,
the trees and bushes were all a glow.
Fire surrounded me!
Ahead, fire burned a great tree.

Then I saw my escape—
my excitement was great,
an old troll tunnel,

which allows travel,
inside a great hill.
   Then suddenly
a wall of flame,
leapt up in front of me!
   It blocked my way.
I could not enter—
it kept me at bay.
   I heard the dogs behind
getting louder;
it seemed I had no time!
   I had to run through,
be burned, or be doomed."

   Tom closed his eyes and took a deep breath. No one said anything. Each one thinking over the story they just heard. Now they understood the fear they could see in their father's eyes.
   After a few minutes Tom said, "I know what has to be done. Gather in close. As far as time goes,
we have none."

Chapter 2

It had taken Eli two days to get as far as he had. The map his father gave him proved very accurate. It was a good thing too, as Eli had never been so far from home. As Eli trotted along the path, he noticed the snow was beginning to get deeper. To keep dry Eli started jumping over snowdrifts and moving along under the protective branches of the Evergreens. It made the trek a bit windier but he was still moving at a good pace. He had to get to Troll's Pass as soon as possible. That's where his father said the dogs' camp was.

Troll's Pass was located along the Border Bush of Catland. The Border Bush was a magical bush said to be fifty miles thick separating Catland from The Rest of the World. Father Time had put a magical enchantment on the Border Bush that made whoever came close to it, to lose interest and not want to spend any time near it.

It was also said to be a very dense bush full of thorns and poisonous plants. Plants that would sting and plants that would treacherously hold you so you couldn't get away. Most cats could get out of a Holding Bush because once a cat decided it didn't want to be held, it could twist and turn with so much speed it was near impossible for the bush to hold on. Other creatures weren't so fortunate. The Holding Bush was a true threat to them, and never let go.

Eli's father told him Father Time and the rest of the Royal Monarch employed spy cats who could travel through the bush into The Rest of the World. There had to be trails through the Border Bush but for some strange reason Eli had absolutely no interest in those trails and didn't even want to spend time thinking about it, let alone go there.

According to the map, Eli had about two days left to travel. Eli's mission was to locate the exact position of the dogs' camp because they would have moved on from where his father had seen them. Once he located them, he was to go to Whisker Creek and wait for Elliot and Samantha to show up with the Monarch's army. This way, the Monarch's army wouldn't have to waste time searching for them. Turning the dogs around and getting them out of Catland as quickly as possible was of the utmost importance. It sounded easy to Eli, but his mother and father were very reluctant to let him go.

"It's the most dangerous mission, Eli. If you get caught you could die," his father warned. Once Eli located the dogs, he was to leave immediately. He wasn't to get close to them. His father had been very adamant about that. "Whatever you do, don't be seen. Those dogs are bred to be mean."

His mother really didn't want him to go. She said there were other cats that could do the job. But Eli's father stressed time was crucial. They needed to be stopped dead in their tracks. If the dogs reached their cities they would wreak havoc on everyone and everything. And unfortunately, there was no one else nearby to do it.

"Don't worry, Mother,
they won't catch me.
I know how to sneak undercover," Eli had said trying to reassure her.

Sneaking undercover was a natural thing for a cat. It was something cats didn't have to be taught. The same went for hunting and climbing. Every cat was good at it.

What cats did need to be taught however, was not to get too confident in themselves. That was when mistakes were made. When a cat started thinking he was too good to get caught, he almost always found himself in a nasty situation. Eli's mother had taught this to her kittens. But now she questioned if Eli was going to remember it.

"Nine lives can go pretty fast.
You're young, Eli,
you need yours to last!" she had replied.

All cats are born with nine lives. That's what they called it when a cat should have died from a life-threatening situation but didn't. Eli knew his father had three of four lives left. This last encounter with the dogs had taken another life from him.

But Eli wasn't that young. He was a teenager almost of age for the royal guard and he wanted his mother to give him some credit. He knew getting caught could snatch all nine lives from him.

"I'm not a baby!
This mission's dangerous.
Trust me—I'm not crazy!" Eli said, hoping this would help.

His mother said sternly,

"Promise me this, Eli:
you won't get over confident
and think you're a professional spy.
You have no training
and lack experience, young guy."

Eli made his mother that promise and when he first set out, he was really excited to be trusted with such a dangerous mission. But now as he got closer to Troll's Pass, he was beginning to get nervous.

Eli travelled up and down hills, keeping a steady pace. As he thought about what he might find at Troll's Pass, he found himself getting more and more worried.

"Perhaps I should come up with a plan.
An escape route, and then succeed I can," he said quietly to himself as he hopped over a fallen log.

Suddenly there was wind blowing snow in Eli's face. He couldn't see. He heard flapping right in front of his nose. Eli jumped back so fast he did a cartwheel in the air and landed back on the far side of the log.

"Watch out! You clout!" said a French Hen as she flew away.

Her accent was thick but Eli understood her clearly enough. Birds were the only ones who could come and go out of Catland as all they had to do was fly over the border bush. But once in Catland they spoke cattish as it was part of the magical enchantment of Catland.

"Phew! That was close. My heart is pounding like a trapped mouse!" Eli exclaimed.

"And so it should be;
she was in plain view,
anyone could see," said a deep, strange voice.

Eli jumped again spinning in midair to face his foe. Landing back on the other side of the log where the French Hen had been, Eli peered wide-eyed into the face of a large male white cat. For a moment they stood there staring at each other.

The large white cat had yellow eyes and as he stared at Eli, Eli began to feel uncomfortable. Like he was staring right into Eli's soul. He had scars on his face and part of his left ear was missing. And being white, he was hard to see in the snow. It wasn't any wonder Eli hadn't seen him.

Then, the white cat took a long blink, a sign that he was no threat.

"Relax friend.
To scare you,
I did not intend," the white cat said.

"Where did you come from?" Eli asked.
My heart's pounding like a drum!"

"So, I can hear
but you have nothing to fear.
My name is Striker.
Are you lost little hiker?" asked Striker.

"I'm Eli and I'm not lost.
I'm on a mission of great cost," Eli replied.

Eli knew there was nothing to fear. All cats work together to keep Catland safe and happy. He was just a little jumpy that was all.

Raising an eyebrow, Striker asked:
"What kind of mission
is there for a kitten?"

Eli frowned. He wasn't a kitten. Then he lifted his chin and proudly answered, "My father sent me.
He's border patrol
and respected as can be."

"Your father?
Tell me his name—if it's no bother," Striker asked grinning.

"Tom of Sphinxville,
border patrol,
stationed at Lynx Hill," answered Eli.

Striker's grin widened into a big toothy smile.
"Tom? I know Tom!
How is he?
How is your mom?"

Eli didn't answer him right away. He didn't know if he should tell him about the dogs. His father hadn't said anything about sharing the news with anyone. Then he realized the dog invasion was not a secret. Besides it was going to take a lot of cats and the Monarch all working together to get them out.

"They're not so good.
Catland's in trouble.
I'm helping, as I should."
"What's going on?
Fill me in, Eli.
Tell me what's wrong," Striker inquired.

Eli was only too happy to tell Striker what was going on. As Striker learned of the dogs and their beast, his ears began to flatten lower and lower, giving the white cat a menacing, angry scowl.

Eli decided it was good to have Striker on his side. He sure wouldn't want to be the one against him. Striker looked like he was used to fighting and coming out the winner.

"Troll's Pass you say?
I better go with you.
Sounds dangerous,
and it's along my way," Striker told Eli not giving him a choice.

Striker turned taking the lead, leaving Eli to follow behind. Eli was actually glad Striker had decided to join him and followed happily along. There was something about having a big menacing cat on his side that comforted him.

Troll's Pass was still a long way from them and so Striker chose a fairly fast pace to get there sooner. Eli didn't say anything but he wondered if he would be able to keep this pace up the whole way.

After some time it began snowing pretty heavily, but at least the wind had died down, which Eli was grateful for. As long as they stayed under the evergreens travelling wasn't too bad. In between the trees was where it got difficult. Sometimes the snowdrifts were too big to jump over. Eli didn't mind climbing them at first but soon it became tiring.

He worried the snow would get through his dense coat. If that happened, he would get wet. Getting wet was an awful experience. It happened to him once when he was much younger.

He had been chasing a pretty butterfly and had leaped very high into the air to touch it. When he came down, he landed in the middle of a brook. He hadn't noticed how close he had gotten to the brook, which was near their little farmhouse.

As he stood there looking around, a cold icky feeling began to seep in through his coat, first little spots by his toes, then another spot under his belly. Then all of a sudden this cold icky feeling was coming in from all sides—touching his skin. It was pricklish feeling. It was awful.

He had to get out. He had jumped and jumped until he was free from the brook. As soon as he was clear of the water he had ran as fast as he could—straight to his mother.

She helped dry him off and explained he had gotten wet. She told him that he could become very sick from getting wet and he must take better care in the future.

Though Eli had not become sick, he knew he never wanted to get wet again. Eli remembered how cold he felt when it was still warm outside and thought it would probably feel even worse to get wet while it was so cold out.

As they traveled, Eli and Striker got to know one another a little better. Striker was a lot older than Eli would have guessed. He had grown up in Purring City and had seen all the members of the Royal family at one time or another.

Striker told Eli how nice they were. They always had a smile on their face or something nice to say. Everyone liked them and it was always a joyful time when they came out of the castle. The merchants were happier, the entertainers would put on special shows in the streets for free, and even the fang cleaners were known to give a few cleanings for free.

As Eli listened to Striker, something began to bother him.

Finally, Eli said, "But not Winter, right? He's mean and gives everyone a fright."

There was no way Eli could believe Winter was nice too. Not the way Winter was storming about and making their travels so difficult.

"Oh, don't let Winter get you down.
He's just doing his job.
And, he enjoys a good frown.
No cat likes Winter's reign.
Cats like it warm and dry,
not the cold that gives Winter fame.
But Winter . . . nah, he's not so bad.
If you met him . . . you'd like him and be glad."

Eli in disbelief said, "Nobody likes Winter!

They say he's mean.
And unpleasant like a splinter."

Striker knew Winter personally, and it always bothered Striker how unpopular Winter was in Catland, all because it was his nature to be cold and icy.

Winter did his job well, but the citizens of Catland didn't appreciate it. They were always complaining and whining about Winter. Sometimes, Winter would get mad at the citizens of Catland and give them a good storm. But most of the time, he just ignored them.

"No, no—you don't understand.
It's Winter's job and it's unpopular here in Catland.
But in The Rest of the World, many creatures like the cold. Some like the snow, some like to get burrowed."

Eli thought about it for a moment. What kind of creature would like the snow? Eli just couldn't imagine.

"That's crazy talk!
No one likes the snow.
You make it sound like they flock."

"Well, it's true.
But how could you know?
Unless you've been there, you have no clue."

Striker sighed. Poor Winter always getting picked on, even when he was gone.

It was getting late. Striker looked around and realized they were about a day away from Troll's Pass now. If the dog pack was still there, it might be a good idea to find a good spot to hide in case they got spotted. It should be a place where the dogs couldn't get into.

Striker thought about the tunnels the trolls had dug out. There were lots of them around. The problem was if there was a troll in the tunnel it could be just as bad as facing a dog.

Trolls were nice enough as long as they were not in their homes. You could have a nice conversation with a troll when it was outside, but never ever enter a troll's home uninvited. They called it break-ins.

One time an old cat sought shelter from one of Summer's rain storms by crawling into a troll tunnel. The old cat wasn't even very far in the tunnel when the troll caught him. The old cat must have had only one life left, because he didn't live through the experience.

If Striker remembered correctly, there was an abandoned tunnel nearby. It didn't go very far into the mountain, but it could be just what they needed for a safe spot to hide. And being in a tunnel gave them two entrances to choose from.

Eli was exhausted. He had been trotting all day, stopping just long enough to eat some of the food his mother had packed for him. Eli wanted to stop and check his map when Striker took a turn to their right.

"There's a spot up ahead, it's not far and it's a good spot to make a bed," he said.

Eli was relieved.

Striker finally slowed down and walked over to a bush. He searched through it; not finding whatever it was he was looking for, he went to another bush and searched through it too. Striker went from one bush to the next. Eli sat down to watch him. It felt so good to sit down.

Letting out a big yawn Eli said, "What are you doing? Aren't you too tired to be fooling?"

"Shh, keep your voice down.
There could be dogs around.
I'm searching for a tunnel—
a place to rest and huddle."

Eli crouched down, resting his body on his haunches while he waited for Striker to find this tunnel. The snow was letting up. Eli was glad about that then he heard a noise behind him. Eli listened carefully but he couldn't see anything. He took some deep breaths but he didn't smell anything out of the ordinary either.

The forest always had a variety of smells. Every type of tree had a scent and every bush did too. But the smells weren't very strong during Winter's reign because the trees would go to sleep or dormant as some cats called it.

With the exception of Striker fooling around in the bushes, it was fairly quiet. All he could hear was the usual forest sounds, the wind, the creaking of trees. An owl hooted far off in the distance.

Eli strained to hear the sound again. He wished he knew what it was that made the noise he was listening for. But whatever it was, it didn't make the sound again.

Eli went back to watching Striker. After a few moments he heard it again. It was behind him. Standing up, Eli turned to face the direction the sound came from. He stretched his neck high up sniffing and listening.

Striker caught Eli's movement out of the corner of his eye and stopped his searching. He quickly and quietly stepped over to Eli.

From behind him, Striker whispered, "What is it? Do you hear something? Did you see it?"

Eli spun toward Striker. He hadn't heard him come over. Cat Alive he's quiet, thought Eli impressed, I should definitely practice it.

"I heard a noise.
But to hear better,
I'm trying to poise," Eli whispered back.

"Try standing like this,
to help hear the noise and not miss." Striker jumped up, standing on his back legs, he looked around.

Looking at Striker, Eli smiled. Then, lifting one front paw and one back paw he said,

"Maybe if I stand this way,
my hearing will improve,
and not decay."

Eli looked ridiculous. Striker came down on all four paws chuckling. Apparently Eli had his dad's sense of humour. The thought of standing a certain way to hear better suddenly struck Striker as funny and he started laughing out loud. In spite of his efforts to be quiet, so not to draw any attention their way, Striker couldn't stop himself. It had been a very long time since he had broken into an outright laugh and there seemed to be no stopping now.

Striker's laughter got Eli laughing too. Just giggling at first but then he let his guard down and joined in with a good belly laugh. Being exhausted from travelling in combination with the stress of the situation, the two of them fell to the ground and laughed until their bellies hurt.

After a bit, Striker got up. Still smiling he said, "Come on, I found it, and it will do for a bit."

Striker led Eli to the last bush he had been searching through. There, behind the bush, was a hole that led into the mountain. Striker went in first and Eli followed. It was dark inside and smelled of stale air.

"This tunnel is abandoned.
I saw no tracks and that's not random," said Striker quietly.

Eli yawned. "I'm dead tired, beat.
I just want to sleep."

"There's a spot, go ahead;
rest your eyes.
It will make a good bed."

Eli looked at the spot Striker pointed out. It was a pile of old grass. Someone must have made it long ago. Eli walked over sniffing the grass. It smelled musty and dusty. It was old all right, but it would work.

He climbed on to the pile and curled up. He no sooner laid his head down and he was asleep.

Striker looked around. He smelled the air for any scents that might belong to a troll or any other creature. Satisfied they were alone in the tunnel, Striker headed for the entrance. With one last look over his shoulder at Eli, he headed out and disappeared into the night.

Chapter 3

Eli

Eli woke with a start. The tunnel was freezing. He looked around, it was still dark out so he switched to his night vision, which all cats have and naturally use at night. He could see quite well with the little moon light that was coming in at the entrance.

He didn't see Striker anywhere. Just as he was about to call out for him Eli heard a noise. His hair stood on end. It seemed to have come from the darkness within the tunnel.

Eli sniffed the air to find out what creature was there. But he couldn't pick up any scent. Someone was there, he knew it even if he couldn't detect them. He had heard trolls have a terrible smell so it couldn't be a troll.

Then a soft wind blew through the tunnel and the temperature dropped even lower. Now it felt colder than ever. Suddenly Eli realized something—the source of the cold and the wind was not coming from outside, it was coming from within the tunnel. Eli had been in cubbyholes and small tunnels before so he knew something was unnatural about this. It was time to leave.

With one powerful leap and with all the speed Eli could muster, he raced as fast as he could to the entrance. Just as he was about to break outside—ker-thump! He ran into something head on.

Eli flew through the air into the outdoors and through the bush that covered the entrance. Whatever he hit went rolling along the ground under him and got caught up in the branches.

Eli hit the ground hard. Dazed he ran for the first tree he saw and climbed up as high as he could safely go. When he reached the top he closed his eyes and waited for his senses to comeback. He had hit his head pretty hard.

Eli knew his senses lived in his head and didn't like to get knocked around. He had heard how they would leave and never come back if they had been hit too hard. That was where the saying "he's lost his senses" came from.

Hearing a groan come from the bush, he looked down but he wasn't able to focus properly. His head still felt dizzy.

"Eli?
Oh my" came a weak voice from the bush. It was Striker!

"Striker get out of there!
In the tunnel,

there's a monstrous scare!" Eli yelled franticly.

Eli could see the bush wiggling. He heard groaning again come from the bush. Then slowly emerging out of the bush Eli saw Striker. Striker limped over to the tree and sat down. He lifted his front left leg to get a better look at it. The dizziness was going away so Eli figured his senses must be coming back, slowly, maybe one by one.

Then from inside the tunnel came a loud wind-like howl. Without hesitation Striker leaped up the tree. Striker climbed as if he had no injury to slow him down. From the other side of the tree Eli looked Striker in the eyes; he was amazed at his speed.

"Wow, you're fast.
With speed like that,
you're nine lives should last," he said very impressed.

"Wasn't fast enough to avoid you.
This huge bruise makes me want to mew." Striker lifted his paw and made circles with his left shoulder in effort to work out the soreness.

That's when Eli saw it. Striker's claws were made of metal. The tips were slightly longer than would be naturally and the undersides were as sharp as a knife's edge. No wonder he could climb so fast. Eli bet he could do a lot of things with claws like that.

An eerie howl came again from inside the tunnel. Strangely it sounded like it was calling Striker. Then something even stranger happened; the bush covering the entrance turned white, frozen stiff with ice crystals.

Eli was scared. Wide-eyed he turned back to Striker but he was gone. Looking down Eli saw Striker climbing down the tree as fast as he could.

"What are you doing?
Where are you going?
How could you leave me without knowing?" Eli called down frightened.

"It's Chill!
He's my friend,
Oh what a thrill!" exclaimed Striker excitedly.

"Are you sure?

I'm not moving until I see his fur," said Eli.

Striker didn't reply, he just continued working his way out of the tree.

Eli felt safest high in the tree with the snowy branches hiding him. He wasn't going anywhere until he knew for a fact it was safe. He watched Striker limp over to the tunnel entrance. Eli noticed it wasn't snowing anymore. It must have quit sometime during the night.

"Chill, my friend, is that you?
Come on out before I turn blue," Striker called into the tunnel.

Eli wondered if it was possible for Striker to actually turn blue.

Then another bush right next to the entrance stiffened and turn white with ice crystals. Since Eli had never seen Chill, he watched with a combination of fear and fascination.

A transparent shape appeared at the tunnel entrance. It was glowing white and blue. As it came out of the tunnel hole, Eli saw that it was a young man bent over. As he came clear of the entrance bush he stood up straight.

Eli was amazed at his height. He seemed to grow as he straightened up to his full height. When he was finished stretching up to his full height, Eli wondered how he ever fit in to that tunnel.

He was tall with blue hair and glowing skin. Eli knew Chill was one of Winter's helpers but what was he doing here?

"Striker, my dear friend.
You're hard to track
but I caught up a while back." Chill's voice had a wind-howling sound.

He was hard to understand. Just listening to him made Eli feel cold.

Striker smiled. "I thought something was on my tail.
I couldn't see though.
Were you wearing your veil?
I circled around to get a better view.
I sure am glad it was you.
But why were you in the tunnel?
You know you caused me some trouble." Striker moved his shoulder around some more. It was clearly hurting him.

Wherever Chill went, everything around him turned white

with frost. Even Striker had frost on him, but because he already was white, he just looked fuzzier. Except his whiskers, his whiskers looked oddly thick. The strange thing was—Striker wasn't shivering.

"You were not alone,
or I would have let you known.
I hoped to get your attention
from inside the tunnel.
Quietly was my intention," Chill answered.

Eli wondered how long Striker was gone. It was just about dawn. A bit of light was beginning to show on the horizon so Sun was waking up.

"Well after I circled around,
I headed to Mew View,
to over look the ground.
A camp had been there
but gone now I found," Striker told him.

Chill stood very still, he had a look of peace about him. Eli felt calmed watching him. He had a blue white glow around him and Eli thought he might be seeing right through him. Eli strained his eyes to see if he could make out the bush on the other side of Chill. Or was Chill reflecting the bushes on this side of him—like a mirror. It was hard to figure out which one he was: transparent or reflective. Either way, Chill was beautifully serene.

"So you know dogs have broken through the border.
They've come to steal, destroy, and loiter.
The rest of the Monarch needs to be informed.
We need to know their order." Chill's voice sounded like the wind but strangely beautiful.

He continued, "Winter sent me to find you.
When did you return?
Your report is due."

Striker glanced at Eli then continued,
"Tom of Sphinxville sent his kittens
to the Monarch with bid'ns.
We'll meet them at Whisker Creek
and bid those dogs good riddance.

But first we must locate these hounds

before they cover too much ground.
We'll locate their hiding place
then we'll run them out of town.
   Where is Winter now?
Please, do tell.
Does he require assistance?
I will help somehow."
   Chill didn't answer right away. He lifted his head and stood perfectly still like he was listening to the wind. Eli noticed his ears were large like his but flatter and the tips were curved.
   "Winter is busy fighting,
a forest fire—very frightening.
   This situation is despairing
How these dogs got in needs repairing.
   Winter wishes to speak with you.
When we see him,
he'll tell us what to do." Chill turned to walk away but when Striker didn't follow he turned back.
   Then he looked at Eli in the tree and back again at Striker. "Send him home. It's not safe for him to roam."
   Eli suddenly felt embarrassed. It seemed Chill knew he was there the whole time. Eli didn't know what to do.
   "Eli, come down.
I won't leave until your paws touch the ground," Striker said.
   Eli started making his way down the tree. It was always much more awkward going down than going up. He wondered how Striker managed it so quickly. Maybe those knife-nails helped descending too. When Eli finally reached the bottom he walked over to where Striker and Chill were patiently waiting.
   Eli was in awe of Chill. As he had approached the temperature got colder and a frost formed on his body. Soon he was encased in frost like Striker was but strangely he was warm inside. It was like wearing an ice blanket.
   Striker then said,
"Let me introduce you, Chill,
Eli is from the town of Sphinxville.
His father is Tom
and a grave mission he is on.

Tom sent him to track those wild dogs.
Find them, and report those polliwogs."
    Chill looked surprised.
    "He is still but a kitten!
What is Tom thinking?
His judgment is bitten!"
    Eli was shocked and blurted out,
"I am not just a kitten!
I am almost of age
as it is written!" Eli was indignant.
    Chill didn't know the circumstances surrounding his father or why Eli, his brother, and sister were sent out before reaching the proper age. It was only another few months before they could join the Monarch's royal defenses but that didn't mean those not employed were useless. Eli knew joining meant there would be lots and lots of training and studying before given a posting. But cats had a survival instinct that was natural and they didn't have to join if they didn't want to.
    Chill looked over Eli, inspecting him with his cool gaze. Then his voice took on an icy tone.
    "You *are* a kitten,
as it is written.
You are not of age.
You will come along.
And Winter will decide what to do at this stage."
    Eli felt a chill go through him, different from before; it was an emotional chill. He looked at Striker and back at Chill. Clearly Chill was not asking him. Suddenly Chill did not look so enchanting. He looked frightening, towering over him.
    Eli didn't dare cross him. He nodded his consent and they turned and walked away. Eli followed behind silently. He was afraid to meet Winter. Striker was the first cat to ever say anything nice about him.

Chapter 4

"Elliot, wait up, I've dropped my turn-up." Samantha shoved the rest of her breakfast in her mouth as she ran back down the cobblestone street to where the turn-up lay.

They had arrived at Purring City yesterday afternoon. But so far they had not gotten in to see the Monarch's magistrate. The guards told them the magistrate was too busy and no one would send a message regarding them.

One guard told them, if he let every little kitten in, who wanted to meet one of the Monarchs, they would throw him in to a bin. Elliot and Samantha had a hard time believing him but nonetheless they had to leave to find a different way in.

Their father had warned them if they encountered problems getting in, to find a cat named Scratch, he would help them. So far no one knew where Scratch was. They had asked around and had discovered his house but he wasn't home.

It had been pretty late so they stayed at an inn called the Wild Cat Hotel. Elliot thought the place sounded exciting but as they soon discovered, it wasn't. There had only been one other customer in the lounge. So it made for a very quiet evening. Samantha was just as happy about that as she was tired from the journey and looking forward to getting her rest.

This morning however, they were up very early eating breakfast on the way. Elliot had said he didn't want to miss Scratch in case he came home last night and was planning to leave early again today.

Elliot and Samantha turned down the street that led to Scratch's house. The street was lined with a wall of houses. The homes looked like they were all one long building but each home was painted a different colour. It made the street very pretty with all the different colours. Yellow, blue, red, purple, all the colours reminded Samantha of a jar of jellybeans. Samantha felt cheerful walking down this street. Maybe when she grew up she could live in a neighborhood as cheery as this one.

They arrived at Scratch's home and knocked at the door. They heard some bumping noises coming from the inside and waited patiently for the door to open. When it did, an old orange tabby cat met them. He had a patch over one eye and a few scars here and there on his body.

"What do you kittens want?
To sell me something I want not?
Go away you annoying tot!" Scratch grumbled and swung the door shut but just before it closed Elliot stopped it.

Elliot and Samantha were surprised by his grumpiness. Elliot pushed the door back open saying,

"Please, Mr. Scratch, hear us out.
Our father Tom sent us to the Monarchs.
We have news to tell them about."

"Tom who? And why tell me? I don't care what you do." Scratch tried to shut the door again but Elliot held it open.

"Tom of Sphynxville, border patrol stationed at Lynx Hill," Elliot said quickly.

"We have a very important message.
But the guards won't give us passage," Samantha added just as quickly.

"Tom of Sphynxville you say?
It's been a long time since I've seen that crazy half-grey.
But why send you to me?
Why send you my way?" Scratch asked.

"Father said you'd help us get in.
With your aid his message won't come to ruin."

"He did, did he?
What is this message?
I want to know before I agree," Scratch replied.

Elliot and Samantha started to tell Scratch all about their father out on patrol when Scratch interrupted them.

"Hold on, Hold on.
You better come in before you go on." Scratch stepped back to let them in, then shut the door.

He led them to his living room where they all sat down. The kittens sat on the chesterfield and Scratch sat on a big chair facing them.

He said, "Ok, go on. Sounds like this story might be long."

After Elliot and Samantha were finished telling him everything that had happened, and what their father's plan was, Scratch sat back and took a deep breath. He was shocked to hear about the dogs and very distressed to hear about the strange beast.

"Well," he said, "we need to tell the magistrate.
Why he'd send kittens, I can't get straight.
But we'd better get going, don't want to be late." With that he got up and walked out of the room.

Elliot and Samantha got up and waited for him at the door. When Scratch came back he was wearing a purple robe and carrying a basket with nothing in it but a red and white-checkered napkin. The kittens looked at each other, Elliot shrugged and walked outside. Samantha followed with Scratch behind her shutting the door.

"Okay. Let's go this way," Scratch said taking the lead.

Samantha and Elliot followed him admiring the city. Elliot hadn't noticed very much of the city the last two days because he was so concerned about their mission. This trip was his first time to the big city and for the first time he took notice of the buildings, how the streets were laid out and the various signs along the way.

Most buildings were two storeys high but some were three and four storeys. He had never seen such tall buildings. Some of the buildings had a narrow walkway in between them separating one from one another but most were attached. Each one was individually painted or decorated.

All the storefronts had signs, each one presented in a fashion unique to the store itself. Elliot noticed a fish store had a sign hanging in the shape of a fish that said "Bobby's Fishery," another store that had a kitten wearing mittens playing with a ball of yarn on its sign that said "Mittens for Kittens."

Elliot had lost his fair share of mittens so he made a mental note of that store for future reference. It might help keep him out of trouble with his mother if he had some mittens to spare.

They walked on for a bit before Elliot noticed they weren't headed directly to the Monarch's castle.

Frowning Elliot said,

"Umm, excuse me, Mr. Scratch,
but isn't the Monarch's castle that way,
past that cabbage patch?" Elliot pointed to his right over a small barren cabbage patch field. Over the tops of buildings he could see some of the castle's towers.

"Yes, yes, come on, this way is best," Scratch responded.

They followed Scratch for a while longer before Scratch stopped in front of a yellow store. The sign was in the shape of a muffin and read "Marvin's Muffins."

"Come on, come on. We won't be long," Scratch said.

Without looking at them he walked into the store. Elliot and Samantha followed him up to the counter where he ordered a dozen salmon-fish-filled biscuits. The clerk took Scratch's basket and started filling it with fresh salmon-fish-filled biscuits.

The aroma of the biscuits was overwhelming, they smelled so good. Samantha could feel her mouth beginning to water.

"Mmm, those smell delicious.
But my tongue isn't convinced,
I think it's suspicious," said Samantha hopeful to get one.

Scratch glanced at Samantha but she didn't see him roll his eyes to the clerk.

"You better give me two more,
wouldn't want these kittens to drool on your floor," Scratch said.

With a smile the clerk finished filling the basket and covered them with the red and white napkin. Then he took two more biscuits handing one to Samantha and one to Elliot.

Samantha sunk her teeth into the biscuit. Delicious salmon flavour filled her mouth. Scratch paid the clerk. The kittens thanked both of them and they left the store.

The biscuit was still warm from the oven. In the center was a burst of juicy salmon. It was truly the best biscuits Samantha had ever had. She tried to remember where this store was so she could bring some biscuits home to her mother when their mission was all over.

"Thank you again for the biscuit, Scratch.
I think I had the best one in the batch," Samantha said quite satisfied.

"Yes, it was a delicious detour.
But shouldn't we hurry? Our safety isn't secure," said Elliot worried that they had wasted too much time.

Scratch looked at Elliot, nodding he said,
"This way now, it's the quickest way, I vow."

Elliot and Samantha followed Scratch through the city. The castle became bigger and bigger as they headed toward it. The castle was laid out in the shape of a square. There were four gates, one in the center of each wall. When they reached the castle wall, Scratch turned away from the big gates of the southern wall and went around heading toward the gates of the west wall. But when they reached those gates, Scratch walked right by not even looking in.

Elliot was beginning to wonder if they were going to walk by all the gates. It was a huge palace and this could take all day.

Just as they reached the northern corner of the west wall, Scratch stopped and knocked on a doorknocker. There wasn't any door to be seen just a doorknocker on the huge stone wall.

Samantha and Elliot glanced at each other. It seemed weird that there was a doorknocker with no door. Suddenly a small stone was removed from the wall and two eyes appeared.

"Who goes there?
Remove your headdress
and state your affair.
If you have business
be prepared to share," a voice said from the other side of the hole in the wall.

Removing his hood, Scratch replied,
"It is I, Scratch.
I have warm fish-filled biscuits
to which there is no match."

Scratch held the basket up to the little hole for the eyes to see. Immediately there was a big rolling sound and a door opened out from the stone wall. They all had to step back to let the door open.

Elliot and Samantha were amazed because they had not seen any outline of the door when it was shut. As they walked through the entrance Elliot and Samantha took a close look at the doorframe. The door shape was cut around each of the stones, which gave it a crooked wavy shape. The door fit so closely into the wall the outline was hard to see. But now that it was open they could see where a thin crack had been.

Inside was a room with an open door to a courtyard. There were two other guards in the room and a couple of wooden chairs along the wall.

"What brings you in today, Scratch?

Surely, it's not just to bring us this fresh batch," The guard said after shutting the door behind them and reaching for a biscuit. Scratch held the basket up for each of the guards to have one.

"Not at all.
I have grievous, dreadful news.
News that will appall."

"What is it?
Don't just give us that tidbit," the soldier said wanting more information from Scratch.

"I must first report to the magistrate.
Then I can elaborate," answered Scratch.

"Scratch, you're retired.
Technically, your report time has expired," the soldier told him.

"I'm out of retirement with this one.
This is important and we must run." Scratch gave a little bow of his head and headed toward the palace.

The guards stepped aside to let them through. Scratch and the kittens entered a garden. There were vegetables plants, fruit trees, and flower bushes everywhere. There were also plenty of paths in various directions. Scratch led them along a wide path heading directly to the palace. They came into a clearing up close to the palace and walked along the side of the castle's great stone wall.

There were cats working everywhere. Some were cleaning windows, some were working in flower gardens, everyone had a job to do. In a large grassy area Elliot and Samantha saw what looked to be a class learning some battle skills. Elliot watched them intently. He wondered if he would be in a class someday.

The palace was in the center of the yard with four large courtyards between the gates and the palace. Scratch led them around to the front of the palace. There were two huge doors wide open in the front. Scratch led them through and up to a cat dressed in formal wear. After a brief few words with him, they were led to a room to wait.

Chapter 5

It seemed like their walking would never end. Up and down the mountainside they traveled. After a while the scent of smoke began to fill the air. At one point the trail overlooked a valley. Eli wasn't sure which valley it was but he could see smoke, lots and lots of it. The smoke was dark and reached as high as the clouds. Along the valley ground he could see flames of red and yellow.

Eli wondered if this fire was the same fire that burned his father. He hoped not but a part of him suspected it might be. He sure didn't want to get too close to it.

As they continued to travel it started snowing again, big heavy flakes. "Oh great, just my fate," mumbled Eli.

"What's that, little cat?" asked Chill, stopping to look at Eli. Striker looked over his shoulder at him.

"It's snowing.
I wish it would stop.
It's hard going," said Eli.

"Humph!" said Chill turning back to lead the way.

Striker shook his head following Chill. Eli had the feeling he just did something wrong. But what was wrong with wishing for easy travels?

The smell of smoke was beginning to get stronger. Where were they headed? It was getting late and hard to see. There was a smoky haze settling in. Sun was going down again for his rest and the snow was falling heavily now.

Chill suddenly stopped and made a loud cracking type of call. Eli had never heard anything like it. It sounded like frozen branches snapping off trees. Chill went on for a few minutes, with his hands cupped around his mouth making this loud strange noise.

Was he speaking some type of language Eli wondered? When he stopped everything was quiet. There was no noise at all. Not even a bird. Then faintly, in the far distance Eli heard a reply. It was different from Chill's but it had the same cold cracking sound. Then he heard it again louder, and again louder. It was coming toward them fast.

Eli stepped closer to Striker, huddling in close to where he was sitting. Wide-eyed he listened to the sound closing in on them. It sounded like ice breaking and it moaned. Similar to the way ice sounds when it is breaking up on a frozen lake—ice rubbing against ice.

"What's he doing?
I feel so vulnerable, I might start pooing," whispered Eli to Striker.

"Winter's coming," said Striker with a smile. "They're talking to one another. They're very cunning."

"You can understand that? So it's not a trap?" asked Eli cautiously.

"They're speaking Winterish.
I know a few words.
Winter's unhappy and sounds offish.
I just overheard," Striker answered reassuringly.

Eli started to shiver. A tree beside him, white with frost from Chill's passing, began to form thick clear ice on its branches. Eli looked at an evergreen nearby; it was doing the same thing, each needle becoming encased in ice. Eli was becoming colder too. The frost blanket he wore from Chill was no longer keeping him warm.

"You'll warm soon. As he appears you'll become immune," Striker told Eli as if he were reading his mind.

Through the trees Eli could see a light. It was illuminating the forest as the source of it drew nearer to them. Then as if someone turned on a light, Eli could see all around.

Winter appeared then. He was taller than Chill, and older. His hair was white and he was dressed in white and blue robes, which sparkled. He had the same type of appearance as Chill only everything seemed more—much more glow, more size, more hair, more iciness to him. Even Winter's eyes were an icy pale blue, which contrasted with Chill's large dark blue eyes, which had a coldness to them but now seemed warm in comparison.

Chill and Winter talked in their winterish language. Eli listened to the cracking, moaning, and wind blowing sounds of their speech. After a while they turned their attention to Striker and Eli. Eli wanted to shrink back and hide behind Striker but he sat perfectly still, too afraid to move a muscle.

"So, Striker, you have returned.
The Rest of the World is a huge concern.
What have you discovered?
What have you learned?" Winter asked him.

Striker stood up to give his report.

"The Rest of the World is in chaos.

The peacemakers are at a loss.
Everyone is out for selfish gain.
I've seen kittens and cubs abused and in pain.
   The inhabitants have forgotten the ways of peace.
No matter where you turn wickedness does not cease.
Very few remember what it is to love.
How can we help them without the big cat above?
   Yet, I can still say there are a few;
who believe in love and know what to do.
They run in small bands giving out a kind word,
or an act of kindness it's almost unheard.
But they hide for safety and safety they need.
For many seek to destroy them and they're kind of weak-kneed.
   My report is disturbing that I know.
What can be done their happiness is low." Striker sat down looking very sad.
   Winter gave Striker's report some thought. Then with his face downcast he said gravely, "Then it is time.
The messengers have warned them and still there is crime.
The inhabitants will learn no other way.
Now their children and the whole world will pay."
   With a tone of determination Winter continued,
"But first things first:
these trespassing dogs they are accursed.
They play with flame.
They started this fire I can barely tame.
I snowed and blowed and still it burns on.
This flame of theirs—something is wrong.
   Tell me, Striker, have you seen any trace?
How these dogs got here, how they were graced?"
   Winter was fighting the forest fire with snow? Eli had no idea that was why Winter was snowing and blowing so much. It made sense now. Eli felt bad he had wished it would stop snowing.
   "Until I met Eli, I was unaware of them.
I don't know how they got in or from where they stem," Striker answered.
   Winter looked at Eli,
"Eli, son of Tom from Sphinxville

I will get to you still."

Eli wondered what that other thing was they were talking about. "The Rest of the World was in chaos?" There was only one way Striker could know that. He must be a spy cat sent out into The Rest of the World to report on the status of the inhabitants there. But why? Eli suddenly had a lot of questions for Striker, but he would have to wait for the right opportunity to ask them.

"Striker, I know your rest is overdue.
However, I have a new mission for you to ensue.
Discover how these trespassers got in.
We must stop their progress before their crimes can begin.
Catland must remain wholesome and clean,
A place of love, peace, and beauty serene.
You must understand,
it is of utmost importance,
in preserving Catland." Winter spoke with an intensity that made Eli think he was worried.

"I do indeed,
I will not stop until I succeed," Striker responded giving Winter a small bow.

Winter then turned his attention to Eli.
"Where is Tom now?
I have not seen him,
he should be on the prowl."

Eli took this opportunity to tell Winter everything that had happened. How he and his brother and sister wanted to help his father. He told of the plan and meeting up at Whisker Creek with the Monarch's army. Then he sat down and waited to hear what Winter had to say.

Winter quietly pondered Eli's story. Finally after what seemed like quite a while he said,

"They have a beast you say.
If they have the beast I think, then there is no time to delay.
That creature explains this fire.
Only sulfur could burn so entire.
Spring and I will band together.
Be warned ahead of time, the ferociousness of our weather.
Tom has come up with a decent plan.

You will continue tracking that evil dog band.
But now you will report a number;
by how many are we encumbered.
 They are no longer at Troll's Pass.
They've gone to the Dead Mouse Mountain Bypass.
 Follow the old Cat Tooth trail.
Knowing their number will help us not fail.
 But Eli you need to be warned,
leave as soon as you find them, you are an untrained greenhorn.
Should you fall into their paws,
there may be no rescue from the clamp of their jaws.
Should you become treed,
they will not let you be freed.
 Do you understand the danger you face?
One wrong move and your life misplaced?"
 "I do. I won't disappoint you," said Eli with renewed fear.
 "Then rest tonight
for tomorrow you depart.
But first let's have a bite,
it will give you a good start."
 Winter turned and walked between two iced-up trees into a clearing. Striker and Eli followed. In the clearing was a big table with a bunch of chairs around it. A feast was prepared with all sorts of meats, cheese and warm milk—to Eli's delight.
 Eli wondered how it got there and who set it but he chose not to say anything.
 As they ate Eli observed Winter and Chill chatting quietly amongst themselves. Perhaps Striker was right about Winter. He didn't seem so mean here. Although, Winter seemed to be all work and no play, and Eli could see that Winter had a presence about him that was frighteningly icy. He determined it was probably in his best interest to do nothing that might make Winter angry with him.
 After eating Eli was shown to a cozy little bed made up for him under a fir tree. As he lay down, Eli wondered who made up the bed for him? But he was too tired and somewhat afraid to ask. He would probably learn all these things once he joined the Royal Monarch's army. He fell asleep within minutes.

Chapter 6

Eli

Scratch, Elliot, and Samantha stood before the Magistrate Spring. He wore brown and glittering green robes. His skin was a pale golden colour, which glowed. His eyes were a dark chocolate in colour and his hair was a long glimmering brown with streaks of blond, dark brown, and red. The look of his eyes was soft and gentle but there was an unmistakable alertness to them that seemed to not miss anything.

Elliot and Samantha stood in awe of Spring. Never in a million years would they have imagined him to look as beautiful as he did. There was also a sweet freshness around him like the smell after a rain. When he spoke his voice was calming. It reminded Elliot of the sereneness of a babbling brook.

"This is disturbing news you bring.
I knew of the dogs, but this beast is a new thing," Spring said.

"Our troops are gathering now.
I thank you young kittens.
Tell your father we're going on the prowl.
We'll proceed to Whisker Creek.
Pray Eli's news isn't bleak.
    You have brought valuable information,
when you come of age,
I hope you'll choose to serve your nation.
    You've proven yourselves trust worthy and loyal
these are traits that keep Catland royal.
    But, for now you shouldn't roam,
it is best you return,
to the safety of your home.
    Scratch, your service, like a good comb,
has been invaluable.
The kittens need an escort home.
Are you expedition-able?"

"Excuse me, Mister Spring,
but we know the way home.
We can handle such a thing," Elliot said respectfully.

"You may know the way
but this is a time of danger.
In respect to your father this day,
I would send you with a good ranger.

Should Scratch be willing to go that way?"

All eyes turned to Scratch waiting for his response.

The look on Scratch's face was one of surprise and disappointment. Scratch swallowed rather loudly answering, "I have served Catland for sixty years.

I have experienced things in my career,
that would leave most cats frozen in fear.
If you only want me to escort these kittens home
I will surely do it,
and keep them within the safety of Catland's dome," he answered.

Samantha and Elliot felt bad for Scratch who was clearly disappointed that he wasn't going to be reinstated to service.

"Thank you, Scratch.
With you, their safety could not be matched." If Spring was aware of how Scratch was feeling, he showed no sign of it.

Elliot, Samantha, and Scratch made their way out of Purring City. They had stopped at Scratch's house so he could pack a few things for the journey. Then Samantha insisted they go back to the bakery so she could get salmon-filled biscuits for her mother. She suspected her dad would be quite pleased with them too.

As they traveled, Scratch was quiet, keeping to himself. Once in a while the kittens would hear him mutter under his breath. The kittens decided to leave him alone and chatted amongst themselves, admiring the scenery. They stopped once in a while to sniff wild flowers or pounce on a bug that happened to be along their way.

"We best keep going.
It could be dangerous,
there's no way of knowing," Scratch said urging the kittens to keep moving.

Scratch and the kittens had traveled the majority of the day when Scratch decided he best find them a place to camp for the night. He knew Tom was from Sphinxville but other than that he had no idea where exactly these kittens lived. He wasn't worried about it though, he figured they would direct him the closer they got.

Never before had he experienced such disappointment with the magistrate. He really believed that at such a time as this he would be reinstated to service.

Unaware he was muttering to himself, he mumbled, "I can't believe I'm a babysitter. I never even had a litter."

He was beginning to believe the magistrate thought him too old to be reinstated. Well, he'd show them; after these kittens were safe at home, he'd do some investigating on his own.

He led them down a path that was beginning to fill in with wild plant life. Scratch knew of a secluded little clearing he had camped at many times when he had traveled this way.

Once they had their camp set up, they sat down to enjoy a bit of supper. No sooner had they gotten comfortable than they heard someone heading their way through the bushes.

There wasn't much of a wind blowing so Scratch wasn't able to pick up any scent. But by the sound of it, whoever it was they were a good size.

Scratch directed the kittens to hide just as a precaution while he waited to greet whomever it was coming. There had never been any serious dangers in this part of Catland. Maybe a warthog searching for food or a troll in a bad mood, if you stayed out of their way, they were likely to leave you alone. Scratch decided it was still best to be safe than sorry.

Whoever it was sure was noisy. Cats prided themselves in their stealth movement; the goal was always to be silent even in fall when fallen leaves crackle and crunch under paw. But this creature didn't seem to care about how much noise they were making; it was probably a hog, they were very noisy.

Just then the wind blew and Scratch caught a whiff of who was. Scratch hissed spinning towards the noise, arching his back, a moment later a big brown dog broke into the clearing.

Seeing Scratch the dog came to a stop. He quickly glanced around the clearing and then his eyes fell on Scratch again. He licked his lips.

"Well, well, well," he said.
"Look what my nose did smell,
I thought I was on the trail of something malicious,
Here it turns out to be something delicious."

Scratch looked at the food he and the kittens were about to eat, willing himself to calm down. Scratch growled, "Help yourself as you may and then please, be on your way." It was hard for Scratch to use his manners but he managed it.

The dog looked at the food. "Yesss," the dog drooled out, "I may eat that too." He barked out a laugh and sat down on his haunches. He sniffed the air. "Is that all you have on your menu? I've been on my paws for days with very little to chew."

Scratch growled quietly. He could see their small lunch wouldn't be enough to satisfy the big dog. Scratch had no intentions of becoming the dog's next meal. It had been a really long time since he had interacted with dogs in The Rest of the World but he knew dogs couldn't resist a good chase. Especially if they thought they would get to devour their prize. He had to lead the dog away from the kittens. Just thinking about what the dog would do if he discovered them was unspeakable.

It never occurred to him that what the dog smelled was Samantha's salmon-filled biscuits. She still had them with her in her backpack.

Without taking his eyes off the dog, Scratch slowly walked away from the food, deliberately circling around in the opposite direction from the kittens.

"I don't have much food, but what I have isn't crude, help yourself, I won't be rude," Scratch growled out.

"Indeed, it calls me like a bell." The dog drooled again, and trotted over to the food, with two gulps the food was gone. The dog's stomach rumbled. He sat down again, sniffing the air he cocked his head to the side and lifted his ear.

"Is that fish I smell? Oh fish would be swell." The dog sniffed the air, looking in the direction of the kittens, "Oh do tell, are you holding . . ."

Scratch didn't wait for him to finish speaking. He let out a wild hiss and leaped for the bush, crossing directly in front of the dog's path. As predicted, this motion proved too much for the dog to withstand. He immediately gave chase snapping his large jaws behind Scratch.

Scratch ran straight thru the bush, dodging trees, jumping fallen logs, ducking under low branches, running as fast as he could. He took the easiest most direct route he could find. The dog came crashing along right behind him. Scratch could hear his snapping jaws very near to him. He had to lead the dog as far away as possible to allow the kittens a chance to get out unnoticed.

Scratch deliberately ran under low-lying branches and small bushes to give himself an advantage from the big dog but he didn't have the strength of his youth. The dog was able to run around these obstacles, or jump them and still gain on him. He wished he could just climb a tree but not yet. Scratch ran as hard and as long as he possibly could but his old body was beginning to falter.

After running for what felt like an eternity, he knew he couldn't keep it up any longer. He was tiring. He looked for the nearest tree to climb and leaped for it. In midair the dogs' jaws closed around his chest.

Scratch screamed in horror and twisted in the dog's mouth trying to scratch the dog's face. The dog tightened his grip and shook his head. The shaking made Scratch dizzy. He closed his eyes. He couldn't breathe. The dogs grip was too tight. There was a cracking sound and a sharp pain as a number of Scratch's ribs broke.

"This is it," he thought, "my last life gone, lickety-split."

Scratch kept his eyes closed. He was losing consciousness. There was a buzzing sound in his ears and it was getting louder, drowning out the dog's heavy breathing. Faintly he heard. "Don't kill him, Rex, the captain will question him next. You know the lack of animals has him perplexed." Scratch fell into unconsciousness.

Elliot and Samantha were frozen with fear. Wide-eyed they glanced at each other and strained to hear where Scratch and the dog had gone. It was quiet now but they were still too afraid to move. After quite some time passed with no return of Scratch, Elliot finally spoke.

Whispering he said, "What do we do?
I have no clue.
Go home as planned,
or save Scratch and pursue."

"Save Scratch? Are you insane?
Did you see the size of that thing?
Pursuit would be in vain!" Samantha was horrified at the thought of going after that huge menacing creature.

"Well what should we do?

Go home and tell Dad?
He's not healed.
He's already been had." Elliot was frightened but he had to do something.
    "No, we shouldn't tell Dad.
He'll just worry,
and Mom, she'll get worked up in a hurry.
No, we can't leave Scratch; the thought makes me teary.
But pursuit I fear is far too eerie."
    "Well what should we do?" Elliot got up and walked over to where the food had been.
    "Go back to Purring City?
We could tell Spring of this horrid little ditty."
    "Spring's not there.
He's gone to Whisker Creek,
and I fear he won't care," Samantha said quietly.
    "Oh, I think he'd care.
But you're right,
he's left and not there," Elliot said and then he got a thought. "Maybe we should go to Whisker Creek too.
    We can inform them and they can pursue."
    "That is a good plan!
And we'll meet up with Eli,
and help if we can!" Samantha wanted to do something too but there was no way she wanted to see that big creature again.
    She and Elliot started walking down the trail they had come in on. Even though Sun would be setting soon, neither of them had any intentions of spending the night there.
    "I'm so scared, my head's in a fog. Do you think that's what they call a dog?" Samantha asked. Wide-eyed she glanced back in the direction Scratch had run.
    "I think so. Sure wasn't a hog. At least that I know," Elliot answered.

Chapter 7

Eli yawned and stretched standing up on his bed under the fir tree. He looked around and saw Chill waiting for him. Eli walked over to him looking around for Striker and Winter but he didn't see them.

As if reading his mind Chill said, "Striker is gone.
Tracking the dogs backward,
from where they came upon."

"Winter has returned fighting the forest fire.
A relentless fire that just won't tire." Chill sat down on a fallen tree and handed Eli a warm cup of milk and two hot hard-boiled eggs. Chill waited for Eli to get comfortable and start eating his breakfast, then continued,

"You'll follow Cat Tooth Trail.
The dogs have been on it;
though, their scent maybe stale.
Trust your senses, they'll help you prevail.

As Winter told you last night,
you'll have to find them outright.
Once found, count them right.
But do not delay in this plight.
You do not want to feel the sting of their bite.

Then race to Whisker Creek with all your might,
the troops there prepare for a fight."

Chill then reached into a pouch hanging from his hip and pulled out a small raincoat.

He placed it beside Eli saying, "Eli, you should know,
Winter will make it snow.
And Spring will make it rain.
Your travels will be a strain.
So beware of the weather,
the storm that Winter and Spring will brew together,
It may interfere with your directional senses.
Just know, it's an attack on the dogs' defenses."

Eli gulped rather loudly as he swallowed the last of his breakfast. He took the raincoat and looked it over. It was an off-white colour matching Eli's fur. The coat was light in weight and the material was unusually quiet for being a raincoat. It was also lined, which Eli was pleased about; he could use all the warmth he could get in these mountains.

Chill got up and said, "If you are done, then come.
I'll show you the way,
there really is no time to delay."

Eli pulled on the raincoat. It fit perfectly, as if it was made just for him. Grabbing his backpack he noticed his food supplies had been replenished. Putting it on Eli followed Chill down a path that led them northeast winding its way around the mountain.

He followed Chill quietly, thinking about the task before him. He was glad for the silence as, he was becoming increasingly more worried.

What if he couldn't find them? He'd let everyone down. Or worse, what if he couldn't find Whisker Creek? Well, he had a map so he should find it but he better start paying attention to where he was to help keep his directions straight.

As they traveled, Eli took mental note of the new smells around them. He tried to remember the various rock formations and unique trees. The smell of smoke was strong but Eli could make out the faint scents from the plants and trees. There were plants he hadn't seen before but mostly he wanted to remember the direction they were coming from just in case he needed to back track.

It wasn't long before Chill came to a stop at a fork in the trail they were on. Turning to Eli he said, "This is the old Cat Tooth Trail." Chill gestured to the trail on the left.

"May Cat Above be with you,
May you prevail," Chill said with reverence and gave Eli a little bow.

"Umm, thank you, Chill,
but I was wondering, still,
while I'm tracking the dogs,
and Winter and Spring are creating fogs.
What will you be doing?
I mean, to help fight these polliwogs?"

Chill looked at Eli for a moment then replied,
"The mission set before me,
relates to The Rest of the World,
Catland must remain free,
but The Rest of the World is in the midst of debris.

And if The Rest of the World cannot live under its decree
It may be determined that no one will be free."

Eli didn't know what to say so he gave Chill a little nod. Chill gave Eli another bow and with a gust of wind he was gone.

Eli looked down Cat Tooth Trail. The trail was covered in snow and there wasn't any paw prints to be seen anywhere. Wondering what Chill meant when he said "No one will be free," he trotted down the trail.

It was getting close to noon when Eli began to feel edgy. He had never seen a dog but it might be a good idea to make sure they didn't get a jump on him by surprising him from out of seemingly nowhere. He decided the best way to make sure that didn't happen was to scout from a tall tree once in a while. It would give him the lay of the land and hopefully reveal any dogs that may be hiding around a corner.

Upon doing this, Eli discovered he had to be choosey about which tree to scout from. The big pine trees, which were the easiest for him to climb, were also the worst to see from because their branches were thick and full of pine needles blocking his view and snagging his coat. It turned out that the sparser the tree was, such as the ones that lose their leaves in the fall, gave the best vantage point. But the down side was Eli was visible in those trees and he felt vulnerable in them.

However, it wasn't long before scouting from trees paid off. Eli stood on one of the top branches from a tree he was scouting when he saw in the distance a clearing. The area looked well trampled. Eli looked around from every direction but the clearing seemed to be abandoned. Eli climbed down for a closer look.

He approached the area very cautiously, listening for any sounds that didn't belong and smelling the air continuously for the scent of anything unusual. As he made his way into the clearing, he could smell many animals had been there. It didn't seem like an overly large group although it was hard to tell just how many.

The scents were days old maybe even a week or so. But at least now he had an idea of what these dogs smelled like. He determined they were a messy animal, not cleaning up after themselves.

New snow was laying over their tracks but he could still make out which direction they had gone. Eli quickly gobbled down his lunch and followed the tracks.

Now that he had found their trail, Eli decided he better go quickly to catch up to them. He also needed to be as quiet as possible. Even if he was sure there wasn't anyone around to hear him.

Eli followed the trail noting the way the snow laid on the ground, bumpy from filling in tracks. He noticed bushes that had lost the snow off the branches from being rubbed against. Although new snow had fallen, there was a clear difference to Eli, which branches had been bumped and which had not. Eli decided he would have to be careful he didn't do the same thing and leave such an easy trail to follow—just in case.

Eli had followed the trail most of the day. It had started snowing about midafternoon but now it had picked up its pace. And the temperature was warmer too. It wouldn't be long and it would be raining as well.

Eli took his map out to see how far he was from Dead Mouse Mountain. He should reach the bypass late in the day tomorrow, if he kept traveling throughout the night. He wondered if dogs had night vision like he did.

So on he went, carefully checking for scents, tracks, broken branches, and fallen snow patches. Eli climbed trees once in a while to check his surroundings. He wasn't sure how far the dogs traveled or how long it would take to catch up to them but he was sure that he was on the right trail.

Sometime in the middle of the night the weather started to get really bad. As he was warned, it rained and snowed but it was the wind that caused the most problems for him. Eli started to experience difficulty following the trail. Even with his night vision it was difficult to see much further than a few feet in front of him. Eli was warm and dry within his coat but his paws were feeling pretty wet and cold.

Winter had said they were last seen at the Dead Mouse Mountain Bypass but he wondered if they were still there.

He came across a rock jutting out on one side making a sheltered area beneath it. Eli was tired and his body was aching so he decided it was time for a rest. He crawled beneath the rock grateful once again for the dry warmth of the coat he was wearing.

He slipped off his pack and curled up.

Eli dreamt he was running. He could hear voices; someone was after him. He tried to run faster but the voices were getting louder. He couldn't seem to move fast enough. It was as if he was running in slow motion then he jerked himself awake.

Eli glanced around himself, nothing looked familiar. He could hear deep low voices, two of them, talking to one another. Then he remembered where he was. He was snowed in under a rock with only a small opening to the outside.

It was daylight outside and judging from the brightness it was well into the day. The wind had died down quite a bit but there was still some blowing going on. Eli strained to listen to the voices. They were faint but getting louder. That meant only one thing; they were heading toward him.

Eli's body tensed. He positioned himself so he could leap out from under the rock if he needed to. Hopefully, they were cats and not dogs. And if they were dogs, maybe they would just pass him by. Eli listened carefully.

"I smelled something,
but my memory won't ring," one voice said.

"You don't smell it now?
'Cause you need a snowplow?" the other voice joked.

There were sniffing noises and some snorting. They were definitely not cats! They were getting closer.

"No, but give me a minute.
If I can pick it up again the snow won't limit." the voice, although delayed, answered anyway.

They were getting louder, easier to hear.

"What do you think it is Earl?
Do you think it's a squirrel?
I'm so hungry, I'd give a whirl eating a squirrel."

"I don't think so, but you never . . ."
The other voice cut him off,

"Can you believe the captain?
'Fetched a resident or I'll feed you plantain!'" the other voice had changed his to mimic someone else.

"Plantain! I might as well as suck on satin."

Eli could hear them making sniffing noises and rustling about.

They were right outside his rock. He didn't dare move. His hair stood up. He hoped they didn't find him. His heart started to pound. Eli closed his eyes and tried to make himself breath normal and quietly. His heart was beginning to pound so hard he could hear it in his own ears. Maybe if he could get himself to breathe normal it would calm his heart down. Could these creatures hear his heart pounding? Striker had. It was so loud.

"I got it! I got it! I'll have it in a minute split! Then we'll bring it to captain and he'll feed us a bit," the voice declared excitedly.

Suddenly, there was rustling, then rapid digging and then a big wet nose pushed its way under the rock. From that point on everything happened fast. Without thought he hissed. The creature yipped with glee and started digging again to get in to his hiding spot. The other creature made a joyful howling noise and joined in with the digging. They were going to get him! He couldn't stay here!

Eli saw a small opening off to the side of them, where the snow had dislodged from their digging. He bolted through it into the daylight. With lightning speed, he ran as fast as he could to escape the creatures.

The snow was cumbersome with a thin layer of ice over soft snow. The ice layer was thin but it mostly supported his weight. Every now and again he'd break through into the soft snow beneath but it didn't slow him too much. He just had to leap higher to get out. He could hear the creatures behind him were breaking through with every step.

Then he saw a bit of a trail where the snow had been slightly trampled. He took that hoping to gain speed and some distance from the creatures. It was still raining and snowing. He could hear barking and howling behind him. The creatures were chasing him and getting closer.

Eli didn't look back. He knew from seeing their noses and their digging paws that they were bigger than he was. Longer legs meant they could run faster through this icy snow.

He thought about climbing a tree to get out of their reach but maybe they would just follow him up and get him in the branches. Also he remembered Winter's warning. "Do not let yourself become treed. They will not let you be freed."

He was going to have to outrun them to escape and find safety.

Eli leaped snowdrifts running faster than he ever had. The trail he was on although icy, was getting easier to run on. The creatures behind him were getting closer.

Suddenly Eli found a burst of energy within himself and he ran faster than he thought was possible. The trees blurred by him, his eyes teary from the wind, snow, and rain. He was putting some distance between himself and the creatures. The trail was getting wider and more packed. Eli used that to his advantage, digging his claws in for more traction. It was working! The creatures were getting left behind. Eli saw an opening up a head, an escape route with options.

Eli put his head down and ran straight into it. The snow was icy, packed down here from many paws. Suddenly there were creatures in front of him. Eli slammed on his brakes. He slid while looking around for another route. There were strange creatures on both sides of him.

Everyone stopped what they were doing and stared at him. Using his claws to slide to a halt, Eli spun around looking for somewhere to go.

He was surrounded. He could hear the creatures he had left behind barking and howling as they were nearing. Frantically Eli looked for somewhere to go. Two was better than hundreds. Just as he was about to head back from where he came, the creatures broke into the clearing and slid on the icy path trying to come to a stop. Their tongues hung out the side of their mouths. Once they spotted Eli they jumped back into pursuit of him, never taking their eyes off him.

Just to the right side of them was an opening into the forest where no one stood. Some of the creatures saw where he was looking and moved to block him. Eli bolted into action, running for the opening hoping to outrun the strange creatures and escape back into the trees.

All at once the creatures all around him dropped what they were doing and leaped toward him, closing in on him. Eli saw jaws open, mouths snarling as they raced to catch him.

Suddenly there was a shadow overhead, a gust of wind and someone said, "No you don't. Let you go, I won't."

Eli

Out of the corner of his eye Eli saw a strange claw come down on him from above. With a blur of motion Eli was in the air and being held by some sort of powerful paw. It held on to him so tight it was hard to breathe.

As Eli was taken up into the sky, he looked down and saw that he had run straight into a huge camp. There were tents and creatures everywhere. Eli saw smoke coming from small campfires scattered here and there within the camp. Never in Eli's life had he seen so many strange creatures. These must be the dogs, he thought. Too many to count, he was going to have a guess.

Eli looked up at the creature that was holding him. No one had told him dogs could fly. Eli tried to wiggle free but the grip tightened making it even more impossible to breathe. This dog's grip was like iron, unbendable. It tightened some more. Eli couldn't breathe! Didn't the dog know it was holding him too tight? Feeling the breath being squeezed out of him Eli panicked. He fought to get free but the more he fought the tighter the flying dog squeezed. Eli began to see big black spots. Then from lack of oxygen Eli fainted.

Feeling the cat go limp in her clutches Ruby loosened her grip. It wouldn't be a good idea to deliver a dead cat.

Chapter 8

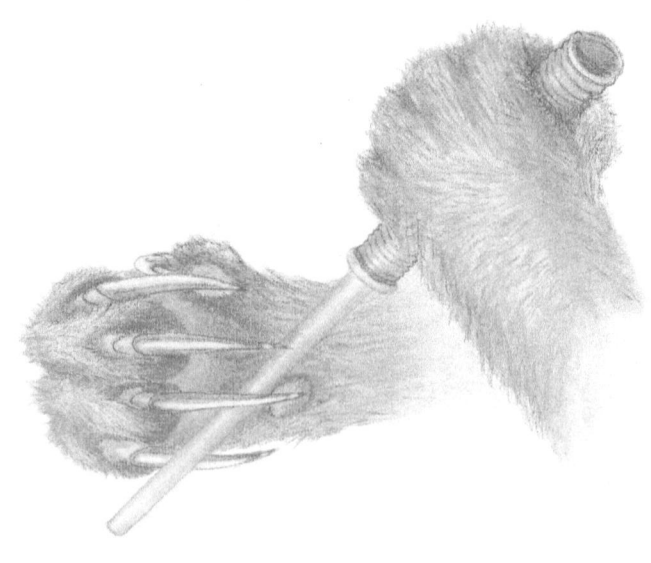

Samantha and Elliot had been traveling a day and a half. The path they were on was well traveled, which made it easier for them to go with some speed. Although it was snowing pretty heavily, they had run nearly the whole way stopping only for short rests under thick evergreens. They hoped to get help to Scratch as soon as possible. However, the weight of the situation caused them to travel mostly in silence.

Worriedly, they approached Whisker Creek when all of a sudden about half a dozen guard cats surrounded them. The cats all wore winter camouflage coats, which blended into the forest so well that neither of them had any warning that they were even there.

One cat stepped forward saying,
"Two young cats traveling alone,
neither should be here,
both should be at home."

He was blocking their way, not that Elliot or Samantha minded, they were both glad to see the guards. They were still shook up from what had happened the other day and for the first time they felt a bit of relief that they had reached some help.

Elliot spoke first,
"Sir, we seek Spring,
dire news we bring.
Our guide, appointed by Spring,
has been chased by some dreadful thing.

We don't know his fate,
nor where is his current state,
But Spring we trust,
and our hope is in the magistrate."

The guard cat sighed. He had the look of someone who had heard plenty of bad news, he replied.
"Kittens we are on the verge of war.
Sighting of beasts we hear galore.
By what lucky streak,
did you know to come to Whisker Creek?" he asked but then giving Elliot no time to respond he added,
"Never mind little scamp,
Rigger here, will take you to camp.

The officials will listen to the wiles of your tramps."

He turned to the guard on his right, gave him a slight nod, then stood tall on his hind paws and made some motions with his front paws. Silently all the guard cats disappeared into the brush including himself.

Rigger motioned with his head that indicated a "come-with-me" look. Elliot and Samantha followed him. Rigger didn't speak to them but he very quickly picked up his pace listening closely to make sure they were keeping up. They were half running and half walking for a couple of hours when they broke into a clearing.

It was a frozen marshy meadow with tall grass and snow that had been trampled down and cleared to accommodate the huge amount of tents. There were what seemed to be hundreds upon hundreds of cats and tents.

For the first time Rigger broke his silence.
"The officers' tent is this way,
they'll listen to what you have to say.
Keep close though, don't stray.
No one wants to listen to a lost kitten's bray."

He said the last part quieter, more to himself than to them. But they heard him and exchanged a lowered ear glance with one another.

They followed Rigger through the camp. Weaving around tents this way and that. There seemed to be no particular road or path to follow. Elliot wondered why they wouldn't just make a path to go straight there? He was tired of traveling.

Looking around he saw all the cats were wearing some sort of white camouflage. Males and females all dressed the same. Most were sitting around sharpening their metalized claws.

Metalized claws? Elliot and Samantha looked a little closer at the army cats' paws. Then they glanced at each other to see if the other one had noticed. Then they both checked out the paws again. Indeed all the army cats wore shiny silver metalized claws on their paws.

As they walked through the camp they saw the arm cats either sharpening their specialized claws or chewing on dried meat. In the distance there were groups of cats fighting each other in paw-to-paw combat. Throwing one another around. But those cats were a fair distance away and they couldn't get a good look at what they were doing.

Most of the cats they passed seemed relaxed although not too chatty. Some glanced their way upon their passing but none gave them a second look. Which was a little odd because cats were curious by nature and usually like to get a good look at anyone new.

Closer toward the middle of camp they came upon some tents larger than the rest. Rigger led them up to one of them. There was a guard cat posted at each of the tent doors. Rigger nodded to the guard at the tent they approached. He nodded back.

Then Rigger stated rather plainly, "Two kittens wandering, found not far from the Great Tree of Pondering. Say they've encountered a beast but they've made it here at least."

The guard nodded to Rigger and Rigger took his leave without so much as good-bye or so-long. Turning his attention to the kittens the guard said, "You may rest here, until Officer Hiss can give you an ear." He indicated to his left where a fluffy mat lay in the snow. Elliot and Samantha wasted no time curling up on it. They were so tired.

The guard made no motion of letting the occupants in the tent know that they were waiting outside. He just kept sitting there staring straight ahead.

They watched him for a bit, waiting to see when he would notify someone of their presence. When it became obvious he wasn't going to, Elliot spoke up,

"Excuse me, sir, I don't mean to irritate,
but how will they know we wait,
if you do not relate?"

Drawing a breath, the guard answered,
"No need to woe,
they already know," He answered without moving.

"Oh," Elliot said quietly then shrunk down into the fluffy mat. He wasn't going to ask "how" since he felt like he was disturbing the guard from doing something important; although he couldn't see what that might be. He let his eyes close to rest for a bit. His body was tired and achy from almost two days of running with little sleep.

After a while Samantha sleepily whispered, "Do you think he gets bored? It couldn't be a job anyone adored."

Elliot looked at the guard who was unmoving, except his ears. He moved them around listening to the various camp noises.

"I wouldn't want it.
Do nothing but sit?
Think I'd rather knit,
and I'd hate to knit," he whispered back just as sleepily.

Elliot wished he could see the army cats practicing their fighting. He could hear them off in the distance so he closed his eyes again and tried to imagine what they were doing with each sound he heard. He wished he could have watched more of that class back at the Monarch's Castle. Maybe he would join the Monarch's defenses so he could learn how to fight like they could. He always had so much fun play-fighting with his brother and sister.

"Officer Hiss will see you now." Both young cats jumped to their feet, wide-eyed looking around.

"Take it easy you're safe, I vow." The guard looked amused that he had scared them awake.

Elliot and Samantha looked at each other. When had they fallen asleep? Elliot couldn't remember doing so. The guard cat was standing and holding the tent door flap open for them. So they walked through into the dark interior.

Inside there was another guard who stood aside to let them pass. There was a number of cats all dressed in winter camouflage standing around a table located at the back. Their clothing was more formal than the guard cats they had seen so far. They wore medallions and patches of symbols on their shoulders and sleeves. Only the tips of their metalized claws could be seen, as they were not extracted. So it would be easy to miss that the army cats had specialized claws. There were also a number of tables and a few wooden chairs around. From here Elliot could see they were looking over a large map.

"Hello, I'm Officer Hiss.
How may I be of service?" Asked a voice to the right of them. Elliot and Samantha turned seeing a cat behind a desk in the corner with a couple of chairs in front. They went over and sat

down on the two chairs. The officer cat moved some papers aside then gave his attention to them.

Samantha started, "We seek Spring, sir.
The ranger he appoint"—she choked off then continued—"tragedy did occur." Then she choked off again.

Elliot seeing his sister struggling with her emotions spoke up, "We were on our way home, sir, accompanied by Scratch,
a retired old cat.

With our lunch laid out flat,
we heard from a long way off, a pit-a-pat.
Someone was coming, not a cat, we were sure of that.
So to be safe, my sister and I scat.
Hiding under a bush, we laid flat.
That's when we spied a most fearsome creature, more hideous than a rat.
It was big and brown, with huge teeth; it looked ready for combat.
    It said it was hungry and down it sat.
It ate our food! In two gulps, that was that!
It sniffed the air and looked our way; 'I want more,' out it spat.
    That was when Scratch screeched and ran like a hellcat.
This creature gave chase, like a noisy howling prat.
We waited for hours, but no return of that old cat.
    Finally, greatly distressed there at,
we came looking for Spring; a friend of our guide Scratch."

Officer Hiss sat back into his chair, looking at them he gently told them, "Well, I'm sorry to inform
but Spring isn't here.
He's away conjuring up a storm."

Officer Hiss let that information soak in before he added, "It is unlikely your friend survived this confrontation.
But tell me your location.
Where were you at when occurred this delation?"

He could see the hope rising on their faces. He knew they thought he was going to help them find their friend. He decided not to tell them otherwise.

"We were a little under halfway still,
from Purring City to Sphinxville."

Purring City? Did he hear that right? Wondered Officer Hiss.

"Sir, my worry sinks me like bog, could this creature be a dog?" Samantha's question broke into his thoughts.

Looking at her Officer Hiss answered, "Possibly little cat, but without seeing my guess is flat."

Sitting forward he asked, "If I showed you a map, do you think you could narrow the gap?"

"I think so. Yes I think I could show," Elliot said hope clearly in his tone. He'd do anything he could to help find Scratch.

Officer Hiss got up.

"Come with me, let us see," he said.

He led the kittens over to the table at the back where his fellow officers were.

As the kittens got close they could see a map of Catland with Xs marked down on various locations along the east side of Catland. Most were concentrated along the border about two-thirds of the way down. Elliot and Samantha got in close.

Looking at the small trail indicated from Purring City to Sphinxville Elliot put a paw up to a thickly bushed area he thought they had set up their camp. He glanced to Samantha for reassurance. She nodded her approval. Then looking to Officer Hiss he saw worry seep in on his face. Looking at his paw he realized there was no other Xs in the area. In fact, no Xs were this far inland. One of the officers reached over and placed an X where Elliot had indicted.

Elliot glanced around the table. All of the officers looked unhappy with this new information. Some looked angry, some looked worried, one cat caught Elliot's attention. He was standing back a bit from the table. A little more in the shadows, he was a big strong grey tabby cat but it was his cold features that made Elliot look twice at him. He wore no expression at all. He looked menacing.

"Well that's not good.
Not for our nationhood," Officer Hiss finally said.

"Kittens, I'm going to send you to the mess tent for some chow. I'll have Mistress Long-Tail tend your needs for now.
If I could spare a cat to see you home I would, I vow,
But in light of this infiltration going so deep,
unnecessary travel I cannot allow."

Officer Hiss looked to the guard at the tent door who nodded his head in acknowledgment.

Seeing they were about to be excused from the tent Samantha and Elliot both spoke at the same time.

Samantha blurted, "So you'll send rescuers to find Scratch? He's a bit old but he's from a good batch."

Elliot blurted out, "What about Eli?
What news does he supply?
These dogs he's scouting out,
has he discovered where they lie?"

Officer Hiss, taken back a little from their outburst, looked from one kitten to another sorting out who said what. "Wha...," he began to say but stopped looking directly at Elliot. He squinted his eyes and asked, "How do you know of Eli? Is there more you know or do I have to pry?"

Elliot suddenly felt all eyes on him. Officer Hiss looked annoyed.

"Eli's our brother,
He was sent by our father.
Tom of Sphinxville,
stationed at Lynx Hill.
Our father sent him locating dogs
then he's to report here; to this swamped out bog.
Spring knows this already.
His report would be heady.
Has Eli returned?
Will you tell me what have you learned?"

Understanding the connection now, Officer Hiss said, "Ah, so Eli is your brother,
that explains your bother.
We know Tom, we know your father.
Well there is no word from Eli yet.
But there's no need to fret.
Our scouts are informed and to him they'll get.
Now if you...," he began to say but Elliot cut him off.

"What do you mean 'No word from him yet'?
He should be here with a location set.
How else will Spring know,

where to give chase; where to go?"

Elliot was suddenly worried for Eli. It was bad enough Scratch was missing but what about Eli. Where was he? Why wasn't he here? Had he located the dogs? What if something happened to him? Questions filled his mind.

Officer Hiss was now openly annoyed, annoyed at being interrupted, annoyed at Tom for sending out his kittens, and most of all annoyed at the dogs for infiltrating Catland. These kittens had to go now. There was planning to be done.

"There are more cats than just Eli.
We have more than just one spy.
And we have a good idea of where the dogs lie.
Now on you we have to keep an eye.
As I said before, to the mess tent for a good fry."

With that Officer Hiss motioned to the guard at the tent. The guard came over saying, "Come with me, kitten, before you push your luck and get bitten."

"But, sir, what about Scratch? Will a team detach?" Samantha didn't move to follow the guard. She searched Officer Hiss's face looking for any sign he that would help find Scratch. He never looked all that friendly but now he wore a scowl, closing his eyes he turned his back on her. Looking at the map he began discussing plans with the other officers.

Samantha's heart sank. They weren't going to send anyone to find Scratch.

Slowly she followed Elliot and the guard cat out of the tent. He led them to the place Officer Hiss called the mess tent. Once they entered the guard cat found a female and introduced her as Mistress Long-Tail. Both kittens looked to see if indeed she had a long tail. They couldn't help themselves. Mistress Long-Tail must have been used to kittens checking out her backside because she turned slightly and waved her tail in front of them.

She did have a long tail but neither of them said anything about it because that would be rude. Besides everyone knew that long tails were better than short. Long tails helped to maintain one's balance when perched on precarious objects. Mistress Long-Tail quite likely had excellent balance.

Mistress Long-Tail took one look at the two of them then said,

"Well you two look beat,
Come with me, I'll get you some meat.
Then I have a place where you can get some sleep."

There was something about her that reminded Samantha of home. She didn't look like her mother but there was something mothering about her. Samantha relaxed for the first time in a couple of days, grateful to have Mistress Long-Tail take them into her care. She was hungry, tired, sore from all their running and after meeting Officer Hiss she felt like crying too.

She looked at Elliot, she knew from his expression he was worried for Scratch and now Eli. So was she but the difference was he looked like he may try to do something about it.

Chapter 9

Ruby flew over the encampment, circling it until she picked her location to land. She hoped the little cat she was holding was going to survive. It wouldn't be the first time she accidentally squeezed the life out of someone. She cringed at the thought of what they might do to her if she delivered it to them lifeless. Blasted canines! If they didn't have her heart in their clutches she'd destroy them all.

As she landed she held her front foot up so as not to put any weight on it. Once she had her three other feet securely down, she gently laid the cat on the ground. Curling her long neck around, she bent her nose over it and sniffed. Holding her breath she gently touched her sensitive nose against its body.

Good! She could feel its heart beating and there was breath in its lungs. She relaxed then lifting her head. She had just managed to get herself out of chains. She wasn't about to go back in.

"Well what do we have here? What gift is this, Ruby, my dear?" A voice said coming out of the big tent she landed beside.

Ruby looked at the big Mastiff dog. She had known him for a year. He was tolerable when things went his way but he turned mean and calculating the instant they didn't. Well actually, he was always calculating.

"It appears to be a resident, Captain, sir. Not much of one, that's to be sure."

Ruby nudged the cat carefully with her big clawed foot.

The cat groaned.

"Well let's take a look. Oh wouldn't he be delicious cooked? Too bad I need him alive. From where was he took?"

The captain bent over the little cat for a closer look and a sniff. It seemed to be in good form. No bleeding or twisted limbs indicating broken bones. Knowing Ruby it was likely bruised but that was nothing to him.

"He ran into camp with two troops on his tail. Lucky I was there or he'd be nothing but entrails. The boys frenzied to an unreasonable scale."

Seeing the little cat was slowly coming to, he stood and motioned to a couple of guards to come with a cage. Maybe this one would tell him what he needed to know.

Taking a few steps back he said, "It appears to be healthy enough. Although, I think you may have been a bit rough."

The captain gave Ruby one of his piercing stares. Most dogs cower when he looked at them that way. Ruby turned her head away not wanting the captain to see the worry in her eyes, nor wanting to challenge him. To the captain, turning away was a sign of submission. Something the captain seemed to thoroughly enjoy.

Eli could hear voices talking talking about him. He tried to open his eyes and get up but stumbled down again. He lay there trying to wake up. He felt some paws lift him. Then he was placed on something. He heard a clang. He tried again to open his eyes with success but everything was blurry. He blinked a few times trying to bring his surroundings into focus. Maybe he was in something.

He saw a large muscled creature talking to the big flying dog that had captured him. The muscled creature was probably a dog too. He wore some type of green clothing and had light brown hair all over his body but his face was black. Its eyes were golden and drew Eli to them. Eli had seen plenty of yellow eyes before but these were different. The pupils were circular and there was something about them that was intimidating.

Eli looked up at the flying dog. It was huge in comparison to himself and the muscled dog. It towered over both of them. But strangely, it seemed afraid of the muscled dog. It didn't wear any clothing and had neither fur nor hair. The weather did not seem to bother it. Its body was a deep red color, which shined in wetness from the snow and rain. It had powerful thick legs with strange paws. They looked more like Winter's or Spring's hands than they did paws. It also had a long tail, which frayed at the end. Its neck, very long led up to a long face with huge teeth. The only thing that looked the same between the two creatures was the teeth. Both had really big teeth.

The muscled dog bent down, peering into Eli's cage. Its golden eyes staring harshly at him. Eli decided the dog was ugly.

"Oh good, you're coming to and all nice and mellow. Tell me, from where did you come little fellow?" The dog's voice was low and smooth as honey.

Eli wasn't fooled by the sweet sounding voice. His menacing

eyes gave him away. He held the big ugly dog's gaze. The big dog licked his chomps and said silkily, "Don't worry, you'll tell me all I want to know. Two minutes with any of my troops and all your words will flow." He barked out a laugh and stood up.

Eli was petrified. What had he gotten himself into by running here? What a mistake! With his ears flattened, he laid as low as he possibly could, trying to make himself as flat to the floor as he could. He wished he could turn invisible. Eli didn't know what to do. The past events were all a blur. He looked around. The cage had bars on all four sides. There was nowhere he could hide. Only the top and bottom were solid.

The muscled dog and the flying dog continued talking with one another.

"The troops grow tired of dried food.
The way they frenzied speaks of their mood," Eli heard the flying dog say.

"This I know.
We'd be on the go
if it weren't for all this snow.
And you've said yourself there's nothing to hunt,
not even a doe.
But enough of this chatter!
Heal! We have a troll matter." The dogs walked away toward the largest tent Eli had ever seen. Two other dogs stood guard on either side of the tent's door.

Eli checked out his surroundings. He was in the middle of the huge camp. There were many dogs here, all wearing green coats. It was still snowing pretty heavily and the rain mixture from overnight had left an ice layer over everything. He could see dogs slipping and sliding as they walked.

Eli's cage was approached by a couple of big dogs. They lifted his cage and carried it a different direction from the big tent. There were a few other large tents but the one the flying dog and the muscled dog had walked into was the largest.

He watched the strangers through the bars. It seemed that dogs came in all shapes and sizes. Some were tall, some short, some lean and others completely bound with muscle. The only thing completely similar between them was their large toothy snouts and wet noses. All of them seemed busy but would stop what they were doing to stare at Eli as they passed by. One or two of them even licked their lips after seeing him. That gave Eli a very uneasy feeling.

Then Eli saw them. Trolls! There were trolls wandering about! The muscled dog was right! Eli wasn't sure if he had heard that correctly. They didn't seem bothered by the dogs at all. In fact they looked to be getting along with them! Scattered in various areas talking with the dogs in small groups. Eli was disgusted. How could this be? This was troll territory too. Why would the trolls be getting along with these dogs?

He was taken to a tent not too far from where the dog with wings had landed. More guard dogs were posted on either side of the tent opening. Eli saw that not all the tents had guard dogs, just a few of them. This one did. He was taken inside and set down beside a bunch of other cages.

Most of the cages were empty, but the one beside him had a cat in it. The cat was an orange tabby and looked to be in rough condition. He was lying on his side, his breathing labored. He looked to be asleep. On the other side of the cat, a few feet away was a large cage with a troll in it. Eli was surprised to see the troll caged. Considering the trolls outside seemed pretty content with the dogs' company. He wondered why this one was in a cage.

In between them was a small cage. Eli almost missed seeing it with the large troll catching his attention. The small cage had a bird in it, a grouse Eli figured. It was brown with some speckles throughout its body. One of its wings was hung down oddly.

Eli looked at the troll again.

The troll was in rough shape too. He looked to have been bitten and beaten. His clothes were torn and he had dried blood on them. One of his eyes was swollen shut and his hands looked swollen too. Eli looked a little closer at his hands. He had bite marks all over them and a finger or two seemed oddly bent. But this was the first time Eli had seen a real troll, maybe they were supposed to be that way.

Eli waited for the dogs to leave then he turned to the troll.

"Dare I ask what happened to you?
The trolls outside seem a friendly crew.

Yet here you are, all bloodied and blue."

"You know nothing stupid cat!
If I not caged, I make you splat." The troll turned his back to him.

Eli was taken aback by the troll's threat. He had never been threatened before today and never expected it from a fellow citizen. He suddenly remembered he had been taught trolls had a volatile temper and he should be careful around them.

Eli looked around the tent. He had to figure a way out of here. Like most tents it only had one door and the walls were sewn together to the floor. The wind outside was blowing the walls in and out making the room seem eerie and unstable. He didn't know what they intended to do to him but judging from the condition of everyone else here, it was going to hurt.

Eli took a closer look at the cage door. It didn't seem complicated. He reached over and gave it a little push to open it. It moved slightly but then stopped. There was something on the other side preventing it from opening.

The troll gave him a side-glance, snickered and turned away again when he saw Eli look at him.

Eli took a closer look at what was on the other side of the cage door. He saw a metal hooked item with a square bottom hanging through a loop of the cage. It was preventing the door from opening. Eli stuck his paw through the bars and lifted it a little. He could see an odd shaped hole in the center of the square part.

"It called a lock.
You never seen one?
What a shock," The troll said dryly.

Eli looked up to see the troll watching him. The cat beside him groaned then fell silent again.

"If you're so smart trollmen,
tell me, how does it open?" Eli asked.

"It require a key. The fact that you not know, say a lot to me."

Eli knew the troll was insulting him somehow but since the troll was right, he had never seen this mechanism before he didn't know what the insult was.

"Where is this key? Unlike you, I intend to flee," Eli informed him.

"Good luck with that. Guard's got it, little brat."

Eli got that insult.

Eli looked at the lock again. Just an odd shaped hole in the middle of the square part. Then extending his special claw, he looked it over. It was worn down some, likely from running on the ice earlier, but it was still a good size.

"Does the key go in here?" Eli put his claw into the odd shaped hole and felt around with it. He could feel various things in there. He pushed on something. Click. The lock popped open. "Ah-ha! Lookie here!" Eli beamed at the troll proudly.

The troll gasped, eyes wide he urgently whispered as loud as possible, "Undo my lock too! I know a way out! I will show you!"

Eli dropped the lock to the ground with a soft thud. Pushing the door open he quietly crept over to the wounded cat's cage first. "Pisst, hey can you wake up too? The troll here says he'll help us shoo."

The troll shook his head, "Not him! He too broken for travel. Just us or departing plan unravel."

"Everyone should be set free. I'd want to, if he were me." Eli grabbed his lock and stuck his claw into it. After wiggling it around for a bit. The lock clicked open.

The bird in the next cage fluttered its wings catching Eli's attention. Eli left it on the hook but moved over to the bird. The bird eyed him nervously.

"If I open your door,
you must remain rooted to the floor.
An escape route we'll quietly explore.
Understand, you're not allowed to soar."

The bird flapped its wings again and jumped toward the opposite side of the cage. It was clearly terrified and didn't trust Eli. Eli couldn't blame it since he knew cats ate birds. But he had no intentions of hurting this bird or eating it so he softened his tone.

"It's the quietness I implore.
If we rouse suspicion we'll face dogs galore.
Once we are all safe, you'll be free to soar.
My promise is to the core.
I don't want to see anyone's gore.

Will you agree or need I say more?" Eli asked the bird.

Eli could hear the birds rapid breathing. He sat down and watched the bird who was clearly weighing its options. Finally, the bird calmed down a bit, without saying anything it nodded its head in agreement.

Eli inserted his claw into the birds lock.
"Don't do it!
She not stay quiet.
She fly a fit.
She make a riot.
Birds are dumb.
To noisy ignorance, she succumb." The troll sounded desperate.

Eli checked the bird over. She was still at the far side of the cage watching his every move.
"She hasn't said a word yet.
I don't think we need to fret," Eli whispered to the troll.

He opened her lock with a click and laid it gently on the ground. He then walked over to the troll. The troll was most eager now.

Never being this close to a troll before, Eli looked up at him closely inspecting him. He could see how anxious the troll was. Suddenly he started doubting the troll's promise to help. There was something about the troll's behavior that made him stop.

Searching for some truth he asked,
"How do I know *you* won't give us away?
Your eagerness might mean you'll be the one to stray.
Besides, how will we escape with all these dogs in the way?"
"Oh I know way all right.
But don't get me wrong,
I do this out of spite."

Well that might be the truth but Eli still hesitated. There was something about the troll that didn't look trust-worthy. He looked . . . rough. Maybe nobody had ever been nice to him. He had scars and marks on his body from long ago that had healed but still showed. The new bites on him looked bad, they needed to be cleaned.

Eli remembered his mother cleaning a scratch he got as a kitten. She had stressed the importance of cleaning wounds so they wouldn't infect and fester. Perhaps this troll did want to help out of spite. "Judge by action, not attraction" was what he was taught, besides, what other choice was there?

"Hmmm, out of spite? I wonder what that might ignite." Eli pondered out loud as he lifted the lock to insert his claw.

"I'm free! I'm free! I'm free! Look at me! I'm free!" Suddenly the bird was flapping around in the tent awkwardly with her injured wing, squawking at the top of her voice. She was trying to find the opening.

Eli gasped! Just then two huge dogs ran into the tent. With the tent door open the bird flapped wildly over the dogs heads.

"I'm free! I'm free! I'm free!" One of the dogs jumped up trying to catch the bird in his jaws but he missed and she flew out of the tent and out of sight still squawking excitedly.

"What's going . . . you!" Spotting Eli by the troll's cage. One of the dogs growled at Eli. "Out that bird flew because of you!"

Eli immediately put his hair on end and arched his back. "Always make yourself look bigger. In the face of danger, fear you'll trigger." It was one of the very first lessons taught to all kittens. Eli backed up unaware that his jacket prevented them from seeing his hair standing on end. Only his tail looked poofy.

Slowly he maneuvered himself around the side of the troll's cage attempting to put it between him and the dogs. Both dogs had him in their sights now. Both dogs lowered their heads baring their teeth. The hair on their backs stood up. Very slowly they crept toward him. They did not look afraid of his size.

Eli hissed, "Stay away from me or sorry you'll be." The dogs did not seem bothered by his threatening hiss either. They crept closer. They really were big, Eli noticed.

"You know what that means?" the other dog growled. Eli stepped back further.

"We get to break your legs into smithereens!" The two dogs exchanged glances and then slowly separated one creeping one way around the cage and the other creeping the other way.

"I told you so. Birds are dumb. Now you know," the troll grumbled quietly to Eli.

Eli slowly backed up some more. He backed into a wall of

empty cages. With both dogs closing in on him there was nowhere left for him to go. So with one loud screeching hiss he leaped forward jumping on top of the troll's cage leaping again for the open tent door. But both dogs were anticipating this move and leaped toward him in unison.

The dogs being bigger had less distance to cover and they were fast, very fast. They had him in an instant. The dog on his right snapped his jaws around Eli's neck, front leg and chest. The other dog got the opposite side, back leg, and tail. Eli howled in pain as the dogs' teeth closed down on him.

Eli attempted to free himself by swinging his free front paw around and digging his claws into the neck of the dog on his right. He also simultaneously brought up his free back leg sinking his claws into the other side of his face. The dog let out a whelping cry but did not let go.

Just then more dogs rushed in. Eli couldn't see how many as his eyes were watering. He was being pulled tight from both dogs who jumped off the troll's cage together.

"Don't damage him! Or your own survival will be slim," a voice warned the dogs.

Eli dug his claws further into the dogs face in a vain attempt to be freed. The dog on his right gripped tighter with his teeth and let out a warning growl not to do that again. Eli didn't know the dog was using every ounce of self-control not to rip him apart. The pain in his face was searing and anger filled the dog.

"You better put him back in here. Then go see the medic, those scratches look severe," the voice said.

Eli was hurled viciously back into his cage by the two dogs. He hit the back of the cage so hard it tipped the cage up a bit before dropping to the ground with a thud. Eli was too stunned to move. The cage door was slammed shut and the lock replaced.

"Oh he got you good, Rad. Those scratches are bad," the other dog said.

The dog named Rad glared at Eli. Baring his teeth he growled, "You're lucky to be alive. Next time you won't survive." There was blood running down his face and neck. Eli's claws had gone deep into his flesh. It was likely the dog's face would be scarred.

"I warned you.

Now shoo," Eli replied defiantly.

Rad instantly lost control of his rage. He dove at the cage attacking the door with all his force. Snarling he viciously tried to rip the cage apart with his teeth. Eli watched in horror as blood mixed with saliva and froth from the dog's mouth went flying toward him. Seeing he was getting nowhere, Rad let go of the cage door and flew round to the backside where Eli was. Eli scrambled out of reach.

The other dogs surrounded Rad. Working their way between him and the cage. They gently forced him away from the cage. Using calm tones and rational protocol on how he had to submit or face his superiors, they managed to calm him down. Reluctantly, he backed away, although, fury still gleamed in his eyes.

Eli was shocked at the dog's response to his snide remark and decided from now on he'd try to keep his mouth shut.

As most of the dogs escorted Rad out of the tent, one of the dogs turned back to Eli.

Walking over he said almost in pity, "Foolish little cat, you may pay harshly for that."

He stood there for a moment or two just looking at Eli. Then he turned and said to two dogs still remaining.

"Guard him from in here. We don't need another fiasco to appear." He then left the tent.

One of the remaining guard dogs was the same one who had caught Eli on his left side but a new dog had taken Rad's place. The two dogs took up positions on either side of the tent door, sitting down at first, then lying down to a more comfortable position. Eli wondered how long it would take for them to fall asleep.

Eli gingerly moved his limbs beneath him. Silently checking his injuries. He was very sore where the dogs' teeth had grabbed him but remarkably there were no broken bones. There was some blood and bruising though, lots and lots of bruises. And his new jacket was torn! His brand new jacket torn from dogteeth, now Eli was really upset. But no matter how much he wanted to cry, Eli would not let himself make a sound.

Chapter 10

After what seemed like hours and hours the orange cat next to Eli began to stir. Outside the tent the wind had picked up. The top of the tent began to sag from the weight of the ice-snow forming on it. But then the wind would blow knocking clumps of snow off. The dogs had long since fallen asleep, but it was a light sleep as they woke easily to the sounds outside.

As the cat became conscience he began to moan with each of his movements. He clearly had broken bones but Eli didn't know which ones. The dogs lifted their heads to watch the cat as he came to. Once the cat was fully awake, he realized he wasn't alone and fell silent.

Eli watched him get himself into a position that didn't hurt too badly and check out his surroundings. Then he looked at Eli. Both cats gasped.

The orange cat was missing an eye. It looked like an old wound but it was grossly scarred with a hole where the eye should have been.

The cat looked like he recognized Eli but then he narrowed his one eye as if he was suddenly angry at Eli. Eli wondered if the pain was making him mad. He knew now that the orange cat was awake; he wouldn't voice his pain again if he could help it. Everyone knew voicing pain showed weakness to the enemy and enemies were not nice. They would just hurt you more.

The cat looked around some more, when he saw the troll he stopped. The troll fidgeted under his gaze. From behind, Eli saw the orange cat's ears flatten then after a moment or two of what Eli could only guess was some serious staring, the cat decided to look away without saying anything. Gently repositioning himself again the cat turned to Eli and in a low quiet growl he asked,

"Where is your sister?
I told you to hide mister!
Now you're here?!
I swear, if this isn't a twister . . ." Then as if a tap of anger was turned on the orange cat let his anger pour out all over Eli.

"What were you thinking?
Have you even an inkling?
All my trouble for your safekeeping,
all gone, all undone, all wasted, everything for nothing!

Eli

The chasing, the capturing, the questioning, the beating, the wreathing, the screaming, all this is mind sweeping.
And here you are,
just sitting there unblinking, unspeaking, and most of all unthinking!"

Eli stared at him. His mouth hung open. Confused.

Grumbling to himself the orange cat turned his head away and quietly started muttering, "Wretched kittens, each one is brow-bitten, and they never listen. So glad I never had a litter, I'd never stop being a spitter, just the thought makes me jitter, what was he thinking making me a sitter, never in my life have I ever been a hitter but I think now I could be a committer . . ."

Eli didn't know what to make of the orange cat. Clearly he was a mad cat. Eli wondered if he still had all of his senses, maybe some got out from that hole where his eye use to be. In spite of his injuries he had a lot to say.

Licking his lips, he shyly interrupting the cat's mumbling, "Excuse me, mister, you know my sister?"

"Know your sister? What are you a trickster?
Or did you hit your head you foolish little inbred,
come closer so I can see where you've bled."

"I didn't hit my head and I'm definitely not an inbred.
My name is Eli, I don't know what information you've been fed but clearly you've been misled. Or maybe it's you who's hit his head."

"Elliot why . . . wait, did you say Eli?" The orange cat looked Eli over from head to tail.

"Oh. Mistake you for your brother did I?
Well, suppose that could happen to a cat with one eye.
You both look the same, don't deny.
Been roughed up some, I spy.
You all right? You can tell me but don't you cry."

Eli looked over at the guard dogs who were listening intently. He didn't want to talk about what happened.

"You know Elliot too?
How do you know those two?
Tell me, did they accomplish what they set out to do?"

The orange cat shook his head in disbelief. Where was his

head? He had already said too much.
  Ignoring Eli's question he said,
"So you're not who I thought you were,
Well that's slightly better than a burr in my fur,
but not for you, that's for sure.
  What was your father thinking sending you here to rot?
Of course you're caught.
Now I'm going to have to plot."
  The orange cat got up, aiming toward his cage door but grunted and lay down again.
  "Rats, Bats," he cursed unable to mask the pain he was in.
  The guard dog who had replaced Rad snickered. Eli could hear the crunching sounds of someone approaching on the ice-snow. Then both dogs suddenly alert, stood up, also listening to whoever was coming this way. A few moments later the tent door opened blowing in icy snow and four snowy dog soldiers.
  "Captain's ordered prisoner interrogation," one dog announced. "Hope you like intimidation," the dog said to Eli as all four dogs approached his cage.
  Picking up Eli's cage they walked out into the blizzard.
  The one guard dog who had snickered followed quietly behind.

Chapter 11

Elliot and Samantha woke to the smell of food cooking in the kitchen. A small spot had been cleared in the back for them with beds made up. Mistress Long-Tail explained there weren't very many spare tents left and what there was, was needed for the troops. It was a secluded little spot, which gave them some privacy and since the kitchen was one of the warmest tents around with all the food they could eat, neither of them minded at all.

They had been in the camp for a couple of days now and they each had been given chores to do to pay for their keep. The kittens did them cheerfully, as there were many benefits to being part of the kitchen staff.

Aside from all the food, they got to hear parts of conversations from the soldiers as they cleared tables and wiped up messes. They learned much of what was going on with the dogs and some of the plans of escorting the dogs out of Catland.

They also learned that there was a blacksmith on sight who kept a pot of molten metal available for the soldiers to dip their claws into. This is how their claws were metalized. Since claws were always growing, they had to keep up with periodic dipping.

Unfortunately for Elliot and Samantha though, they weren't allowed to metalize their claws because the metal was saved for only the Monarch's army.

Elliot became fascinated with the troops and started looking for opportunities to ask them about their jobs or training. Some of the soldiers took time for Elliot but most were preoccupied with current affairs. It seemed some big plans were under way.

Elliot and Samantha learned that Winter and Spring had stopped the dogs in their tracks. They knew the location and it was just a matter of time before they would push the dogs out of sacred Catland. It seemed like they were waiting for something though.

Elliot wondered how the dogs got into Catland and how were they going to get them out.

Elliot and Samantha still hadn't heard from Eli. No one had. Both kittens were sick with worry for him and for Scratch. Eli should have been here by now. But the more they asked about him or Scratch, the grimmer the faces became until they stopped asking.

"Rise and shine young ones.

We got mouths to feed and battles to be won."

Samantha and Elliot woke one morning to Mistress Long-Tail bustling around in the kitchen with her kitchen staff coming in to prepare breakfast for the soldiers.

"Today is the day,
they go on a dog hunt.
Many may stray,
if they do not confront."

Samantha and Elliot jumped out of bed and started helping with the breakfast routine. Excitement combined with nervous anxiety was in the air. Everyone could feel it.

"How are they going to do it? I'd like to help, I admit," Samantha asked Mistress Long-Tail as she placed full containers onto the buffet table. Soldiers were pouring in and filling their plates with breakfast. Within minutes the mess tent was a loud racket of chatting and clanging of dishes.

"You're helping them right now, dearie.
Without a big healthy breakfast, they would grow weary.
A weary cat may go splat, and the thought of that is far too dreary," Mistress Long-Tail answered.

Samantha wasn't really satisfied with that answer but she continued to help by filling empty containers with fresh cooked food or taking dirty dishes handed in by the soldiers and stacking them by the sinks to be washed. After a while she looked around and noticed many of the soldiers had finished and had left. With empty spots increasing at the tables, she looked for Elliot. He usually was out there mingling with the soldiers and cleaning messes made. But she couldn't see him. He was missing. Growling to herself she muttered,

"Just like him, I'm stuck in here cooking
and he ducks out when no one's looking."

Elliot decided to quietly follow some soldiers that had finished their breakfast. He had to help somehow. Not knowing what happened to Eli and Scratch was all he could think about. Kitchen duty was fine but he wasn't getting any answers to what happened to Eli or Scratch. And he couldn't stand it any longer, there had to be something he could do to help find them or maybe he should just go find them himself.

He watched the soldiers pack from a distance. He didn't want them to send him back to the kitchen so maybe if they didn't notice him it would be okay. Although it was snowing and he was leaving tracks, no one paid him any attention. It didn't really take them very long to gather their gear. They didn't seem to need much. Once they were ready, they headed to a large field at the west side of the camp by the creek. Elliot continued to follow, making every effort to be unobserved. He crouched near some large barrels and watched as they got into their respective groups.

There seemed to be a commander of some title with every group discussing plans and giving orders.

Suddenly from behind a gruff voice said, "What are you doing here? State your intentions clear!"

Elliot sprang into the air landing several feet away from the voice that startled him. Turning around he saw the large grey tabby cat from the officer's tent from the first day they arrived. He looked just a menacing now as he did then. Elliot saw he had a number of badges on his coat signifying he was a major. Elliot had learned the ranks from the soldiers in the mess tent and knew the Major Cat recognized him too. The major wasn't the ultimate cat in command but he was up there with the Lieutenant-Colonel Cat.

"Admiring the hard work, sir!
They're like *ants* all a stir;
preparing for a sugar march.
Gearing up, to taste some sweet action for sure!" Elliot sounded overly excited and unsure of himself at the same time. He felt like he had been caught with his paw in the cookie jar. He slinked down a little, under the major's scrutinizing gaze.

The Major Cat stared at him quietly for a moment or two. Elliot hoped he wouldn't send him back to the kitchen. Then as if sensing Elliot's reluctance to go back, he said, "Make yourself useful, gather that gear." The Major Cat motioned to an area where gear was being loaded into a sleigh. Elliot breathed a sigh of relief. "And put on a jacket! You'll find one in the rear."

He then walked away, with his tail down, twitching slightly at the end, indicating he was irritated or anxious about something, maybe both.

Elliot ran over to the cats loading the gear. He told them what the Major Cat said. They accepted his help with a nod.

Grabbing a small jacket out of one of the duffle bags in the sleigh, one of the cats introduced himself, "I'm Jack, this should fit and you can start by loading that sack."

Elliot put on the jacket. It was one of the older green army jackets, a little stiff and it smelled funny but now he looked like he belonged. It was water proof too Elliot noticed. He liked that. Elliot was quite pleased with this new job.

There were quite a few sacks lying around, ready to be loaded. He grabbed one, it was heavily loaded with blankets. He looked at the sleigh, which was actually a small cart on skis. It still had its wheels only they were attached to the skis with a rope in front and a rope behind securing it in place.

The walls were over his head so he heaved it with all his strength. It hit the far wall and dropped spilling some of the contents on the sleigh's floor. He grabbed the next one and heaved ho with the same result. This was fun.

"Whoa, wait up, wait up young fellow,
too much zeal, you need to mellow."

"Like this, see?" Jack picked up a sack, lifted it high and carefully set it down over the side checking to make sure it was secure in its location. "Nice and careful, gentle as can be."

"Sure thing, boss, watch this toss." Elliot picked up another bag. Even though it was tied shut, he could smell it was filled with dried meat. Since the walls were still over his head, he swung with all his might to get it over the edge, but instead of letting go he waited until it banged on the other side of the wall then he let it drop to the floor with a plop.

"Umm, still a little rough.
How about you get in and I'll hand you stuff."

"Okay, anything you say.
I'll do what I can to make your day," Elliot said smiling. He was just so happy to be out of the kitchen and doing something with the soldiers.

Jack wasn't so sure he wanted Elliot to make his day but the kitten sure was eager to please so he let it go. Together and with the help of the other soldiers assigned to packing, they loaded three sleighs.

One was full of food and medical supplies. Another filled primarily with ropes and chains. The last had a combination of supplies such as bedding, tents, and items that may be needed on the battlefield.

Each sleigh was rigged with harnesses for eight cats to pull. The harnesses were simple in design fitted with soft wide leather around the cats' chest and back for pulling and a soft wide strap around the rump for stopping.

Stopping could be very tricky especially if they were heading down a hill. Cats' claws were useless in stopping because of their curved design whether or not they were metalized, so the sleighs had a braking mechanism. However, the brakes could only be applied from within the sleigh. So either a cat was quick to jump in and apply the brakes or ride along. Unfortunately, the harnessed cats tended to resent other cats getting a free ride from them so unless a cat was injured, the braking cat almost always walked along side and jumped in when needed.

Elliot was slender and a little shorter because he wasn't completely grown so he was selected to be a brake cat. Elliot was thrilled with this new job. Now he could go with the soldiers and look for Eli and Scratch.

A high-pitched whistle was blown. Elliot looked out over the field. There were hundreds of groups of soldiers; each lined up in blocks of Elliot guessed twenty cats. The blocks of cats then were lined up with each other spanning across the field giving it a huge tiled look. Except, the cats wore white camouflage coats which was more like a bunch of tiled floating heads, paws, and tails out there. A little freaky Elliot thought.

The snow falling was nearly stopped. Just the odd snowflake fell now so they were off to a good start. When the whistle stopped blowing the soldiers began their march. Although it was still overcast, Elliot noticed the clouds were even darker over the mountains in the direction they were heading.

The cat army took a trail heading east. Of course the trail was too narrow to accommodate such a large volume of cats marching in a row so they headed out two columns at a time. Starting with the two columns on the far right side of the field. Once the last row passed the first row, the second set of two followed behind the first. This was how every section of soldiers left the field. Elliot had never seen anything like this march. And in spite of the large number marching, there was very little noise coming from them.

Once the last row of cats left, the three sleighs followed behind. Elliot was so excited to be marching with the soldiers; he had butterflies in his stomach or at least that's what he had heard that funny feeling in the pit of your tummy was called. He didn't think there were any real butterflies in his stomach, as he hadn't eaten any in a long time.

Elliot didn't know he was being watched. Outside the mess tent stood Samantha, Mistress Long-Tail, and the rest of the kitchen staff watching the soldiers go off to war. Other cats who were not part of the march were watching too.

Samantha glowered at Elliot. He never came back to tell her he was leaving. He didn't even look back, not even once. Samantha watched them go. Once the army was well on their way, the cats left behind started to head indoors. Samantha didn't. She just stood there.

Mistress Long-Tail gave Samantha a sympathizing gaze as she turned to head in. She could tell Samantha was upset.

She put her paw on Samantha's shoulder as she passed her by, "He'll be all right. You'll see. He'll return from this plight."

Samantha ignored her. She was so angry, too angry to even spit. So she said nothing. Even after the last sleigh was long gone she just stood there. After quite some time Samantha couldn't ignore the cold any longer, she was shivering. She turned and joined the others inside the warm mess tent.

Elliot was enjoying the march through the forest even if it was a bit of a struggle for the harness cats. He could keep a sharp look out for either Eli or Scratch in the forest as they traveled the trail. Of course, coming among the last in a large group like this meant, it was unlikely he'd be first to spot them but he'd try anyway.

Elliot noticed the two by two marching cats kept the exact same distance from each other as the skis on the sleigh. Elliot wondered if this was on purpose. He suspected it made it easier for the harness cats to pull with two definitive tracks to follow.

It didn't occur to him until they were well on their way that he should have let Samantha know he was leaving with the army. He completely forgot about her. Now he felt bad but there was little he could do at this point. He hoped she wouldn't be too mad at him.

Elliot's sleigh was in the middle. It was a good spot. He could watch and learn from the brake cat ahead of him when to jump in to apply the brakes. And he had the security of having a few others behind in case there was a sneak attack. Now he was beginning to get the hang of how to apply the brakes.

At first he would hit the brakes too hard causing the sleigh to stop suddenly. That angered the harness cats, both his and the ones behind him. Not to mention, it stopped the procession and jostled the loads. Next he didn't apply them hard enough causing his harness cats to run off the track to avoid hitting the sleigh in front and being run over.

After that, he'd hit the brakes too hard again, jerking them to a stop. They were all really furious with him. One even talked about having him fired but stopped when he saw the fear in Elliot's eyes.

Elliot couldn't believe they would actually set him on fire but he promised and promised and promised that he wouldn't do it again (even though he did two more times). Now he knew how to apply the brakes slowly to get the correct braking speed. Not too hard, not too soft, just keep the sleigh at an even pace with the march.

They travelled up and down hills but mostly it was uphill as they were heading into the mountains. As they continued on the weather began to change. The light small snowflakes became heavier and bigger sized. A wind blew in just a light breeze to start. The clouds overhead were dark and appeared darker still ahead. Elliot sensed they were heading toward a snowstorm. He hadn't experienced a snowstorm before and he had the feeling he wasn't going to like it. But he was with the monarch's army of cats so he wasn't worried.

They travelled all day like this with the weather increasingly getting worse. Small gusts of wind would blow causing the snow to twirl. At times getting into their eyes making it difficult to see. The mountains on either side of them slowly became taller, seemingly closing in around them as they gained ground.

Jack and Elliot talked quietly on and off along the way, well

Jack mostly just instructed. Elliot learned they were heading toward Claw Canyon and they wouldn't stop until they got there. Except they would take short breaks to rest, but no unpacking. Only a couple times was food handed out from the sleighs. As day turned into evening and evening turned into night they trudged on. The mountains got taller and the valleys they travelled in got narrower.

Elliot didn't mind traveling with little breaks but he was pretty tired now. So were the harness cats he noticed. Secretly, he was glad he didn't have their job. They traveled all through the night and into the dawn with the wind and snow picking up. It was really beginning to take a toll on them. Elliot wondered if Winter and Spring knew they were on their way because it sure seemed like they didn't.

About an hour after Sun got up (not that anyone saw him through the clouds) many of the army cats took off at a run. Heading straight ahead up the trail into the blowing snow. Elliot looked to Jack alarmed!

"No worries, little buddy.
They haven't fled.
Claw Canyon's up ahead.
It's known to be a bit muddy.
Maybe in this weather just rutty,
but they're headed there to make up a bed." Jack reassured Elliot.

Elliot sighed in relief. Ooh a bed would be nice. He'd run up ahead too if he could.

After quite a while they broke into a clearing. There was a little stream, half frozen in, flowing along the side of a steep mountain face. Rock stretched straight up from the stream to the top of the mountain. It had three large gouges in it like a huge paw had clawed it from the top down. The mountain on the other side also had a huge rock face reaching up to the top but this side a nice meadow part. Although covered in snow, they could easily camp on it.

The troops had cleared an area for the sleighs to park near the center of camp and were pitching tiny white round tents in the snowy meadow. Elliot noticed the placement of the little tents gave the camp a sort of triangle shape. With the snow falling heavily and the wind blowing in short but powerful gusts, the little white dome tents made the meadow look bumpy but otherwise blended into snowdrifts—a perfect camouflage should it be needed.

Once the sleighs were parked (and the parking brake set), the harness cats immediately unharnessed themselves and went to work. First fires were made, then food was pulled from the sleighs and heated up. Large pots melted snow into hot water. A long table was set up and the army cats lined up anxious to receive their hot meal.

Elliot assisted with the unloading and helped the cooking cats anyway he could, fetching items as they were needed. He was fed his portion from behind the table not having to stand in line. He was also provided a drink of hot water to warm his insides. It worked really well. The army cats ate anywhere they happened to be. Often just stepping out of line long enough to devour their food.

Jack told him, "The greatest benefit to being a pack cat, is not having to wait, to eat from the sack."

Once Elliot had finished eating his hard-boiled egg and delicious heated canned meat, Jack showed him a small tent set up for him and Jack to share by their sleigh. Jack told him to go ahead and get some rest. He and the others would clean up the mess.

Elliot eagerly crawled into the little white dome. Inside was a blanket to curl up on. Outside the sound of wind blowing lulled Elliot to sleep.

Chapter 12

Eli was taken to the large tent the flying dog and the ugly dog had disappeared into upon his capture. The wind blew the tent walls in and out with each gust. But the tent held firm. As soon as he entered the tent, the pungent smell of dog and troll body odor filled his nostrils.

Inside, curtains were hung in a row parallel to the left side of the tent to provide some privacy in four makeshift rooms. Along the right side was one long horizontal curtain dividing the tent in half creating two large rooms. The huge flying dog was in the first large room open to the tent door. A number of large trolls were there as well engaged in a heated conversation with the ugly dog.

Eli was carried down the center hallway to the third makeshift room on the left. Just before turning into the room Eli saw a number of dogs in the second large room guarding some shiny bright stuff and what appeared to be a huge green glowing egg set on a very long table. The scent of something delicious also emanated from the table but it conflicted with the scent of something rotting, which as they turned to enter the third room, seemed to be coming from the fourth makeshift room.

A curtain was drawn behind him in the small makeshift room and he was set on the floor between two long poles near the back of the room. The five dogs that brought him in remained, talking about him quietly. The guard dog who followed behind from the other tent informed them of the conversation Eli had with the orange cat. Since none of them were saying anything nice Eli closed his eyes and tried to think of something happy, like home, and warm milk with fish.

Eli heard and smelled a dog come into the makeshift room and approach his cage. He opened his eyes to see an old, thick-skinned, grey-faced, pug-nosed dog peering in at him. This dog's odor smelled stronger than the other dogs. None of the dogs smelled good but this one had a really bad scent, like he had been wallowing in a stale, manure-filled, slime-infested swamp. He also had old scars on his body round his chest and neck. Clearly bite marks.

Circling and sniffing through the bars the dog opened his mouth to speak; a long string of drool fell from either side of his cheeks.

"Hmm, you're just a little speck,
and look at that scrawny little neck.
We'll have to take care it don't get wrecked,
but I got something to fit a little dreck.
You stay here while I go check."

He licked his cheeks to wipe the drool but instead caused saliva to splatter in all directions. Eli cringed away in an attempt to avoid getting dog spit on him. But a few splatters still managed to hit him through the bars just before the dog turned to walk away.

The stinky slobbery dog went to a box sitting by the entrance of the makeshift room. He dug around in it making all sorts of clanging noises. Then he held up a small iron ring with a loop on the side. Eli couldn't see how he did it but suddenly the iron ring sprang open from a hinge set beside the loop. Walking back to Eli's cage he took a cable that was hanging from above the cage and snapped it on to the loop of the iron ring.

"Okay, boys, it's show time,
and missing this show would be a crime." The stinky slobbery dog announced.

Before Eli knew what was going on all the dogs surrounded the cage. The cage door was opened and four of the dogs including the stinky slobbery one had their paws on him. Panic and fear seized him.

Eli fought with every ounce of strength he had. Hissing, spitting and scratching for all he was worth. Clink! The iron ring was around his neck and the cage was pulled out from behind him.

The dogs quickly backed off but Eli continued to fight. Twisting this way and that. Only now he wasn't fighting the dogs he was fighting the ring around his neck and the cable. Eli jumped high in various directions trying to get away. But all his fighting was only causing him to choke and to swing violently back and forth.

Eli stopped, trying to get a grip on the situation; he looked up. The ring around his neck was attached to the cable that ran up to a pole connecting the two side poles together. He was tethered. But he could touch the ground so he pulled back from the ring on his neck as hard as he could but it wouldn't come off. It was on tight.

All the dogs were watching him from a safe distance with

great amusement. They were all much bigger than he. He couldn't let them touch him again; there was no telling what they might do to him.

Eli looked at the structure holding him again. There was nowhere he could go. It was too strong for him to break. Then Eli got an idea. With a huge leap Eli jumped toward one pole landing two thirds of the way up. Without stopping he climbed to the top. He walked along the top to the center where the cable was fastened, crouching down there to rest and catch his breath. His body really hurt. But now he was a safe distance from the dogs, and bonus! He could see over the curtain walls!

"Well I didn't expect that," said the stinky slobbery dog. "Guess I should have, considering it's a cat."

Eli was pretty close to the tent ceiling. It blew violently in and out from the powerful gusts of wind outside. Eli could see the stitches holding the panels together, stretching; but they looked strong and didn't look to be fraying.

Whatever was rotting in the last makeshift room smelled even worse from up here.

The guard dog who had followed them here stood up.

"I am so glad I am not you.
I don't know what you're going to do,
but I no longer want to be seen with this crew." He turned and left the makeshift room.

"I'll get him down," the stinky slobbery dog said to the remaining dogs, "if my name isn't Chopper Brown." He stood up; slowly walking closer he eyed the cable that hung down in a loop.

Eli seeing what he was looking at, reached down and gently pulled the cable up out of the dogs reach.

"Good one, Chopper.
You never could have reached it,
you're not a good hopper." One of the four dogs chided the stinky slobbery dog Chopper.

"Well, if that don't beat the bush.
Fine! Stay there for now little puss.
It's a matter of time before I give you a push." The stinky slobbery Chopper glared at Eli.

"What are you going to do?

If captain finds out, it will be Chopper stew." Another dog asked Chopper.

"I think, Chopper Brown, you're going to have to chop-her-down," Said another dog.

"No no and ruin my . . ."

Just then before Chopper could finish his sentence a big gust of wind picked up the massive tent's opposite side causing the straps holding it in place to pull free. The front corner by the entrance collapsed inward. Dogs in that area were buried beneath the collapsed tent. Others ran toward it in efforts to fix it, including the dogs with Eli. Eli could hear dogs scrambling beneath the fallen tent ceiling trying to free themselves.

Barking and yelling filled the air both from within the tent and from the outside. The wind continued to howl and blow, shaking the tent violently, threatening to take down yet another side of the tent. Eli dug his claws deeply into the pole to steady himself.

Then Eli saw the huge flying dog stand up, spread her wings and stick out her neck to hold the tent up for the little dogs. In spite of the fierce wind outside, Eli could see the dogs would be successful in restoring the tent structure with that big flying dog helping. It was now or never if he were going to escape.

Eli braced himself with his back paws and felt around the iron ring with his front. He had to find out how it opened. The iron ring was fairly smooth all around, and fairly thick. No levers or buttons on it that he could feel. There was a small hole by the part that latched together on the opposite side from the loop and hinge. Eli wondered if it was like the keyhole on the cage. But he couldn't see it. It felt circular in shape and was placed squarely in the center beside the latching part. That made it very awkward to insert his claw into.

Eli took a quick look at his front claws, they were all worn down some from all that running on ice but still had a nice curve, unfortunately, too curved to get them into this hole. Eli looked around for something he could poke into the hole. There was nothing. He looked behind himself then noticed his back claws dug into the post. They weren't as curved, they were thicker and shorter from all the running on ice too. But they might do. Eli switched his bracing paws to free up a back paw.

The wind howled fiercely again shaking the tent once more. Eli grabbed the post with all four paws. It seemed the entire structure might collapse if the wind continued on this way. Eli suddenly realized Winter was doing this on purpose. Maybe Winter didn't know he was in here. He had to get out.

He carefully moved the ring around his neck so the hole would be more accessible by his back leg. Then Eli extended one of his back claws and slid it around on the ring trying to find the little hole through touch. Where was it? He slid his paw this way and that searching. Then he found it!

Just then a huge gust of wind picked up the tent on his side causing it to lift up and cave in on top of him. The structure he was on tipped sideways. Eli was thrown down with the tent ceiling collapsing all around him. The structure didn't fall though; it rocked back into place jolting Eli off his paws by the cord attached to the top. Eli swung by his neck. The cord was caught around a bolt at the top taking several inches away from the ground. Eli could only stand on his back paws.

This was not good. The loop was now at the back of Eli's neck meaning the little hole was in the front under his chin. There was no way he could get his back claw into it now. Eli had to somehow turn the ring again.

Dogs barked orders and raced about inside the tent and out. The huge flying dog moved to the center of the tent to support the weight of the newly collapsed side. Although this did lift part of the tent ceiling off the structure, it did not lift all of it.

Eli smelled the stinky slobbery dog make his way into the fallen saggy room. Eli spun on his back paws to glare at him.

"Oh good! I see you're down.
And I'm glad to see you're hanging around.
That's a relief for me 'cause I'd hate to see the captain frown."

Chopper trotted over to give Eli a slobbery sniff. Eli hissed at him in warning not to get too close. He stopped. Chopper looked unusually cheerful given the circumstances.

"Hint taken," he said.
"Just didn't want you think'n you been forsaken."

Chopper left then probably to go help right the tent. Eli didn't really care as long as he just left.

Hanging by his neck and careful not to choke himself, Eli lifted his back legs and pushed against the loop and cable. Keeping his weight along the back of his neck, he slid his paws along the cable until he hooked a claw into the loop. He pushed and twisted his body until the loop part was under his chin. Then kicking with his other back leg he tried to find the little hole, which was now at the back of his neck.

It took him several tries until he found it. Once found he inserted his claw. Nothing happened. So he pushed harder wiggling his toe around, until pop! It sprung open.

Eli fell to the ground but too quickly for him to right himself. He landed on his side. It really hurt, reminding him how severely bruised he was from the dogs jaws. Eli took another moment to catch his breath and looked around to see if anyone had seen him. No one had. He was glad about that. It wouldn't do for anyone to find out that cats didn't always land on their feet.

Very quietly, and gingerly, he walked over to the saggy curtain door. It actually hurt to breath now that he was on the move. He lowered his head to the ground and peaked out the bottom. He didn't want to catch anyone's eyes by being at eye level. There were a couple of dogs across from him watching the commotion at the tent's entrance.

At the entrance, dogs were working together to get the tent upright. From outside, the tent was being pulled out so the fallen poles could be righted. The side with all the makeshift rooms was still down so Eli crept along the bottom of the saggy curtains toward the back of the tent. He was careful to stay out of the fourth room. He didn't want to know what was in there.

Once he reached the back wall he darted across the hall to hide behind some crates. He was in the big second room here. There were crates stacked along the back wall and piled up in the far corner. As he moved along behind them he could smell some type of dried food in them. It reminded him that it had been quite a while since he had eaten. But there was something in the air that smelled better than the dried food.

Peering into the large room from between the crates, Eli saw a light shining down on the green egg he saw earlier. The egg was very large and seamed to radiate that light making it glow. A mound of shiny gold rocks mixed with large bones surrounded the green egg. The smell was coming from one of these things.

The guard dogs Eli saw earlier watching the commotion were the only ones left. Their backs were toward him so Eli crept closer to the egg to get a better look and smell of it.

The egg was a deep emerald green with a smoky glass like transparency to it. The egg wasn't transparent though. There was something inside of it. And the smell wasn't coming from that. The smell was coming from the bones mixed in with the shiny metal stones.

The smell was alluring, drawing Eli in; maybe he could take just one little bone. Eli slowly reached up to touch a bone. Something moved. Eli snapped his attention to the egg. Something inside the huge egg moved. It looked like a baby flying dog in there. Could that baby flying dog see him?

To check, Eli cautiously reached up toward a little bone along the edge of the table but kept his eyes on the baby. His stomach gurgled in hunger. The little flying dog moved again. Eli could make out one of its eyes through the green shell. It blinked. The baby's eyes were open inside the egg! It could see him! But since it was inside the egg, Eli knew it couldn't hurt him. In fact, Eli wasn't sure but he got the sense the baby flying dog was warning him not to touch the dog's treasure.

Eli took a deep breath, inhaling the aroma. It smelled so good.

The guard dogs said something to one another. Eli ducked down. He looked back over his shoulder around the room. Maybe this wasn't a good spot to be. Quietly he ran over to where the dividing curtain hung sagging along the outside wall. Eli crawled under a fold.

Hidden from view Eli thought about the egg. He was glad the baby couldn't alert anyone from inside that egg. But, could or would, that baby flying dog actually try to warn him? It was weird. He definitely needed to get out of here.

He peered out into the big open room with the entrance. The huge flying dog took up a lot of space with her body. Her wings were outstretched holding up the tent. Her long neck was close to the center of the tent supporting its weight. Eli's gaze followed her neck to her head. She was looking at him.

Eli froze. She was watching him. Just like the baby inside the egg had been. How long had she been watching him? He hadn't noticed her way up there. He ducked back beneath the curtain fold along the outside wall. Then he peeked out at her again.

Yep. She was watching him. Why didn't she sound the alarm? Eli ducked back. He looked behind him into the room with golden treasures and the big egg. Eli knew that big emerald egg belonged to her. The baby wasn't even born yet and he could see the similarities. He turned around and glanced up at her from this room. She could still see him if he stepped out from the partly fallen curtain. There really was nowhere he could go without her watching.

Eli turned around again, looking toward the entrance door for any hole or opening he could dash through. Dogs were everywhere straightening the tent. This side was just about up. Then the big flying dog dragged her tail in front of Eli, blocking him from the entrance. Eli looked up at her again. She looked amused. Was she toying with him? Nobody paid her any attention thinking she was just adjusting her position as she held up the tent. Eli crouched back closer to the wall. He could smell the freezing cold great outdoors just on the other side of the wall panel.

Actually, he sniffed again, the outdoor scent was coming from the seam where the wall panel met the floor panel. Eli smelled the seam again. Looking carefully he could see the material was being stretched tight in effort from the dogs working on securing it to the corner poles. Eli extended his special claw and inserted it into one of the seam holes ripping the material open. Perfect. All he needed was a hole big enough for his head and the rest of him would follow.

CHAPTER 13

Elliot woke up to sounds outside his tent. It was dark out again so he left his night vision on. It no longer sounded windy but the shape of the tent ceiling indicated it had a fair amount of snow on it. He could hear the army cats were bustling about. But being cozy and warm in the tent, he wasn't ready to get up. No sooner had he closed his eyes to go back to sleep when Jack stood, stretched and gave him a slap.

"Get up little buddy.
Gotta put the tent away.
Supper has to be served,
and we'll be on our way."

Elliot hadn't even heard Jack come in this morning but now that he was standing, Elliot realized Jack had helped keep him warm by curling up beside him. Now there was a cold spot.

Groaning Elliot said, "Just another minute, maybe don't set a limit."

"That won't do, you're part of our crew.
So get up, so I can let up. I got other things to do."

"Fine, I'll do as you say.
Just give me one more minute
and we'll be on our way."

Elliot rolled over turning his back to Jack. Jack opened the tent door holding it wide open, letting cold air swoop in and steal all the warm air way.

"Yikes, Jack! That's cold!
Shut the door! I've been told!"

Laughing Jack said, "Then my job here is done. Come on, Elliot, they've already begun."

Getting up Elliot helped Jack pack up the tent and head over to the sleighs. There they began preparing supper. Elliot already having kitchen experience turned out to be a big help as he knew water would have to be boiled, dishes would have to be set. He didn't need much instruction and the crew really began to appreciate having him along. Before long, supper was served and cleaned up. The sleighs were packed and the convoy was set to march onward into the night.

The soldiers were aligned in their respective groups however instead of just heading out in a straight march as they did yesterday morning a few small groups were sent out.

Jack explained they were called platoons about twenty cats and within the platoons were even smaller groups called squads. But instead of marching forward, these platoons simply left the camp at a jog. After about five minutes, another set of platoons were sent out. This took place until only a quarter of the cats remained. The remaining cats then began the march same as yesterday side by side with the sleighs bringing up the rear.

Elliot walked along side of his sleigh paying close attention to the trail the cats were making in the snow. Any sign of a downward slope and he was ready to jump in. So far it was fairly flat in the valley.

After some time Elliot noticed there was a smell in the air that reminded him of campfires. It seemed out of place. But it was the quietness around that made Elliot take notice that his harness cats were nervous. No one was talking and all of them were constantly scanning the surrounding area. In fact as he looked around, all the soldiers within sight seemed edgy. Then he noticed if someone had something to say they would sign instead of speaking. Elliot looked for Jack.

He was on the other side of the sleigh closer to the rear so Elliot jumped on the sleigh and over to the other side.

"No one's talking. Is that . . ."

"Shhhh," Jack cut Elliot off and then made some motions with his paws. Elliot had no idea what Jack was saying. Jack must have understood the look on Elliot's face because then he whispered,

"I said, now's the time to use your sign.
Dogs in the area may hear our chime.
So no words spoken, provoke no crime."

"Oh. I don't sign," Elliot said downcast, but then offered, "I could try to mime."

The thought of Elliot miming in an attempt to join a conversation of cats signing would most likely cause problems.

So Jack said, "Aaah, no.
Just be silent as we go."

Jack fell back to walk along side of the rear of the sleigh again. Elliot moved closer to the front where he could watch the terrain.

It was still snowing and overcast so no one could see Moon but

Winter had let up on the wind now that they were on the march again. Or had he? Elliot could hear the wind blowing up in the mountains all around them. But the wind wasn't touching them. It was nice not to have to deal with the wind like yesterday, especially for the harness cats.

Elliot watched them pulling the sleigh. They were doing all right, pulling with ease for the moment. Their metalized claws helped them dig in tremendously as they pulled the sleigh.

Elliot took in all the scenery around him as they travelled. He also kept a sharp eye out for any type of movement within the forests and along the mountainsides.

As they continued on the ground became icier from a previous snow rain mixture. Ice began to build up on the trees becoming thicker and thicker as they marched on. After a while the thick icicles hung on the tree branches encasing them and weighing them down. Many branches had broken off due to the ice buildup and had to be moved out of the sleigh's way. But the fresh falling snow helped with the traction and the harness cats were able to pull without slipping too much. Elliot noticed that even metalized claws didn't prevent them from slipping entirely.

Elliot wondered if it was Spring keeping the wind off the army. He could still hear it up on the mountainsides. It sounded pretty powerful. Whoever was doing it, Spring or Winter, Elliot was glad for it.

As the army travelled along they left Claw Canyon behind and entered the valley of Dead Mouse Mountain. The smell of smoke lingered in the air long before huge blackened trees covered in ice and frost came into view. Clearly there had been a massive forest fire here and no one had to tell Elliot who had put the fire out. Evidence of a freezing ice snowstorm was everywhere. Thick icicles clung to the black trees like a shiny gloss coating almost as big as the trees themselves. Elliot for the first time began to realize just how powerful Winter and Spring's abilities were, especially when together.

Elliot looked in amazement at the black skeletons of what once was a thick and lush forest. Even in the dark the iced black trees stood out in contrast to the soft white falling snow. Any underbrush that may have been there was completely gone and they could see deep into the burned out forest. Even the ground had burned and lay bare beneath a layer of thick ice. Soft snow covered the ground now but a simple brush of the paw revealed the icy truth. So many burned trees stretched to the sky towering above them in shiny blackness. It gave the area an eeriness.

Elliot already knew the cause of this fire. As he looked around he began to realize just how fortunate he was his father had managed to escape.

Wide-eyed astonishment never left the cats as they travelled through the desolate region. Never before in Catland had there been a forest fire. Some areas in the burnt forest still smoldered with smoke. The hissing of fire clashing with snow and ice could be heard coming from those hot spots. The convoy avoided those areas weaving around the valley as needed.

With layered ice beneath the snow, Elliot at times had to apply the brakes especially hard, scraping the ice deeply with the iron drags. The sound carried easily through barren forest. Everyone worried that the wrong ears would hear them and so some of the soldiers fell back to walk alongside the sleighs. They would grab on to the sides of the sleigh and assist in slowing them so Elliot wouldn't have to brake so hard.

"Quietly as can be. Quiet is the key." Jack had whispered to Elliot. It made a difference but it wasn't until that moment that Elliot realized what he had gotten himself into by coming along. Any number of things could go wrong and then what would he do? What if dogs came charging in on them? He didn't know how to fight like they did.

As they continued it began to rain along with the snow, just a drizzle to start but before long they were travelling in freezing rain. And then the wind came in, blowing them around, making their forward march very difficult. With the wind the rain turned to little ice pellets. Hitting them hard on the exposed areas like the face and head.

Elliot wanted to stop and set up the tent for shelter but no one was stopping. He was grateful for his waterproof jacket but he wished it extended a little further over the head and tail area. Judging by the looks on everyone's faces it seemed to him like everyone wanted to stop but no one did. Finally, after travelling in

silence for many hours, he looked for Jack and asked him.
"How far must we go in this ice and this snow?
This weather is crazy, doesn't Major Cat know?" Elliot whined quietly.
"Oh, he knows all right.
It's the nature of this plight.
We all dread Winter's smite,
but there is a goal in sight.
So rest your worries, at least tonight.
For tomorrow will bring a whole new fright," Jack answered him softly.
Elliot was not comforted at all. But to his relief, a couple hours before dawn they reached the end of the burned forest and they set up their tents to rest.

CHAPTER 14

The wind howled blasting frozen little ice pellets against Eli's already bruised body. Thankfully the ripped jacket was still able to provide some protection against the ice pellets. It was dark out and no sign of Moon of course since Winter and Spring were blocking him with their storm.

A steady wind kept the falling snow and ice from settling thus making it near impossible to see more than a few meters even with his night vision. Before this journey Eli had never experienced a snowstorm and found the lack of vision quite disturbing. Fortunately his senses where intact, and he could still make out where he was.

Once Eli had gotten the hole big enough, he had poked his head out to survey his surroundings. There were some dogs outside but they were so focused on refastening the ripped straps to the frozen ground they didn't notice him.

He made sure no one was looking his way when he slipped through. He even believed the big flying dog didn't see him escape. She couldn't see him from beneath the folds of the saggy wall curtain. If she could have, Eli was certain she would have sounded an alarm.

Even through the wind, Eli could hear dogs working on the other side of the tent barking orders to one another. To avoid being seen, Eli made a wide circle around them, careful not to get too close to a stream that ran in the center of the valley. He headed back to the tent where the orange cat was still held prisoner.

Each leap through the icy snow he took was painful to his ribs. Actually, even just breathing hurt. He couldn't walk because the snow was higher than his head and had a crusty top. It would support his weight for a few steps then he would break through banging his ribs in to the icy layer. It hurt less to leap. At first he bounded from tent to tent seeking the sheltered areas but as he hopped to his third tent there had been a dog curled up in that area. The dog would have seen him if its head hadn't been buried under its own furry tail.

So Eli stayed out in the open moving quickly but cautiously, relying on his ears and nose to help warn him of approaching dogs. He had been able to locate a number of dogs by smelling or hearing them and ducked out of sight as they passed by.

The powerful wind gusts both helped and hindered his senses. The wind could either; carry the scents and sounds to him or away from him. In this case, Eli was sort of glad dogs stunk and were noisy. He used their faults to his benefit. It was too bad he couldn't see them though. But, if he couldn't see well in the storm probably the dogs couldn't see well either.

In actuality there also weren't any trolls outside and hardly any dogs. However, Eli could hear them in the tents he passed by. Sheltered from the freezing rainstorm. Eli wished he could seek shelter too but he couldn't, at least not yet. Not without freeing that orange cat, and probably the troll, although he'd have to see about the troll.

Eli found it a bit more challenging to be quiet on the icy snow as he made his way to the tent. It crunched under paw and so he took extra effort to leap gingerly through it, absorbing his weight with his legs instead of hitting the ground hard. In spite of the pain it caused he could do it. It made him wonder why the dogs made no effort to be quiet. It was as if they didn't care. Winter and Spring could mask a lot of noise with their howling wind. But even the dog's breathing was noisy. They huffed and puffed and loudly licked their lips. It made Eli try to be extra quiet. He wanted to be as opposite from them as he could be.

What he could not control however was his own scent, even if he didn't stink like they did. He did have a scent. Which thanks to the first two dogs he met Eli was very aware of now. He just hoped no one picked it up on the wind as he had them. So far, so good.

As Eli zigzagged his way to the first tent that had held him captive, snow was coming in the holes of his jacket, forming ice in his fur and then melting against him. It was very different from the ice that formed with Winter and Chill. That worked like a barrier against the cold, this was melting through his dense coat to his skin. It was a small freeze that was growing into a bigger one and it was becoming painfully cold. At least the jacket still was helping to keep him warm, or mostly warm and it was still buffering the hits from the ice pellets. Eli stopped only once to scratch at the area in effort to loosen the ice away from his skin.

Once Eli spotted the tent, he carefully made his way around to the back. He knew at least one of the dogs was still there. He wasn't sure how he expected to free the orange cat but he had to try. He didn't even know why he felt that way. Maybe it was because he was beginning to understand how vicious these dogs could get. It was unlikely the orange cat would survive another encounter with them. That might also be why he should just leave, locate the Monarch's army and let them rescue the orange cat. But something stops Eli from fleeing. He just couldn't do it. If it were him in there he'd want someone to save him.

Now that Eli was at the back of the tent. He sat there for a bit watching and listening to the tent walls blow in and out with the wind. The canvas the tents were made out of was a noisy material and added to the ruckus of the howling wind.

He knew the back wall in the tent was lined with empty cages so it would be a good spot to break in. Getting out of the other tent through the seams worked well so maybe getting into this tent the same way would work. Only this time there was no fallen curtain fold to crawl under. He was going to have to be extremely quiet and careful not to get caught again. Eli hoped the noisy material would help conceal him. He scratched at the ice in his fur again.

After digging in the snow to locate the bottom of the tent, Eli dug a hole in the snow for himself to work in. Carefully, Eli stuck his sharp claw through a seam and pulled. This tent wasn't stretched tight so at first nothing but pulling the tent toward him happened. So he pulled harder and wiggled his claw back and forth until he heard the little pop of the thread breaking.

Eli listened for sounds within the tent. He didn't hear anything so he carefully stuck his claw into the thread a little further down and pulled the broken end out, thus creating a hole between the wall and floor panels. He did this again and again until he had a hole big enough to crawl through, stopping to listen each time.

Finally when Eli was satisfied there were no sounds inside the tent to indicate someone had heard him, he poked his head in.

He was right, the back of the tent was lined with the cages. But there wasn't much room for him to squeeze in. Then suddenly he felt something pat his back end. Ouch! Someone stepped on his tail. Lighting fast Eli pulled his head back out. Throwing himself backward he bumped into someone, knocking himself down. Eli was up in an instant, all claws and ready for the fight of his life

when that someone whispered,
"Holy smokes, Eli!
It is just I.
Please; settle down,
before these dogs come around.
Shhhh! Don't make a sound." Striker held up a paw and surveyed the area to see if anyone had heard them.

Seeing it was Striker, Eli was filled with relief and then joy. He lunged at Striker with a huge open pawed hug. Hurting his own ribs in the embrace he quickly let go. Striker was wearing a white jacket similar to the one he had been given only the colour matched Striker's fur.

Struggling for breath Eli whispered,
"What are you doing here,
standing on my rear?
If these dogs see,
ripped to shreds you'll be.
They have no fear.
But I'm really glad you're here.
I really want to cheer.
But are you crazy?
These dogs are severe."

"Yes I know. I know exactly how they go.
Why are you here? That's what I want to know.
And you seem hurt, we should go," Striker answered.

"I just escaped.
Their capture is not my fate.
But inside these walls is one of our mates.
I cannot leave him inside that crate," Eli explained. He was relieved to have someone to help him now. Striker would know what to do.

"They have someone in there?
Who got caught in their snare?" Striker was concerned for whoever had been captured.

"I don't know his name.
But bruised, beaten, and definitely maimed.
I cannot leave him, I would be shamed."

"No, I should get him out.
You have a mission to be about.

So you turnabout, and . . ." Striker stopped.

Something thumped inside the tent next to them. Both cats listened for any more sounds coming from inside the tent. The wind blew hard and the tent flapped violently, muffling the sounds from within the tent. The hole Eli made opened in the wind and a bit of snow blew in.

Eli got close to the hole so he could peer into the tent.

"Sweet mother of dog bones!
Look who's come back to our zone.
It's Eli the cat and he's not alone."

Eli and Striker jumped in unison. A dog stood on Eli's side staring at them from around the tent. Then another dog appeared from the other side. Both dogs stopped, knowing they had the cats surrounded. Eli recognized the guard dogs from inside the tent. The one who had spoken was the one who had helped catch him in the tent and then stayed behind when he was taken out.

Eli faced the dog that had spoken. Striker faced the other. Standing side by side they arched their backs and puffed up their hair to appear larger than they were. Of course, only their tails looked puffy because of their jackets.

"Aren't you a crafty little cat?
I know where you're supposed to be at.
And it's not at this little flat.
But I'm glad you brought a friend,
it will make up for all that." The dog on the other side of Striker spoke.

Without looking at him Eli knew it was the dog who had told his captors of his conversation with the orange cat. That conversation was also when they learned Eli's name. It irritated Eli now. He wished they didn't know his name.

"Oh no, don't stop chatting.
Please, continue.
But speak up would you,
with this rat-a-tatting," the dog on Eli's side said.

Eli knew he would not be able to out run these dogs. He didn't know what to do.

Striker whispered in Eli's ear, "I've got this. Run at my hiss."

Striker hissed!

Eli dove into the hole of the tent. Striker leaped into the air. Both dogs dove towards them. Eli felt teeth on his tail as he slammed into the crates on the other side. He ripped his tail out of the dog's mouth as he scrambled along the inside of the tent wall, banging and clanging the cages as he went. Striker was on the top of the tent and the dogs were leaping against the back tent wall, snarling and growling. Eli ran along the cages and out the side to where the troll and the orange cat were held. The dogs ran round the other side of the tent leaping at it to reach Striker.

Striker shook the whole tent as he leaped off the roof toward the dogs. Eli heard a dog yelp and fall silent. The other dog snarled and loudly barked his alarm. Other dogs started barking. Then Eli heard the snarling, barking guard dog race off.

"Run, Striker, run!" Eli thought, "Whatever you do, don't be outdone."

Eli looked wide-eyed at the prisoners. The orange cat was out of his cage and limping as quickly as he could to the troll. Barking continued outside, sounds coming from different directions.

"How did you escape?" Eli asked stunned, "Are your bars misshape?"

Eli looked at his cage bars. The door was open but nothing looked wrong about the bars.

The orange cat snorted and stuck his claw into the lock on the troll's cage door.

"No! Has your head been clocked?
You left my door unlocked."

Working his claw this way and that he added, "Notso, here, informed me of your little walk. We heard you through the walls, all your talk."

The lock on the troll's door popped open. "Now let's go, and no more squawk!"

His name is Notso? Wonder what name the orange cat will tow, Eli wondered to himself. He would ask later when it was safe to talk.

Eli's tail began to hurt. There were streaks of missing fur from the dog's teeth. There was also blood shining through on his skin but he'd have to ignore it along with the other sore spots he already had.

Barking dogs ran past the tent in the same direction the others had gone. The whole camp was coming awake. Barking could be heard near and far.

The orange cat stepped aside of the cage door. Notso took the lock off and opened the door. Stepping out Notso quickly pulled one of his arms out of his ripped shirt. Pushing his shirt up to free his arm he revealed bruises all over his torso.

Just then a dog ran into the tent. Eli immediately arched his back, ready to do battle but before he could extend a claw. Notso grabbed the dog by its mouth; picking it up into the air he held it high. The dog wreathed and whined in his grasp. It was smaller than the guard dogs. Probably sent to check on them.

Notso growled, "You know I can rip you in two. Make one sound and that I will do."

The dog whimpered in response. Seeing a rope on the floor amongst other things Notso set the dog down. Still holding its muzzle firmly Notso let go with one hand and grabbed the rope. He quickly wrapped it around the dogs muzzle securing it at the back of the dog's head. Then he pushed the dog into the cage he had been held in and replaced the lock. The dog immediately went to work trying to get the rope off with its paws.

Eli and the orange cat just stared at Notso. That's when Eli noticed the orange cat had not braced for battle with the dog but had crouched down instead. He really was hurt bad if he was unable to fight.

Notso limped over to the orange cat, bending over, the troll gingerly lifted the cat up then pulled his shirt down covering his arm and the orange cat. It left an odd bump under the shirt but the orange cat was hidden. Notso extended his free arm to Eli in a jester that suggested Eli be lifted too. Eli shook his head and backed away.

Notso shrugged and hobbled over to the tent door saying in a hushed tone. "As long as they don't know who I am, I am free to scram. You, on other hand, they just want to wham."

He stood there, listening to the sounds outside. Eli came to stand beside him listening too.

Most of the barking dog sounds were fading off into the distance west of them. But there was other barking coming from the direction of the large tent.

The tent shook violently from the wind. Winter and Spring were still hitting the camp hard. And although there was barking throughout the camp, Eli thought some of it might be coming from within the tents. Perhaps not all the dogs were eager to run out into the storm.

Notso quietly opened the tent door. Peering out, he stopped then again in a hushed tone he whispered, "See anything, any type of being?"

He held the door open for Eli to take a look. Eli could make out some dark shapes standing by a tent not too far away. They were trolls with their backs toward them. They were facing the sounds of the fading barks. Eli pointed to them.

"Trolls, out of their holes," he whispered back.

Notso led by stepping out and heading a different direction from them. Eli was able to walk along the top of the snow now. The temperature had dropped and the freezing rain had accumulated enough to hold his weight. Notso however broke through with every step. Eli frowned at the noise.

Notso took long strides covering as much ground as he could. However, Eli noticed, he matched his movement with the wind. When the wind blew hard, he moved fast. If the wind slowed, he slowed. At least Notso was trying to hide his crunching steps with the wind.

Notso did seem to know where he was headed. Rounding a tent he turned to his right and headed straight toward the forest. It looked to Eli that they were now taking the shortest route to the forest as possible. They avoided the noisy areas however where voices, barking, and talking could be heard. They wove their way around tents, ducking out of sight when necessary.

As they neared the forest edge Eli could see a couple of dogs slowly walking the perimeter ahead of them. There was a path cut through the snow from many paws walking the perimeter of the camp. He grabbed Notso's leg to stop him. But the troll kept going not even noticing. So Eli extended his claws and lightly scratched him.

When Notso stopped, Eli thought he was going to strike him. Eli quickly pointed to the dogs who were slowly walking past and away from them. Notso squinted, moving his head this way and that in effort to see through the blowing ice and snow. That's when Eli realized the troll's vision was not too good. The swollen parts around his eyes must be causing him problems because trolls were cave creatures and should be able to see well in the dark. Notso took another couple of steps just more cautiously. The forest edge was just ahead of them. But Eli ran in front, stopping him again. Shaking his head Eli pointed to the patrol dogs.

Notso slowly bent down to speak. In doing so Eli could see his movements were not so smooth but obviously pained and jerky. Once he was low enough Eli quickly put his paw on Notso's mouth to keep him quiet. The dogs weren't very far away. Lucky, the patrol dogs were more interested in the barking off in the distance than they were in their surroundings. So far, they were keeping their eyes and ears in that direction.

Eli looked around some more to see if there were any other patrol dogs out. All they had to do was wait for the dogs to continue moving on then they could cross this open section to the forest edge and get out of sight.

After a moment Eli took lead, creeping slowly toward the forest watching the patrol dogs from the corner of his eye. Notso took each step as slowly as he could, breaking the ice layer as quietly as possible. The patrol dog's slow pace never faltered.

About half way across, a new frenzy of barking broke out in the center of camp. Eli suspected those dogs had learned of his escape. The patrol dogs turned toward the barking, seeing Eli and Notso they immediately began barking their alarm and leaped into a charge. Simultaneously, Eli and Notso raced for the forest.

Eli easily out ran Notso entering the forest first. Not knowing where he was going, he just ran straight ahead. But he couldn't out run the dogs. Not this time, he was too injured. One of the dogs was quick to follow him, barking and crashing through the snow at a tremendous speed. The dog was definitely gaining on him.

Eli heard Notso and the other patrol dog behind him engage in a fight of some type. Snarling, grunts, and angry words from both sides faded as he ran into the forest.

The dog behind was catching up. Knowing he would be caught in a few moments, Eli did the only thing he could do. He climbed an icy tree.

Even though Winter warned him not to get treed, Eli didn't see what choice he had. He stopped about half way up the tree before he took to a branch. Looking down at the dog that would have caught him. Eli froze.

The dog had bandages on its face and neck and it was going crazy at the bottom of the tree; leaping and snarling for all it was worth. Eli felt his senses drain out of his head and dizziness seep in. He dug his claws further into the icy branch for fear of falling. Now what was he going to do? It was Rad down there!

Chapter 15

Eli closed his eyes and offered a silent prayer to the big Cat above.

"Oh Cat above, hear my howl.
I'm out on a limb;
my enemy, ready to disembowel.
My survival is looking slim.
I need your assistance,
any thought, idea, or whim.
Anything you offer will make a difference.
Whatever you ask, I'll go the distance."

After a moment Eli took a deep breath, opened his eyes, and looked for Notso and the orange cat. Eli could still hear a commotion closer to the forest edge but there were too many trees in the way to see what was going on. Unfortunately, he could also still hear barking headed this way from the camp. How long did they have?

Looking down at Rad who was now leaping at a branch. Eli watched in terror as Rad reached an icy branch and pulled himself up on it. Balancing precariously Rad looked for another branch to climb. Eli didn't know dogs could climb trees too. It looked to him like their paws weren't designed for climbing. He watched Rad move to another branch slipping slightly as he went. At least he wasn't very good at climbing trees. Eli looked up and down the icy tree for an escape route.

Suddenly Eli got an idea. Where the idea came from Eli couldn't say for sure, it was risky but it might work. Rad managed to get onto another branch then paused for a moment. He looked down at the ground as if he just realized what he was doing. Then he looked up again at Eli. Eli could see the rage in him as he found the confidence to continue on.

Eli suddenly felt pity for the dog. Seeing him from a perspective he never would have ordinarily. It became obvious to Eli that dogs were not meant to climb trees. Rad was so full of hate and loathing it was affecting his judgment. Although Eli also wondered how tightly Rad's bandages were wrapped; he knew Cat Above had just revealed a truth to him.

Rad struggled up onto another branch and Eli made a decision. He needed to be opposite with his emotions and thoughts too.

Rad's anger controlled him. Eli could see clearly now how allowing this emotion to control you was dangerous.

Perhaps, Eli should not allow fear to control him either, although that might be tougher to do. He had heard the words "scaredy-cat" before and now he knew why. He was a scaredy-cat. But from now on, he would try very hard to take extra effort in keeping calm and using his head.

More crashing and barking at the forest edge ensued. Eli's heart pounded harder at the sound of them. Keeping calm was going to be hard.

Eli offered Rad a change of thought,
"Why do you risk your life for me?
You shouldn't be climbing up this tree.
All this effort will gain you what?
I'll just move and you'll have squat.
But if you slip and if you fall,
you'll end up with nothing at all.
So how about you get down,
and I will follow you to the ground.
But with one condition, you must agree,
be my friend and let me flee."

Rad teetered on his slippery branch and barked out a laugh.
"You must be joking.
Your friend? Me?
In a moment I'll have you choking.
No matter how you plea,
you'll just be croaking.
But more importantly,
I'll no longer be hungry."

Hungry? That made sense. He hadn't seen any of the dogs eat since he had been captured. Plus he was hungry too.

"Oh! You're hungry, of course!
I know where there's food, even a full-course.
Plenty for you, plenty for me,
just be my friend and follow me."

"There is no point in trying to connive
I made a promise that you won't survive." Rad sneered at him.

Eli could hear he was running out of time. The other dogs

would be there in a few moments.

"Okay stray, have it your way."

Eli turned around and scrambled up the tree to just about the top, slipping a bit in the icy spots. The tree swayed with the wind. Digging his claws in as deeply as he could into the exposed bark Eli found the rhythm of sway. He then leaned into the sway with all his weight causing the tree to sway more and more with each direction. This was dangerous he could fall doing this. The entire tree began to sway more and more, cracking the ice on the branches. Eli watched Rad struggle to keep his footing while ice and snow fell from the branches.

From up high Eli saw Notso making his way to them. He had a huge tree branch in his hand. And Sun was waking up. It was getting light on the mountain's horizon.

The more the tree swayed the less steady Rad became. The showering ice and snow made it even harder for Rad to hold on. Rad changed his direction and was looking for a way down when he slipped and fell. He yelped in pain as he banged into branches. He hit the ground face first breaking through the ice layer onto the snowy ground below.

Notso got to Rad first. Eli started to make his way down, slipping at times and sliding several inches before scratching the icy trunk to a stop. Notso set the orange cat on a low branch above Rad, then turned to confront him. Rad was on his paws again, however he looked unsteady. The other dogs were just about upon them.

Notso took one look at the dogs headed his way. With one powerful swing of the tree branch, Notso hit Rad crossways. Rad flew several feet away and did not get up. Then Notso turned and ran, still clinging to the large branch.

Eli didn't know what to expect, but seeing Notso hit Rad and run away wasn't it.

Dogs suddenly ran into view, running all around the tree sniffing this way and that. Some of the dogs ran after Notso barking in their pursuit. The orange cat carefully climbed up to a higher branch. Eli worked his way down a few more branches before stopping at what he considered a safe distance. Other dogs surrounded Rad, sniffing and licking his face. Eli saw Rad move.

Then two of the dogs sniffing Rad took off back toward camp.

The orange cat climbed up to another tree branch closer to Eli. Eli watched him carefully choose his footing. When he looked up at Eli, Eli realized he was actually a very old cat, obviously in pain, but clearly he wasn't afraid. There was no fear in his one eye.

"I don't know what to do. All I feel is rue," Eli said to him admitting to the fear he still was fighting. The orange cat nodded in acknowledgment. They could hear lots of barking from the camp.

"Heeeeere Kitty Kitty Kitty,
come on down and we'll perform a little ditty.
It'll be fun, you'll see, it's all witty."

Eli and the orange cat looked down at who spoke to them. Eight dogs sat at the base of the tree staring up at them. Some of the dogs snickered. Many dogs wiggled in their spots like they were fighting the urge to get up.

The dog that spoke stood, walked to the foot of the tree, placed his front paws on the trunk saying, "We've got nothing better to do, than sit around and wait for you. So come on down and we'll talk it through."

The orange cat let out a short laugh then shot back at him,

"First you're going to perform and then we'll talk?
You're out of the norm. What a crock!
But go ahead and do your number.
From up here we won't encumber."

Eli wondered what kind of performance they had.

"Oh no we can't. This show requires a cat. So come on down and lets have a chat," the dog said. He smiled a big toothy smile then let his tongue hang out the side of his mouth all while wagging his tail. It made him look very friendly.

But Eli did not want to be part of their show. In fact he realized, with all these dogs staring at them, perhaps they were the show. Eli wished they would just go home.

Bravely Eli decided they should be told,
"You shouldn't be on this land,
not you or your evil dog band.
If you were smart you would go,
pack your things and end this show."

"And what will you do kitten, if we choose to stay here just a sittin?" The dog sat down still wagging his tail. "Will you come down and lay on a lickin? I'd like to see that with your cute little mitten."

The dogs all erupted in laughter.

One of the dogs in the group added laughing, "Yeah kitten. Come on down and feel what it's like to be bitten."

The laughter stopped immediately, all the dogs looked at the one who had joined in with the taunting. The dog at the foot of the tree let out a ferocious growl and attacked the other dog with such speed Eli's jaw dropped.

The dog from the tree base grabbed the other dog by his throat and threw him down on his back. The dog that had spoken out of turn surrendered instantly. He lay on his back whimpering and crying his surrender. The dog from the tree base stood superiorly over him. His jaws were on his throat but Eli could see he wasn't actually biting him. Slowly the superior dog let go, and then he stood there for a moment, over top of him. The surrendered dog looked away licking his lips, not willing to meet the superior dog's gaze.

All the other dogs had moved out of the way of the superior dog when he had attacked. The superior dog took a quick look around for any challengers. All averted their eyes at his glance. Seeing no challengers, the superior dog returned back to the foot of the tree. Not looking at anyone he sat down and so then did the rest of the dogs.

When the superior dog looked back up at them he wore the most apologetic expression Eli had ever seen.

"I'm so sorry you had to see that," he said apologizing.

"But rest assured,
if I say, 'not one hair, not one matt;
will come to harm on any cat.'
Your safety is secured.
And that's a fact."

The dog looked so apologetic and friendly at the same time. Eli believed him. He looked at the other dogs sitting there. After what he just saw, he truly believed none of the other dogs would challenge him. However, there was still no way he was going down.

Eli stood up to adjust his footing. The orange cat misread his movement and snapped at him.

"What are you doing?
Sit down or it'll be your undoing!
Can't you see he's wooing?
Do we need reviewing?
The corporal said '*If.*'
'If,' he said.
If you go down there,
you'll end up dead."

The orange cat was angry again. Or maybe he was just always angry Eli didn't know. But Eli was indignant. He adjusted his crouch to a more comfortable position.

"I wasn't going to, but thanks for the spew," Eli mumbled sarcastically. "You really saved me, so—Phew!"

"Have we met orange tabby?
You remind me of someone I knew—all gabby.
But not here on this land.
Somewhere else—more grand.
Back home, perhaps the abbey?"

The dog the orange cat referred to as corporal asked. He maintained his cuteness with a big smile and tail wagging.

"Yes, Corporal, we've met.
Years ago, I warned you of a threat.
It appears it's still a message you didn't get," the orange cat answered him.

"Oh now I recall," the corporal said remembering the past.
You're the cat with all the gall!
You entered our pack's great hall.
You demanded we stop all our brawl.
Listen to you or suffer a great fall.
Then you disappeared over a wall."

"And you came again;
you tended me when I was lame.
I never did get your name.
Or figure out your game.
You said, 'peace, love, and forgiveness should be our aim.

Without that our lives were in vain.'
Well I disagree if it's all the same;
only goals and ambitions give us something to claim."

    Eli was amazed at how the dog could look so friendly and happy while disputing a truth.

    "But never mind all that," the corporal continued,
"Besides it's all too abstract.
Come on down, there's no need to have a spat."

    Someone was coming from what was now a very noisy dog camp. It sounded like more dogs. Even with the blowing snow he could hear they were dragging something.

    The two dogs who had run off were first to come into view. They were back with a stretcher. But they weren't the only ones coming. The dogs brought the stretcher over to Rad lining it up beside him. Rad still lay in the snow. One of the dogs had been sitting with him, keeping him company, licking his face now and then. The three dogs helped him get onto the stretcher and then all three headed back to camp.

    "Now see, wasn't that full of love and caring?
That was all kissy, kissy, and hugs just a blaring.
So come on down and together we'll start sharing."

    He whined just a little at the end then sat on his haunches holding his front paws up together close to his chest. He tilted his head this way and that way while looking at them.

    The rest of the dogs Eli heard came into view. They were dragging something as well. It appeared to be a long narrow metal sheet with a jagged edge on one side.

    The orange cat began to growl while watching the new dogs approach. His growl became louder and louder until finally he screeched out,

    "Love and caring?
We've already being sharing.
Now look at that tool!
You are anything but sparing!
And I've been a fool!
To think you'd start caring!
Now I can see,
You'll take this land

Eli

You'll take this tree
You'll take our lives
You'll never stop your tyranny.
What's the point of trying to talk?
You don't hear; you only balk.
So I'm done with you,
I'm ready to walk.
Go ahead and cut us down,
when my paws touch the ground.
You'll get the message and it's profound.
But you'll finally understand; you stupid hound."

    The dogs all looked from one to another. Then the corporal suddenly jumped in a circle wagging his tail faster.

    Excitedly he exclaimed,

    "Oh boy, I can hardly wait!
Cut her down boys!
We've got a date!"

CHAPTER 16

Elliot huddled under the sleigh in effort to keep out of the wind and falling snow. The sleigh was covered by a tarp to keep the snow out of it. Elliot could go in there if he wanted to but this was easier for him. The temperature had dropped which, as oddly as it might seem to a cat, Elliot was glad about. There wasn't any more rain. Winter was still keeping it windy but not as much as before.

He watched the glowing embers of his little fire flicker and sizzle with the falling snow. They had built a barrier out of snow on one side to protect it from the wind. This fire was the only one allowed in camp so it was important to keep it going.

The fire was mesmerizing and the hushed voices of the Major Cat's meeting with the other commanders lulled him. They were under a canopy tent nearby with two sides rolled up but were clearly making an effort to keep their voices down. He fought to stay awake.

It was his job to make sure there was plenty of hot water and tea for everyone. The tea wasn't as popular though; Elliot suspected most of the cats wished it were hot milk like he did. Unfortunately, it wasn't practical to bring milk along.

If the officers wanted more tea or water they would sign to Elliot to bring it over instead of speaking so he had be awake and watchful. Elliot had been watching soldiers use sign language and trying to learn through observation. But Jack had made sure Elliot understood the signs that would involve his duties. Such as bring me a chair, water, tea, or food in sign language.

They had only allowed him three hours of sleep before waking him and assigning this task. He had drunk so much hot tea himself in effort to stay awake it was having the opposite effect. His belly was full and warm. Now fighting sleep was even more difficult.

He had started off paying attention to the conversation of the commanding officers. He knew they were arguing on how to overpower the flying creature. In fact they had been arguing over that the entire time and Elliot figured it was the only reason they hadn't attacked yet. But now he was only catching the odd word and partial sentence. If he weren't so tired he really would put more effort into listening to their plans. It seemed this flying creature really had them stumped.

Seeing his fire was dying a little Elliot stood and stretched. It was time to get some more firewood. The pile he had been using had dwindled down to just a few pieces. He strategically placed what was left into the fire, stoking it up to be sure it was going strong. Then he left to get more.

Elliot looked around for the soldier cat named Gadget. He had been helping Elliot with gathering firewood but had disappeared with Jack somewhere. Maybe it was their turn to sleep. Not seeing him Elliot grabbed the small toboggan they used just for this purpose and wandered into the forest.

Thanks to the ice storm there were plenty of branches on the ground. But thanks to the ice storm they were frozen to the ground with ice.

There was an ax to use; however it was too big and very heavy. Elliot hadn't even bothered to bring it. He could hardly lift it let alone swing it. So Elliot's only other choice was to push and pull at the fallen branches to snap them free in order to gather them up.

Elliot wished Gadget were with him. He was much stronger and could snap the branches or swing the ax whichever he preferred. Elliot had to look for the smaller branches. Fortunately, there were plenty of all sizes. But he did have to move around a lot to find the right ones.

Rarely did anyone ever use an ax on the living trees. They never really had to. There were always enough fallen trees to make do with. Besides not cutting a living tree suited the cats. They needed the trees to climb and it just helped maintain the peace and harmony of Catland.

The toboggan was just about full when Elliot heard sounds off in the distance. They were strange sounds echoing far off. Elliot listened carefully as he slowly headed back to camp. He didn't think he had ever heard this sound before, although, there was something unusually familiar about it. The sounds were becoming louder so whatever it was, it was heading this way.

As Elliot neared the camp he saw the solders running this way and that. They were gearing up to do battle! Then he remembered! The sounds were similar to that dog's laugh he had heard when he and Samantha were hiding. The dogs were coming here!

Elliot let go of the toboggan and ran back to his sleigh. He jumped in to the sleigh up front where the brakes were located.

Pulling the tarp over him he ducked down out of sight there. This was where he was told to go should a battle ensue in camp. He peeked over the edge.

The camp was alive with cats racing about shouting orders to one another. Elliot watched what first looked like chaos turn into an organized army.

As the sounds got closer, Elliot watched as most of the troops and officers disappeared into the forest, some of them formed a centerline on the three sides of the camp protecting the center from whoever ran in.

Major Cat and a few of the remaining officers including Officer Hiss had cleared away their maps and documents. They now took up positions in the center of camp not far from where Elliot and the sleighs were.

A smaller number of soldiers took up hiding in various places around camp. These soldiers Elliot noticed were Jack, Gadget, and other soldiers like the harness cats. Then they waited, all listening to the sounds getting louder.

Suddenly soldiers Elliot hadn't seen hiding in the trees jumped out of their hiding places and rushed into the forest toward the coming threat. The noise changed into a frenzied ruckus. Even from a fair distance away Elliot heard yelps, growls, and howls. The battle was taking place in the forest.

After several minutes, a white cat raced into camp followed by some of the troops. Seeing the line of soldiers in front of the camp he came to a stop panting heavily. After a quick discussion with the facing soldier he was let through the line. Officer Hiss ran over to the cat, exchanging a few words. He then led the white cat over to Major Cat. A few more words were exchanged when Major Cat turned to Elliot and signed for him to bring some water.

Elliot jumped down from the sleigh, grabbed a cup from the table and dipped it into the hot water. Thinking it maybe too hot he threw in a pawful of fresh snow. He ran over to the major and the white cat as quickly as he could, trying very hard not to spill.

The white cat frowned as Elliot drew near to him. Without taking his eyes off Elliot he took the cup and downed the water without stopping. Once finished he gave the cup back, wiping his muzzle with the back of his paw he said, "Thanks for the cooling hit, I really had to belly-it. Tell me, young cat, is your name Elliot?"

Elliot's eyes grew wide. He looked from the white cat to the Major Cat and back again to the white cat.

"Yes, sir, how did you know? I've never met you before now, here in the snow."

"I know your brother, Eli,
He's a brave little guy and last I saw still alive." the white cat told him.

"Thank Cat above Eli's alive! Where is he? When will he arrive?" Elliot was ecstatic! He had been so worried about him but he needed to know more. Why wasn't he here?

Major Cat stepped forward, "Return to your post. I need his report first and foremost."

Elliot reluctantly returned to his post. He was wake now. Wide awake. After washing the cup and putting it away, he decided he could stand closer to the officers without actually leaving the fire. So he moved to about half way between them and the fire.

The wind had picked up a bit more gently blowing the tent walls in and out plus it had changed direction. Now it was carrying much of what was being said away. He was only able to hear parts of their conversation. Enough to know there were a lot of dogs in their camp and Eli was there! In their camp!

It wasn't long before the army cats returned with their dog prisoners.

The dogs were huge in comparison to the cats but all of them had cuts and were bleeding from one place or another. Some of them were limping, favoring a paw here or there. Their tails were down between their legs as they walked huddled together eyeing the cats fearfully.

The cats escorting them, easily outnumbered them, maybe twenty to one. Although not all of the army cats were back in the camp. Some of the platoons that had set out ahead of the march a day ago never rejoined them here. Elliot never asked about them, partly because they were suppose to sign instead of talk and partly because he trusted the army knew what it was doing.

Looking at the dogs now, it looked to Elliot like the dogs never stood a chance. Collars were put on them and then they were chained to trees. Elliot had wondered what the chains were for. One of the other sleighs had carried them. Now he knew.

Food was brought out for the prisoners and their wounds were tended. Elliot was ordered to boil more water as they started watering, feeding and patching up the dogs. Elliot quickly retrieved his firewood and went about his duties all the while never really taking his eyes off those strange creatures they called dogs.

He watched the dogs gulp down the food like they hadn't eaten in days and they lapped up every drop of water they were given. It seemed these dogs could easily gobble up all the food the camp had in it. And in spite of being chained to trees, he didn't go near them. Leaving the serving and tending to the army cats.

Elliot was fascinated; he couldn't seem to take his eyes off these beasts. They had such long legs and muzzles in comparison to cats. Even from a distance Elliot could see they had very large teeth. He wondered how the army cats were able to fight these large opponents. He wished he could have seen some fighting but from a safe place of course.

All of a sudden the air changed. The dogs stood up, faced the forest sniffing the air then they suddenly started barking. Elliot felt a slight drop in temperature. He could hear a wind coming toward them from within the forest but no other sound. Then the strangest thing happened. Trees in the forest already icy and full of snow became frosty too but only in one area of the forest. Frosty ice crystals began to appear all over the trees and all over anyone or anything in that area.

The dogs barking increased into an uncontrolled frenzy, which now included growling and snarling too. The hair on the back of their necks stood up making the dogs appear a bit bigger. They leaped and pulled at the chains that held them to the trees. Elliot hoped the chains or collars wouldn't break. He had never seen such a ferocious animal. Now he was truly afraid of them.

Elliot jumped back into the sleigh to hide. What was coming that caused the dogs to react like that. And however did the cats fight them and win? Elliot peaked over the edge again to watch what was going on.

With wide eyes, Elliot watched a transparent shape emerge from the forest. It was glowing white and blue. As it came forward,

Elliot saw that it was a young man. He was tall with blue hair and glowing skin. Major Cat followed by his officers approached the young man. Their coats became frosty like the trees as they neared him. He obviously belonged to part of the Royal Monarch but Elliot wasn't sure who this was.

When the young man stood still, he stood very still, only his hair and robes blew with the wind. And he was indeed transparent. Elliot could see the trees on the other side of him. He had a look of peace about him though. It was almost calming to watch him. Elliot glanced at the dogs.

He did not seem to have the same effect on them. Although, they had stopped leaping against their chains they were still barking and growling at the young man.

Elliot was a little perplexed, he usually could hear very well from a distance what was being said but for some reason he could not hear the conversation between the officers and the young man. Every time the young man spoke, the wind howled and Elliot couldn't make out what he was saying. After a few words they turned and started heading toward the officer's tent.

Then the young man did something unexpected. He stopped and approached the dogs. As he neared them they became encrusted in a frost. It didn't look like they minded though. The young man put his hands up and the dogs ceased their barking. Although Elliot thought he could hear some low growling, perhaps under someone's breath.

He spoke to them but Elliot still couldn't make out what he was saying. When one of the dogs answered him it was in a loud boisterous voice, it was obvious he wanted everyone to hear. He announced they were here to stay. There was nothing anyone could do, nothing anyone could say. Nothing could make them be on their way.

That was disheartening.

The young man said something else to the dogs that made them back away from him a bit. Then they lay down, curling their lips they let out a few more growls. Elliot saw none of the dogs looked away from the young man to show they wouldn't harm him. It was a common courtesy to look away if your intentions were peaceful. Every cat knows a prolonged stare meant a fight was inevitable. All the dogs glared in defiance to the young man.

The young man turned from them and rejoined the officers who were waiting for him. Together they walked toward the canopy tent. He watched as everything became frosty around the young man as he passed by various objects in the camp. As they drew near, Elliot felt a chill go through him, he shivered. Then it dawned on him this was Chill! Of course! That explained the chill in the air.

Elliot could see Chill was too tall to fit under the tent. But as he got closer to the tent, he began to shrink in size. He shrank while walking reaching the right height just as he walked under the canopied top without ever missing a step. Elliot had never seen anything like it. It was perfect timing and as smooth as can be.

Elliot couldn't help himself. He hopped out of the sleigh and ran over to the officer's tent. Again he stood as close as he could without completely abandoning his post. He became encrusted with frost like everyone else who was in close proximity of Chill but it warmed him instead of making him colder.

"Yes I am back, Chill," he heard the white cat say. "Will Winter join us on this hill?"

When Chill answered the white cat Elliot realized it wasn't the blowing wind carrying away Chill's words, it was Chill's own voice. He sounded like blowing wind when he spoke.

"No, Winter cannot release his hold.
The weather around the dogs is far too cold,
so Spring must stay too,
to temperate the weather so the dogs won't freeze through."

Elliot had to listen carefully to make out what Chill said.

Directing his attention to all of the officers, Chill continued speaking, "The time is now, to enforce your pow,
and leave a permanent impression upon their brow.

While Winter and Spring stand still with their buffer,
The Rest of the World continues to suffer.

In The Rest of the World no winds or precipitation,
will flow without this Monarch's participation.
Without the natural order of the throne holder,
the cold becomes colder.
And the inhabitants will start to lose their water,

as the hot becomes hotter.
They need the winds to blow,
and the rains to flow.
For without their water,
they will undoubtedly increase their slaughter.
   So, Striker, tell me what have you learned.
Do you know how these dogs may be returned?"
   Chill once again turned his attention to the white cat, so then did everyone else.
   The white cat named Striker looked disheveled, like he had been through more than just a run for his life. He had scars on his face and part of his ear was missing. He answered,
   "I tracked the dogs backward.
The trail was easy.
The land was battered.
It led to a hole, the tunnel of a troll.
Within Big Ear Cave I saw the toll,
the entrance, large enough for carts to roll.
On the north side of Jagged Tooth Rock,
I must admit I felt the shock.
For the tunnel belongs to the Blackspear clan,
from where within, out these dogs ran.
I know not if by chance or by plan,
but these trolls knew and allowed entry to Catland."
   Chill looked surprised saying, "I had not thought of the trolls." Then taking a moment he thoughtfully added, "This is bad for all trolls in their holes. Now we must find out, to what extent did they play their roles?"
   Chill raised a hand to his chin and slowly began to pace around the tent.
   "And it explains why we found no entry through the bush;
no broken branches, no trail was pushed.
On all accounts the enchantment stands,
I found no interest of anyone to enter this land.
But what is puzzling still,
is trolls allowing passage;
it goes against their will.
Something must have happened,

because it doesn't fit the bill."

Spotting a trunk, he walked over and opened it. He picked out a map. His transparent hand became solid as he lifted the map. Unrolling it he carried the map to a table saying,

"But if trolls can let them in,
then trolls can let them out.
But first we shall begin,
and then we'll use some clout."

Major Cat and the officers including the cat named Striker gather around the table. Major Cat began to relay the plans they had already agreed upon expressing concern over the flying beast. Elliot was already aware of the various plans discussed and so wasn't too disappointed that he was again too far away to hear everything in their discussion.

Hearing his name being called Elliot became aware Jack was quietly trying to get his attention.

"Elliot, Elliot, what are you doing?
Enough of your viewing.
Come over here.
Dinner should be brewing."

Jack appeared to be annoyed with Elliot. Elliot was so involved in his eavesdropping that he hadn't been watching for anyone to sign to him. Elliot again reluctantly headed over to the fire where Jack stood. He didn't want to leave his eavesdropping. He knew they would be sending the troops out soon and now he was going to miss all the important details.

Getting a big pot out, he and the other cats began to prepare a stew. Who knew, perhaps it would be the last stew anyone had in a while.

CHAPTER 17

Notso ran as fast as his stubby legs would carry him. He knew the dogs would catch up to him in a matter of minutes. But if he could ward them off until he could reach the northern side of Dank Tunnel, he might stand a chance. Provided none of his clan was there. News about what had happened at the dog camp would have spread by now.

Thinking about how his clan turned on him made his blood boil. They were the ones who beat him and threw him to the dogs. How dare they? How could they turn on one of their own? All he had done was point out the dogs had not held up to their side of the bargain.

It was Dicey Troll who had turned them against him. It was always Dicey, ever since they were just trollings. Dicey had always hated him and now he hated Dicey. Long gone was the admiration he once held for Dicey. He was embarrassed at how he use to follow Dicey around like a love-sick little pup. Now all he wanted to do was pound on him.

"Not so tall, not so smart, not so ready for a brawl," Dicey use to tease him just before giving him a good beating. It wasn't Notso's fault he was born smaller than all the other trolls. Notso knew it didn't mean he wasn't as smart as the rest of them. In fact Notso thought he might actually be smarter, smarter than Dicey at least.

"Notso bright, Notso slight, but Notso ready for a fight." He use to counter, but Dicey would just laugh and say, "That what I said, dumb head." Dicey was bigger, stronger and always won those scraps. But not anymore, Notso would see to it this time.

Notso felt the teeth of a dog bite into the back of his leg. He spun around swinging the log at his attacker. The dog saw the thick branch coming and jumped out of the way avoiding it just in time. Notso continued his spin around back into a run, still heading toward the tunnel. But this time he waved the log around behind him in an effort to defend his backside.

There were four big dogs behind him. They were snarling and barking at him to give up and surrender. He wasn't going to. No way was Notso going back into that little cage—no way. He'd do anything now to keep out of it. The tunnel entrance wasn't too far but at the same time it wasn't too close either. He had to keep running.

He hated dogs now. Where were these riches the dogs promised? Only in The Rest of the World did they ever see the riches of food galore, soft beds, and music that moved them. There was nothing here but cats and trees. All the trolls knew that. It was the dogs who wanted the gold, not him or his clan. Gold was everywhere in the mountains but food was not. This land only had rodents and birds, cat food if you asked him.

In The Rest of the World the dogs had food so delicious it made the mouth water just to think of it. What did he or his clan care about the gold in the mountains? Give them the gold if they want it so bad. But giving them this land? Notso didn't think it was their land to give. Besides, they would just wreck it like they wrecked their own land. They had holes everywhere. Senseless holes, at least when a troll dug it had a purpose like going somewhere or enlarging his living quarters.

And the way the dogs fought over territory. They would fight even to the death if the wrong dog crossed a border. Well Notso understood that but at least a troll respected other clan tunnels. A troll always made sure it was okay to pass through first, unless he wanted the beating of his life.

Notso felt the log in his hand get pulled from of his grip. He spun around again, facing the big dog who took it. Notso reached for the log grabbing it again but the dog did not let go of his side. The other three dogs surrounded him growling at him to stop fighting all the while nipping at his legs.

Notso tried freeing the huge tree branch from the dog's jaws but the dog would not let go. Notso pulled on his side and the big dog pulled on his, while the other three dogs took turns biting Notso's legs. Notso tried kicking them in between his yanks. But avoiding their teeth was proving to be too much. He started seeing blood on the ground and he knew it wasn't theirs.

This stupid dog was playing a trolling's game of tug-o-war! Infuriated Notso let go of his side. Oh how he wanted to beat the dog with it.

The dog tossed the tree branch to the side. Now Notso was surrounded. His fists were up and ready to hit the first dog within reach. He looked around for another big log. Spying one, he started working his way toward it. He knew he could hit harder with that than with his bare hands.

From the corner of his eye he saw the blur of the first cat attack the dogs. It leaped down from out of the trees. Just as suddenly cats jumped down all around them. The cats all wore camouflage and blended into the trees and snow so well they were never seen until they attacked.

The first cat leaped onto a dog's back. Then Notso saw it cut through the dog's jacket to his shoulder with its shiny claws sliding down and under its belly. The dog howled in pain and ferociously snapped its jaws trying to bite the cat. As quick as the cat appeared it jumped out of the way avoiding the large teeth of the dog it attacked.

All of the cats attacked in similar fashion. The cats were lightning fast with their attacks, cutting and scratching the dogs. Then with neck-breaking speed they jumped and spun out of the way of the dog's jaws. Some of them swinging over the dogs' backs or sliding out from between the dogs' legs. Then just as quick, retreating to a safe distance and allowing the next wave of cats to attack.

There was no way the dogs could counteract this form of bombardment. They were outnumbered. The dogs crowded together in an effort to protect their backsides while facing their attackers. Soon the cats stopped their attacks leaving the dogs huddled together surrounded by twenty or so cats.

Still huffing from his run Notso leaned against a tree staying out of the way of the cats. His legs were full of bites, blood ran down and pooled around his feet. One bite was particularly bad; blood surged out with each pump of his heart.

One of the cats stepped forward. It was one of the bigger cats and had some stripes on its camouflaged jacket as a sign that it was one of the leaders.

Ignoring Notso the cat addressed the dogs saying,
"By the magistrates charge you are under arrest.
For trespassing on Catland blessed.
For assault on a citizen and causing distress.
Surrender now or do you need to be pressed?"

Notso found himself smiling, in spite of the painful tears in his legs, finally a little bit of sweet justice. He sank down to sit at the bottom of the tree and rested his head against it. Black dots appeared in his vision. The bites hurt but no more than any of the other beatings he had endured. Maybe with all the running, lack of food (he hadn't eaten in days) and now blood loss, it was finally getting to him. He suddenly felt extremely tired.

The big dog that had fought Notso for the huge branch spoke up.
"Is that where we are?
In the land of cats?
This is bizarre.
Well you have us outnumbered so we have no choice.
We surrender, so go ahead and rejoice."

That was all the cats required, thin specially woven ropes were brought out from backpacks and the dogs were tied together from around their necks. A cat brought over a medical pack and started treating Notso's legs.

"Are all these from them? Or are some from your den?" the medic cat asked him searching over all his wounds. He went to work putting on salves, sewing holes, and bandaging up what he could.

"Too tired to talk. Too tired to walk," Notso said wearily. His energy was draining from him. He thought maybe he could sleep here. Perhaps just for a bit. The cats would protect him. He let the exhaustion take over and allowed his eyes to close.

"Not here, troll. Cadbury, fetch me a bowl." The medic cat said to a colleague. Something stinky was shoved under Notso's nose. It was a horrid smell, waking him up.

"Here eat this. You need the energy, and it will make you feel bliss." The medic cat gave him a bowl of goo with finely chopped green leaves in it. Notso looked at the goo for a moment. It did not look good, nor did it smell good, but he was hungry, so who cared what it was. He ate it. Unfortunately, it tasted the same as it looked and smelled, like gooey green leaves.

After tending Notso, the medic cat moved to check over the prisoners. They let him tend their wounds but would snap at him if he agitated a sensitive spot too much.

The medic cat was quick on his paws however, jumping out of their way saying, "I'm sorry if that hurt. Please allow me to continue, so healing will not divert."

Reluctantly the dogs would allow him to continue. It appeared they wanted to be fixed up.

After a while, one dog pulled on his rope and sneered, "You think this will ho . . ."

"Shhhhh!" Another dog cut him off. "Be respectful. What they don't know is neglectful."

The cats hearing this made motions with their paws to one another. Once they had agreed upon whatever it was they were signing, they got out some more ropes. They cut the ropes with their shiny claws into four smaller sizes.

"We know how dogs like to chew.
So for safety, we're going to muzzle you," the leader cat told them.

At hearing this the dogs all bared their teeth and started growling.

The medic cat stepped away from them for his safety sake.

The big log-fighting dog growled out his warning, "I dare you to try. Muzzle me, and I'll let my teeth fly."

The leader cat unfazed by the dog's reaction calmly apologized.

"I'm sorry, it won't be for long,
but as your buddy pointed out,
you're all very strong.

Besides, you haven't any choice.
When we get where we're going,
you can have back your voice," the leader cat reassured them.

The dogs didn't back down. They maintained their growling and lowered their heads to a striking position.

Paws were held up and claws were exposed. The cats claws looked like shinny knives with a razor sharp edge and a needle thin tip.

"Must we do this again? Please, put your teeth away. The medic will start to complain," the leader said swooping his paw in an exaggerated jester toward the medic.

The medic looked up from his backpack not expecting to be drawn into the conversation. Seeing everyone looking at him. He smiled and said, "Yeah, I'm a real whiner. There's no one finer" and went back to packing his things.

The dogs still didn't back down. So from every angle a cat

could safely reach, they moved in close and gently pointed their knife-like claws into the dogs. Only then did the dogs slowly submit and allow the cats to bind their mouths shut. Once the muzzles were secured, the dogs all scowled at the one who had given away their silent plan of escape.

The cats quietly gathered their things then encircled the dogs in preparation to depart. Once they were ready the leader addressed Notso for the first time.

"Do you have a name troll? We're going to need you to come along on this stroll."

Notso stood up; the goo he ate was beginning to take effect. The pain was lessening but he felt funny. He felt energized yet lightheaded and he had a funny tingling feeling throughout his body. The tingling feeling made him want to lie down and roll around in the snow. It was sort of a tickly feeling but not quite the same. Notso grabbed on to the tree trunk to stop himself from doing just that. "What was in bowl and why I want to roll?" He asked clutching the tree harder.

"You are going to be fine," the leader told him. "How much did you give him, of that catnip brine?" he asked the medic.

"Well he's a pretty big size. So twenty times the regular amount I devise," the medic answered.

"Perhaps too much. He seems to need something to clutch," the leader said. With a wave of the leader's paw one of the cats set out to look for something Notso could hang on to.

"Troll, what's your name?" the leader asked again. "Here you go. Here's a cane."

The cat was back dragging a long tree branch with a hooked side. Notso grabbed onto it to see if it would help him stand. It wasn't as thick as he would have liked but it did help—sort of. He hung on with two hands.

Suddenly felt like he had tons energy—tons and tons of energy. He was still lightheaded but he couldn't resist the urge to run, and run fast. Dropping the cane he gave into the feeling and bolted, running a circle around the leader cat and a few others. Around and around he ran until he became dizzy. When he came to an unsteady stop the funny tickling feeling came back. This time he dropped and rolled around in the snow. It felt much better to roll than it did fight the funny feeling.

"Did you leave any of that nip for us? Look at him go, what a wuss!" Notso heard some cat in the crowd snickering.

Notso ignored his audience while he rolled and wiggled in the snow. Slowly he became aware that every eye was on him. So he slowed his rolling to a stop, reached for the abandoned cane and used it to help him stand up. No one said anything. They just watched to see what he was going to do next.

Suddenly his stomach gurgled reminding him he was still very hungry. "Anyone got more food? My stomach really in the mood," he asked them.

One of the cats swung their backpack off and handed him some dried meat. Notso took it but still feeling energized he gave a little hop in the air as he did so. Then remembering he had been asked a question.

He answered, "My name Notso. But before we go, there something you need to know."

Chapter 18

Eli

The tree shook and teetered as the dogs sawed at the trunk. Eli climbed down to the same branch the orange cat was on. The wind blew swaying the tree in addition to the chopping and shaking from the dogs. Ice and snow showered down on them.

"May I know your name?
And may I know this plan you claim?" Eli quietly asked through the wind.

The orange cat was looking around from trees to dogs, "My name is Scratch.

And the plan has yet to fully hatch," he answered him just as quietly. He continued to survey their surroundings.

Then even quieter he said,
"By all accounts, I should already be dead.
But the Good Cat Above, gave me an extra life instead.
He did it, the last time I fled."

He spoke slowly and so quiet Eli wondered if he was still talking to him or talking to himself.

Without looking at Eli, Scratch continued his somber speech, "Perhaps the message of sacrifice is what He wants spread.
Putting others before oneself is taught, not bred."

Scratch fell silent. He just watched the dogs sawing at the tree below. Eli didn't know what to say so he watched the dogs too.

The dog's camp remained noisy with barking. They could hear all sorts of barking through the blowing snow but none of the barking was headed this way, to their relief.

Then speaking plainly again, Scratch looked Eli in the face saying,
"I'm now on my last life so I may not survive,
but you do exactly as I say, and you'll leave here alive."

Scratch sounded so grim. Eli frowned. He didn't want to hear anything negative. He needed to be hopeful.

Scratch asked, "Is that agreed, Eli?
And please, tell your siblings,
I said good-bye," he added softly.

Eli looked hard at the orange cat named Scratch. The wind blew his fur around hard. He was scratched, and scarred, missing an eye. His coat was filthy with ground-in dirt. Eli could smell dried blood mixed into his fur along with dog saliva. His breathing was somewhat labored, he had some broken ribs and his breath had the smell of blood on it indicating he had other internal injuries too. He made Eli's bruised areas laughable. He was in very rough shape, but he had made it this far. Eli could not give up on him now. It wasn't right.

"No, you can tell them.
I went back for you,
to save you from this bedlam."

Eli tried his best to sound positive and hopeful.
"We'll make it out of here.
You'll see, we'll make it free and clear."

Ignoring him Scratch pointed passed Eli's shoulder,
"Do you see that branch over there?
On that other tree, it's fairly bare.
When this tree falls, it will fall by,
you make that jump, while on the fly by."

Eli looked at the tree Scratch was talking about. Even with the wind blowing the trees he believed he could make the jump but . . .
"What about you? That jumps too far for you to do."

Scratch was watching the dogs again.
"Don't worry about me.
I have a point to make.
I must make them see."

The tree shook and swayed again causing them to dig their claws further into the icy frozen branch. They had to swing their tails to counter balance their bodies in order to stay on the branch.

Then Scratch looked at Eli again but his expression changed. It looked like he was pleading with Eli.

"This is important. You cannot stay here dormant.
You are part of my point, Eli,
so don't wreck it by getting caught young guy!
Getting caught would be a breaking point,
a disjoint, a huge disappoint,
and undoubtedly the unraveling of my point.
   Am I being clear?
You are not to get caught
Do you hear?"

Eli didn't feel good about this but Scratch was imploring him to cooperate.

"I understand. Getting caught will wreck your plan," Eli answered him. Scratch's request made it hard to swallow.

"But what about you? Just leave you here for them to chew?" Eli asked, silently searching for another way out of this situation.

"And once I'm in that tree, they'll just chop it down. They won't leave me be."

"No, moron. You have to move on." Scratch snapped at first but quickly softened his tone.

"I'll provide a distraction, a way for you to be gone." He desperately wanted Eli to understand him. He needed Eli to succeed in escaping.

The tree shook and cracked. It started to lean in the direction Scratch said it would. They didn't have much time left.

"Remember, in absolutely no way are you to be captured. Or else my point will become completely fractured."

"Okay. I will do as you say. I'll do my best to be on my way." Eli agreed to Scratch's request. It felt wrong though, leaving him to the dogs. Who really was the moron Eli wondered.

Eli turned around, hopping on to another branch he ran to an open section with fewer limbs and got ready for the jump. The tree leaned and cracked some more. Snow and ice continued to shower and blow all around them. On the positive side, all the ice breaking off the branches exposed the bark providing solid footing for him. Then with a loud crack the tree fell. Eli leaped for the branch as the tree fell by it landing perfectly on the bough. Scraping his claws along the ice on the newly attained branch he ran to the center of the tree. Eli spun around to watch what was happening below.

The tree fell with a loud crash. Branches and snow flew everywhere. From out of the branches, Eli saw the orange cat leaped on to the back of the corporal. The dog jumped sideways and Scratch slid around under his neck.

In a loud voice Scratch declared, "I can rip your throat out but I won't!" He then slid under the corporal's belly. "I can slice your guts out but I don't." The corporal jumped up turning in midair in effort to get away from Scratch's claws. Scratch leaped in unison with him. Making it clear the corporal could not escape him. When they came down together Scratch slid in between his back legs. "I can sever each of your tendons."

A dog nearby rushed toward Scratch with his jaws wide open for a bite. Scratch used his claws on the dog's face to swing up on to his head. "Or take an eye out in my vengeance." Scratched jumped from the dogs back to the ground as the dog dropped his head and spun around to snap at him only getting a mouthful of air. Scratch then leaped toward another dog.

Eli was astonished at how, in spite of all his injuries, Scratch could move like that. The old cat really was giving it all he had. He looked for the quickest way down the tree.

"I can take each of your lives." The dog Scratch attacked next reared up with his chin down and teeth exposed, ready for impact but Scratch vaulted around his side dragging his claws along the dog's body as he went. "As you see my claws are knives."

All the dogs on the ground closed in around Scratch. No one was watching Eli.

Scratch landed on the other side of the dog between the dog and a tree. "But take your life I will not do." The dog whirled around facing Scratch, teeth bared. "To do what's right is what I choose." Scratch leaped on to the tree trunk above their heads and just hung there. With a quick glance to Eli and an even quicker nod of his head to him, Scratch jumped off the tree to the side that was furthest away from Eli. "I hope you take this as a cue."

Eli took this as his cue and dropped to the ground, bolting in to the forest in the same direction Notso had gone. The last thing he heard Scratch say was "And do what's right to whoever you pursue."

A dog on the other side of the tree Scratch had jumped off lunged at Scratch. But Scratch was anticipating this and twirled around the dog's paws narrowly missing the dog's teeth saying, "And do what's right to whoever you pursue." From behind the dog Scratch darted toward another tree still trying to lead them away from Eli. A dog there ran in front of him blocking him from the tree in sight.

"Making the right choice isn't always easy," he said jumping over the dog who twirled around snapping at Scratch's paws, "kindness to a foe can make you queasy." Scratched landed in front of the tree. But just as he leaped again to land on the trunk something happened inside of him. Extreme pain shot through his chest. He hit the tree but was unable to grab it with his claws. He fell to the ground. The dogs surrounded him in an instant. Many muzzles touched his body from all sides. He felt a few teeth scrape him but they didn't bite down. Instead he was getting sniffed. They were smelling him, all over, pushing him this way and that. Surprisingly, no one bit into him. He was sure they wanted to though.

The dogs stopped their sniffing and Scratch slowly pushed himself off the ground. He leaned his back against the tree. He struggled for breath. Through the blowing snow the corporal came over to stand in front. The dogs had opened a spot to let him through.

"But acts of violence, should be silenced." Scratch was determined to get his last say in.

"It has always, and will always,
only beget more violence."

"Do you know how hard it is right now?
Not to tear you to shreds from tail to brow?" the corporal asked.

Shaking his head Scratch said, "When will you dogs learn? You *need* heart-felt concern."

Scratched coughed up some blood. He couldn't see straight. His vision was blurring. He allowed himself to lie down in the snow. The pain in his chest was excruciating.

"So is this your plea? To spare your life is the key?" the corporal asked but then realized, "Except, there is no life here to spare. You are drawing in the last of your air.

And look at your price. All this, just to tell us to be nice."

Scratch really hoped the dogs could understand. Struggling for breath he managed to say,

"If you could remember but one thing,
to this one truth I hope you cling:
Acts of cruelty are outrageous,
but acts of kindness are contagious."

He spoke the last of his message as clearly and as loudly as he could, coughing up more blood at the end.

The corporal scrutinized the cat lying before him. The wind blew through his fur with no regard for the cat's dignity. Snow was falling on him. Eventually, the snow would bury him. He didn't have much time left in this world. There wasn't anything anyone could do for him now. Not that anyone would have done anything anyway. By rights, he should let his pack devour him. They weren't completely starving but the captain always kept them hungry; just hungry enough to keep them from wandering too far off and keep them coming back for another tidbit.

Sitting down in front of him the corporal said,
"Well, you gave us quite a demonstration old cat.
You put on a great show in fact.
You cats always provide the best entertainment.
If only it could have been a better arrangement.
But, if it helps you to die in peace:
we understand your message at least.
I'm just not sure giving the last of your life,
was worth this message of peace versus strife."

Scratch smiled. He had gotten through.

"So I *have* made my point.
And my friend is gone, to your disappoint," he choked out still smiling.

What was this? The dogs quickly checked the tree they had seen the other cat jump into. Rotten dog biscuits! The cat was gone like a bowl of briskets!

Chapter 19

Winter continued on with his howling storm. As Eli raced through the forest, he wondered if Winter ever took a break. Once his paws had hit the ground he never looked back. He knew Scratch was doing his best to keep the dogs attention on himself. The least Eli could do was follow through with the plan no matter how much it hurt his ribs to run.

It helped that he was able to run on top of the frozen snow. The ice layer was still strong enough to support his weight but he had to stay out in the open where the ice was the strongest.

It was easy to follow Notso's trail because he and his pursuers had broken through the icy snow leaving tracks that anyone with eyes could follow. Eli wanted to catch up with Notso. He didn't know why. It had looked to him like Notso had abandoned him and Scratch. But in the back of his mind he hoped Notso would help fight these dogs with the help of the Monarch's Army or perhaps worse maybe he needed Eli's help. Eli didn't know but he thought he should at least find out. Then he would circle round and head to Whisker Creek like he was suppose to. But for now he really had to put some space between himself and the dogs behind.

It wasn't long before Eli noticed there was blood along the tracks. The falling snow was diluting the blood and over time would wash it completely away. However it was still fresh enough to smell. Eli had slowed enough to check it out. He knew right away it belonged to Notso from its scent. As Eli continued his run he began to fear the worst for Notso.

The blood increased his worry for Scratch too. He hoped Scratch would be okay.

So far the dogs had only wanted information and the way Scratch was jumping around gave Eli hope that he would survive. But now seeing this blood and knowing how fierce the dogs could be with one another . . . Eli didn't want to think about what they could do to Scratch. He was going to get help for Scratch. He had to. It wasn't right leaving him behind.

Eli had picked up his pace and tried to focus on what he might find with Notso. He made himself pay attention to the tracks, sounds and smells around him instead of the pain his body felt. He could still hear barking from the camp but it was fading the further he ran. The tracks were leading him upward, up along the side of a mountain. He tried hard to stay aware of his surroundings just in case he got surprised by more dogs in the area.

Not long after discovering the blood a tall slender cat dressed in white camouflage jumped out from behind a tree just ahead of him. The cat startled him, seemly to come from out of nowhere. Eli stopped immediately in front of it. He was relieved to see another cat but he worriedly checked over his shoulder. He wasn't far enough away yet. Those dogs would catch him if he stopped here. He didn't know who this cat was but neither of them could stay here. He was about to say something when she spoke up.

"Are you Eli? The one held captive with a troll and a cat with one eye?" she asked him.

"Yes, but it's not safe here I assess. Come on let's go, lets progress," Eli said urgently. He went to move around her when they heard howling from behind.

They had discovered he was gone! Fear seized his heart. Eli panicked, "They're after me! Come on let's flee! They won't let me be! And the same goes for you! If they discover you . . . you might as well say, 'adieu'!"

The cat jumped in front of him, blocking him. Putting a paw on Eli's shoulder she said, "You're safe now.
We've got this, I vow.
Follow me.
I'll bring you to safety."

Eli looked at her wondering if she was with the army, He had never met an army cat before. The cat immediately spun around and ran through the forest, away from the trail. Without hesitating Eli followed her.

As they ran, Eli took note of her clothes. She had a pack on her back and was wearing clothes that looked like the winter woods. She must be with the army who else would wear that? After racing through the trees for a bit Eli began to notice they were not alone. There were other cats in camouflage scattered throughout the forest. Some were on branches; some crouched low under the evergreens, or were hiding in bushes. The cat he was following slowed down and a bunch more cats stepped into view.

Eli was led to one cat in particular. He was a very big and muscled black and white cat. He looked tough. His coat had some stripes on it. Eli didn't know what the stripes meant but he looked like he was in charge.

"Eli of Sphinxville?" he asked gruffly giving Eli a quick once-over. Eli nodded puffing from his run.

"You're alive so you must have some skill,
but you failed to report at Whisker Creek still.
Now we are out of time.
So you'll stay here behind our line."

This was definitely the army and the big cat was definitely in charge. He seemed kind of mad at Eli too.

"Tell me how many dogs are in that camp?
And what have you learned of that flying tramp?"

Looking around Eli spotted Notso in the distance. He was leaning against a tree holding a long stick. Eli was relieved to see he was still standing.

The dog's far-off barking was getting louder. They were coming this direction. They must have followed his and the girl soldier's tracks. It wouldn't be long before they reached them.

"There are more dogs than I could count.
I'd guess five hundred to be the amount," Eli answered the big soldier.

"Not so many on my tail,
about eight on the trail."

Eli wanted him to know they weren't all coming this way. He didn't know they had already identified the number of dogs by their barking voices.

"The flying dog, she's huge with keen eyes.
Even after I checked out her egg, she let me escape,
and told none to my surprise."

Eli added thoughtfully, "I don't know why she let me go."
"She could have stopped me that I know."

The dogs were running fast. Their barking continued to get louder.

"It's a she and she has an egg?" the big cat asked. Not waiting for a response he looked at a soldier beside him saying, "If the dogs have that . . . they have her pegged."

The cat nodded his agreement.

"Jag report this intel. It is pivotal in quelling the rebel."

The soldier took off at a run heading westward.

Turning to the soldier who led Eli here, the big cat said, "Take Eli to the back. Guard them well, the whole whack."

He made a gesture with his paw indicating there were more to be guarded. And then he and his troops took off at a run toward the dogs. Cats Eli hadn't seen revealed their hiding spots by joining in on the run.

The soldier who led Eli this far motioned with her head for Eli to follow her. She trotted over to a spot near Notso where she could keep an eye out for both of them.

Not far from Notso were the dogs who had chased him down. They were all tied together with thin ropes around their necks and muzzles. They were sitting together in a small clearing with two long ropes wrapped loosely around nearby trees. One Soldier each held on to the ends of the ropes.

Eli sat down close to Notso, glad to have a rest. He still hurt. Looking over Notso's wounds he asked, "Are you okay? They got a few bites in I'd say."

He was patched up but there was dried blood on his legs and frozen blood on his boots.

"Catnip's cheesy. Notso's pleasy," Notso answered.

Huh? That didn't make sense. Eli looked up at Notso. Notso was looking down at him but his gaze wasn't right. He was looking at him and past him at the same time.

"He'll be okay . . . later in the day.
He just needs some more time, to wear off some catnip brine," the soldier told Eli.

The dogs were still coming. The army hadn't stopped them yet. Eli looked around to see how many cats were here to protect them.

"My name is Cheena," the soldier said introducing herself. "Over there: Cadbury, Rumpus, Bluey, and Preena."

Eli looked at the soldiers she pointed out. They weren't paying any attention to Cheena. They were all focused on the sounds of the oncoming dogs.

"Hi. I'm Eli," he said using his manners to greet her back. He heard the captive dogs whine. It looked to Eli like they wanted very badly to bark out a warning.

"Oh we know who you are," Cheena said, "you're part of the reason we came this far."

Oh oh. That didn't sound good. Eli suspected he was in trouble for *failing* to meet them at Whisker Creek.

The sounds changed from the oncoming dogs barking and howling to yelping and snarling of fighting.

The prisoner dogs began whining loudly. They squirmed where they sat. One of them started to paw at his nose trying to get the muzzle off.

"Stop that! You overgrown rat!" Eli heard the soldier named Bluey say to the dog. Glancing over he saw Bluey wave a shiny metalized claw around in a threatening way. The dog stopped trying to get its muzzle off but fidgeted where it sat.

Eli looked a little closer at Bluey's paws. All of his claws were metal. Then Eli looked at everyone's paws. Every soldier had metal claws. They were only really noticeable when extended but shiny tips could be seen between the furry toes.

Eli realized as he examined everyone, that they were all tense. All except Notso, he began rubbing himself against the tree like he was itchy, or perhaps in heat. It was hard for Eli to tell. He had never seen anyone in heat. He had only heard about it. But Notso's behavior was peculiar given the circumstances.

Eli listened to the battle taking place in the forest. He began to feel even more anxious. It suddenly occurred to him that everyone had something to fight with. The soldiers had their claws. Even Notso had a big stick to fight with. He had nothing.

"Is there something I should do?" He asked,
"What if they get through?
Is there a weapon I could use?"

"You are as untrained as untrained can be.
If they get through, you are best to climb the very highest tree," Cheena answered not looking his way.

Eli scoured the trees looking for the tallest one. Then looking into the forest he wondered if he should just run for it now. While he still had the chance. He could still go to Whisker Creek.

"Don't climb tree. If Ruby see; she burn you–crispy," Notso said. "I go to Dank Tunnel. It small like runnel. It safe spot." Then remembering what his clan might do if they found them he added,

"Or maybe not."

Eli looked at Notso again who was still rubbing his back and sides against the tree.

"Are you trying to be helpful, or just add to my befuddle?" Eli asked rhetorically.

"Who's Ruby? Is she that overgrown flying flea?" Cheena asked.

"Ha! Flying flea you wish! That flying dragon make you go squish." Notso laughed loudly.

"Shhhhhhh!" All five of the soldiers said at the same time. The cat named Cadbury made motions with his paws to Cheena. Lowering her ears she looked away from them all. Eli didn't know what was said to her but clearly she'd been scolded.

The battle sounds of snarling and yelping died down. Eli wondered what was going on. They were too far away in the trees to see. Who was winning? He sure hoped it was the army cats. Looking past Notso into the forest again he thought maybe it wasn't too late to still run. Eli noticed the soldiers guarding them seemed to relax a little. Although they continuously watched and listened for any sign or sound that would relay some information to them.

After a bit, Eli saw a cat running though the trees toward them. As soon as he knew they saw him he stopped and signed something with his paws. Cadbury and Preena immediately ran over to join him and together all three ran back into the trees.

"Where are they going? I don't know how much more I can take of this not knowing," Eli asked Cheena.

"They need a few more paws, roping closed the prisoner's jaws," Cheena answered quietly.

They could still hear some form of commotion through the trees but it wasn't the same fighting sounds. Faintly, from far off on the wind Eli thought he could hear the barking of the dogs from the dog camp. Thinking about how far he had run he didn't think he should be able to hear them anymore. Eli checked which direction the wind was blowing to see if it was carrying the sound toward them from so far away. It might be possible but Eli didn't think the wind was blowing quite the right direction. He puzzled over that for a bit, however the sounds were not getting louder so perhaps they were safe here, for now at least.

About five minutes later the cats came running into view towing only four of the eight big dogs that had Scratch and Eli treed. Like the other captured dogs they had thin ropes around their necks and their muzzles. Eli saw lots of cuts and bleeding on their bodies.

They even had the corporal in their ropes. They brought the newly-seized dogs over to the other ones and tied them all together. Eli watched the corporal look over each of the previously captured dogs. They all cowered under his gaze.

The rest of the cats who had participated in the fight came into view. One of the soldiers was limping on his back right leg. He was helped over to a nearby tree where one of the soldiers pulled out a backpack with medical stuff in it.

Eli walked over to the big cat in charge.

"You've only captured four! That means the others have gone to go get more," Eli exclaimed worriedly.

Eli felt the eyes of someone watching him, glancing around he saw the corporal staring at him. No longer did he have that cute playful look about him. Quite the opposite, his stare revealed the same type of anger Eli had seen in Rad. Fearfully, Eli backed up to the other side of the big cat.

The big cat observed the visual exchange between the dog and Eli.

"He's bound up tight.
Don't take such a fright," he said reassuring Eli he was safe.

"But do tell who is this insolent,
and why it looks he's blaming you,
for his imprisonment.

"Scratch called him corporal.
I don't know if he was just being formal.
He had us in a tree.
Poor Scratch and me.
But I got away.
What's happened to Scratch I cannot say.
So we have to go back.
He will be easy to track," Eli told him.

Eli looked back toward the dog camp. He didn't actually want to go back now that he was away from there. However, Scratch still needed help so he would go if they needed him to. But maybe now that the army was on the scene he wouldn't have to. After all, wasn't that what the army was for?

"So you left Scratch behind and now we have another cat to find?" the big cat asked making sure he heard it correctly.

It sounded to Eli like he was accusing him of wrongdoing.

"Scratch told me to go. He distracted them so they wouldn't know," Eli explained defending himself.

Peeking around from behind the big cat Eli said, "What happened to Scratch will have been his decision." He pointed to the corporal. "If we ask him, we'll know with precision."

"I will ask him for sure, but right now we have to move this tour." Signaling to his troops he made a circular motion over his head with his paw.

As soon as he had signaled, the army cats started to move. The prisoners were untied from the trees. Anything lying down was picked up. Many of the soldiers moved over to walk nearby the captured dogs.

When it became clear he wasn't going back for Scratch, Eli asked, "But what about Scratch? Don't leave him he's outmatched."

"I'll do what I can. Right now moving is my plan," he said to Eli indicating he should rejoin Cheena with a head nod. He then turned away to oversee the moving details.

Eli went over to walk along side of Notso and Cheena. He began to feel guilty. Here he was safe with the army cats. And where was Scratch . . . still in enemy paws. He wouldn't risk going back himself though; he knew Scratch would be furious with him.

No one spoke much. They moved as quietly and as quickly as they could. They were heading southwest along the northwestern side of Fur Tree Mountain away from the dogs' camp.

As they travelled through the forest Eli noticed there were far more cats than he had realized. He had seen maybe twenty-five or thirty soldiers but actually there was double that. This army was very good at hiding. He was filled with hope but at the same time he was wondering why they were retreating and why wasn't anyone sent back to go help Scratch.

"Eli, I want you to stay close. You have inside knowledge to expose." Eli looked over to the big cat who had at some point walked over to him.

"Cheena, keep Eli in your care," he said to her. "These dogs have given him quite a scare but I need him close so stay aware."

"Yes, sergeant. I'll guard him like precious argent," she answered confidently.

Eli regarded Cheena, she was a long-legged, orange-and-brown-spotted cat not much heavier than himself. However, she was taller than he was and definitely faster. He knew that from following her to the army cats, she could have easily left him behind. Her body size however, although being slightly longer, wasn't really bigger. She was slender like him only he wasn't done growing, she was. And she was supposed to watch out for him, against these huge dogs?

Eli's stomach grumbled. He was starving. Just as he wondered if they had any food Cheena swung her pack off, reached inside and pulled out some dried meat.

"It's Pheasant and quite pleasant," she said softly handing it to him.

Eli practically swallowed it whole. He was so hungry taste didn't matter.

"Whoa, take it easy. If you upchuck I'll become queasy," she added making a face. She handed him one more and put her pack back on. Eli tried to eat it a bit slower this time making it last a little longer as they walked along.

Eli regarded the big cat, Eli now knew was called sergeant, who had walked over alongside of Notso. Eli watched them for a bit. The sergeant was asking him an assortment of questions not that Eli was listening to them.

Notso still broke through the icy snow with every step. The deep snow plus his injuries made him move slower than Eli figured he was capable of. He was using the stick to help him walk. He seemed to lean heavily on it. Looking at his injuries, Eli wondered what kind of life trolls had. Poor Notso had so many scars on him. Now he would have more.

Eli heard the sergeant say, "Notso, I've had to change my plan. We're moving to a more secure piece of land. I am grateful that you have given us a hand.

If you choose to leave us, I understand.
However, Major Cat may send for you.
So if you are willing to stay, there is more you could do."

Notso didn't answer him right away. He appeared to be thinking.

When he answered he spoke slowly taking his time to form his thoughts into words.

"I pretty sore," he said exhaling, he sounded tired.
"Just walking a chore.
But if I go home, I make uproar.
So maybe I stay and help even score."

Notso never even glanced at the sergeant when he spoke. He just travelled along at his own pace carefully picking out his footing.

The sergeant never rushed Notso although Eli saw he was very watchful constantly surveying their surroundings and everyone in his command.

"We will do our best to protect you," the sergeant promised him.
"You know what happens here affects you.
With your helping, we respect you.
And in the end we will not forget you."

Notso gave the sergeant a long look before saying again, "I so sore. I not take too much more."

"I know. I'll keep you on the down low," he reassured him. The sergeant left him then and trotted over to converse with some of his other soldiers.

Eli watched as he gave out various orders. Soldiers would disappear into the forest then return, report their findings to the sergeant and disappear again. At one point Eli caught the sergeant observing him after receiving a report. He looked troubled but didn't say anything to Eli. He gave the soldier another command and continued about his business.

As they travelled upward along the mountain, the weather worsened with increased wind and snow. But every once in a while Eli could hear faintly on the wind, the barking of many dogs. He assumed it was coming from the camp even if the wind wasn't blowing from that direction.

After quite awhile of hiking, the terrain became rockier with more boulders jutting out of the mountainside. Through the blowing snow Eli could see natural rock formations one could use as cubbyholes. He fought the urge to crawl into one to get out of the harshness of Winter's increasing blast.

The cubbyholes reminded him of the map his father had given him. There were spots marked on it for cubbies such as these. Unfortunately he had left the map and all of his belongings under the rock when he first encountered the dogs. That had been a couple of days ago but it felt like weeks. He decided he better make a mental note of the formations in case they were ever needed.

They came to a spot where the side of the mountain was sheer rock spanning very high above their heads. A little further along its side revealed a cavern where the rock curved into the mountainside. The curved rock face looked like an entranceway to the large cave opening, which was at the back. Upon entering, Eli saw it didn't go anywhere and so wasn't one the trolls had made. It was very large in size easily fitting all the cats of this party plus more if more were to come. Everyone seemed relieved to get in out of the cold.

Eli quickly stepped to the side when they brought the dogs in. One of the dogs who had tracked him from the tree growled at him as he was led by. Eli cringed away and went back to the entrance to rest in an area where he could escape if he needed to. Cheena followed him.

The dogs were put along the far backside. There was nowhere for them to go.

"Don't worry, you'll be okay. They just want your nerves to splay," Cheena said attempting to console Eli.

Eli glanced at her but didn't say anything. If that was the dog's plan, then it was working; his nerves were splayed.

Eli could see down the side of the mountain from here. It wasn't a terribly steep slope but from up here they could see a fair distance down. They would be able to see better if it wasn't storming. However, if the dogs decided to attack them here at least they would see them coming.

Eli saw the last of the soldiers making their way up to them. They had evergreen branches in their paws. It appeared they were sweeping the snow.

"What are they doing?" Eli asked Cheena. "You army folk make pretty strange viewing."

"They're sweeping away our prints," she answered.
"They won't get them all, but they will make a dint.
Our scent will give them a hint,
but it's best to hide our numbers by hiding our prints."

Notso was called into the mountain cavern.

Eli stayed at the cavern entrance on the side out of the wind. From here he could watch both inside the cavern and down the mountainside. Being higher up on the mountain, it was colder, which made the wind seem harsher as it continued to blow.

Looking up at the overcast sky Eli noticed it seemed darker over the valley swirling in a circular motion, specifically darker over the dog's camp. And although the sun remained hidden Eli guessed it to be about midafternoon.

The sergeant had remained outside the cavern until now. He walked passed Eli and Cheena without a glance at them. He was focused on the dogs within. Eli heard him command the soldiers to separate the corporal from the other dogs.

Then the sergeant asked Notso to remove the corporal's muzzle. That caught Eli's attention. He wanted to hear the questioning so he entered into the cave but just a few feet. He didn't dare get too close and he wanted the ability to get out quickly just in case one of the dogs broke free.

A large number of cats surrounded the corporal. They were keeping the ropes on him tight. A few of the soldiers had their claws out as a reminder to behave.

"So, Corporal, here you are on Catland soil.
I assumed you've come to plunder and take your spoil?
But I have since learned, your camp has a huge shipment.
And I ask myself why so much equipment?
It looks to me like you've come here to toil," the sergeant asked him.

The corporal looked down at the sergeant. Lifting his head high he answered smugly, "Is that why you think we're here?
Personally I was hoping we'd find more deer.
So far I haven't seen much of your land,
and what I have seen is pretty bland.
Although I could do without all this snow,

I think a dog city would give it a certain glow.
So I'm glad you've happened along.
With you as our slaves you'll build our city strong."

The corporal looked around the room, proud of himself for being the cause of their distress.

"Oh, the look in your eyes say you object.
I know; it is hard at first to become subject.
But once your paws have built our great city,
you will know your place well little kitty."

The corporal gave the sergeant a contemptuous smile making no effort to hide his condescending attitude.

The sergeant never flinched. He remained solid and unmoving. But he did scowl at the dog. Around the room the cats had nearly all lowered their ears in outrage. One of the soldiers to the side looked like he may hiss at the corporal but the sergeant without looking his way held a paw up to silence him.

"You know, I see you are pretty observant,
so rest assured I'll make you *my* servant.
And I shall suffer no guilt,
in working you to the hilt." The corporal gleefully bellowed out his laughter.

Eli jumped. The corporal's voice was loud and it echoed out the entrance.

The sergeant having heard enough motioned for Notso to put the muzzle back on. Notso went to grab the big dog's mouth but the corporal bared his teeth and with the lightning-quick reflexes Eli had seen at the tree, he snapped at Notso's hands. Notso's reflexes were slow in comparison and he just barely managed to pull his right hand out of the corporal's mouth avoiding the pressure of a full bite. The corporals razor sharp teeth scraped along Notso's skin and blood rose to the surface.

The cats pulled tighter on the ropes stopping the corporal from moving any further.

Angered by the corporal's bite, Notso raised his fists high over the back of the dog's head bringing them down hard. The corporal dropped to the ground stunned from the blow.

Notso filled with rage bent down to grab his muzzle again. And maybe hit him again Eli thought but the sergeant intervened,

"Just a minute, Notso, there's something else I need to know."

"I'll smash in his brain, if he bites me again," Notso said angrily.

"I think he got the message. Your language is impressive. And I do apologize for your hands wreckage," the sergeant said to Notso trying to calm him down.

It took several minutes for the corporal's senses to come back to him. Eli didn't see the senses go but he knew when they did.

When it appeared the corporal was coherent again the sergeant asked him.

"Why bring the dragon? And don't tell me she's just to pull the wagon."

The corporal gave the sergeant a long patronizing stare. Finally he said slowly looking around at his captors, "Forgive me, all you tiny venison. I have a headache and could use some medicine."

"That was your medicine. Bite again and I teach you jettison." Notso threatened him.

The corporal glared at him. He lowered his head and in a very low growl he snarled,

"Next time, go for your hands I won't.
Next time, it will be your throat."

Notso clenched his fists again but before he could make a move the sergeant stepped in front of him and put a paw on his thigh. Several of the soldiers pointed the tips of their claws into the corporal's hide.

Notso looked at his scraped hand and hobbled over to the cavern wall and sat down. The cat with the medical backpack went over to examine his hand.

"Withdrawal your paw-knives and I'll consider sparing your lives," the corporal snarled uncomfortably.

"But not you," he said glaring at Notso. "You're through."

The soldiers pushed their claws just a little more into the corporal's hide. He growled in pain.

"Enough! Muzzle this scruff!" the sergeant ordered.

Just as they finished getting the muzzle on, a soldier ran into the cavern puffing heavily.

"Sergeant, sir, the dog camp is all a stir. The signal has been made and the battle has occur!" the soldier exclaimed.

Eli ran out of the entrance. The faint sound of many dogs barking reached his ears. And swirling high above the trees, in and out of the darkened snow-filled clouds, was the big red flying dog.

Chapter 20

"Notso, if you'll remain here with Bluey's team, you can put an end to any hairball escape scheme."

Eli heard Notso grunt in acknowledgment to the sergeant who shouted out orders as he walked out of the cave.

"Scrapper," the sergeant said to one of the other cats, "your team stays too. The rest of you it's time to shoo."

Turning to Cheena and Eli he said, "Cheena, you and Eli are with me. Eli, I know you desire to flee, but right now is the time to be gutsy. So please try to keep up, for we have somewhere to be."

The sergeant then turned giving other soldiers certain orders.

Eli's heart sank. He had to go into battle too? Why? He just got away from there. Eli trotted over to the sergeant who was walking away from him.

"Sergeant, sir, I just got away from those dogs and barely with my fur." Whipping his tail around Eli showed him the missing streaks of fur in case he hadn't noticed on his own. And then he showed him the holes in his jacket.

"See, sir? I don't want this to recur. And when I run it hurts to breathe. I've already experienced how they teethe." Eli struggled to keep his fear under control.

The sergeant quickly regarded Eli. He was underage for sure, something the sergeant was not too impressed with when he had found out Tom had sent him to locate a dog camp. But here he was, a little battered up but still in one piece and most importantly he had been inside the enemy's camp. The sergeant needed every advantage he could get.

"Eli, son. I know you want to run. But when you were caught, into their camp you were brought. Now you have inside knowledge, we do not. Asking you to help is a lot and clearly you are distraught. But now we have a shot. Won't you help us bring these dogs to naught?"

Eli looked at the ground taking a breath and exhaling slowly he said, "I suppose so. Fine I'll go."

The sergeant patted his shoulder saying, "You are your father's son. So come now, let us run." He turned then and with the rest of the soldiers ran down the mountainside.

It never occurred to Eli that the sergeant knew his father but why wouldn't he? He knew his father was respected among the ranks of the Monarch. Eli felt a bit of pride seep in. He was his father's son. He could do this. Swallowing hard Eli followed the sergeant down the mountain back toward the valley he had just escaped from.

Cheena stayed close to Eli easily matching his pace. As they ran down the mountainside, Eli thought of the dogs and what waited for them down in the valley. It wasn't long before Eli started to trail behind. Slowly Eli and Cheena began losing sight of the sergeant and the army ahead of them.

He didn't really want to run into a dogfight even if he was his father's son. In fact, the last thing he wanted to do was run back into the jaws of his captors. So he lagged behind on purpose.

Cheena interrupted his thoughts, "Eli, I know you don't want to go, but the sergeant ordered so please don't be slow," she said in an attempt to get Eli to keep up.

Eli didn't respond to her he also didn't pick up his pace. When Cheena realized her words where not working she changed her tactic.

"Eli, I promise to keep you safe, okay? Just do as I say and you won't become prey."

"Ha! That's easy for you to say. I have no defense; to them *I am* prey!" Eli exclaimed unable to hold his emotions in.

Cheena understood Eli's distress. He had a good reason to be fearful. The dogs could easily tear him to shreds. She decided she had better give him some helpful tips in avoiding disaster.

"All right I get your drift.
The key here is being swift.
Dogs have good eyes and powerful jaws.
They also have a keen sense of smell that rarely flaws.
Once you are within their paws,
the chances are you won't survive the might of their maws."

Frowning and laying his ears flat Eli snapped at her, "You're *not* helping! Please shut up before I start yelping!"

Cheena ignored him. If he was going to survive he needed to know how to.

"When a dog goes to attack,
he attacks with his teeth.
He has no other tack;

he has only the knack of using his teeth.
But your reflexes are faster,
and they're something you can master.
Your eyesight is keener,
and you can use them to be a gleaner.
So watch how they move.
Anticipate their groove.
Cat Above has given you flexibility,
so use it with sensibility.
Never lose sight of their jaws,
by using agility."

Still glowering at her, "So use my sight, to avoid their bite?" Eli asked incredibly.

"That's all you have to say? Stay out of their way!"

Eli couldn't believe it. He thought she might actually tell him something useful. Like, your claws are like knives, here's how to take lives. Nope. He got don't let them bite you. Step aside to avoid the chew. Like that hadn't occurred to him.

"Gee thanks. Your insight is top ranks."

"It's best you don't try to scratch. It's not a fight you can match. Eli, I'm serious. Your ability to outmaneuver them is not mysterious. And it is your best defense, which makes the most sense."

"See these rips? Tell it to my ribs," Eli retorted.

"I wasn't there for that.
Since you're not trained in combat,
you were easy for them to grab at.
If you want to stop them flat,
then do as I say.
Not only will you live to see another day,
but you'll show them what it is to be a cat."

"Here, I'll show you and you'll see. Now do what you can to avoid me!" Cheena dove at Eli with her mouth wide open.

"Wha!" Eli was completely unprepared. She grabbed Eli by the neck forcing him down the mountainside with her weight and momentum. The two of them rolled through the snow coming to a stop against a tree. Cheena released him so he could get up.

"What are you doing! Knock off your fooling!" Eli demanded

angrily.

Getting up he shook the snow out of his torn jacket. That's just what his sore ribs needed, a hard hit and a roll in the snow. Her pretend bite didn't hurt but it did annoy him.

"I said, 'Avoid me'!"

Cheena dove at him again but this time Eli jumped out of her way bending backward in the snow to avoid the collision. He hissed at her angrily. Cheena completely ignored his hiss like it never happened.

"That's good. You're learning. I knew you would. Again! Time is turning," Cheena told him.

Cheena playing the role of a dog simply charged him with her mouth open and teeth bared. Eli with his ears laid flat to his neck judged her angle of direction, the speed she was coming from and made a split second decision to duck under her left side. She tripped over him but neatly rolled back onto her paws, spinning around to face him.

Smiling she said, "See you're getting it, pretty quick I admit."

Baring her teeth again, she charged for his throat. This time however she watched to see which way he would go.

Eli saw instantly she was aiming for his throat. So with the lightning-quick reflexes he was born with, he tucked his chin down and leaped high swinging his body around to his right narrowly missing the impact of her charge.

This time however, at the last second, just as she missed him, she leaped up matching his direction. She grabbed for him in midair pulling him close with her paws, careful not to extend her battle claws, and reaching for his throat with her teeth. Eli braced his paws against her body and pushed. He rolled away from her twisting around and almost landed back on his paws. He landed on his rump instead but with the momentum from his push he continued the roll back onto his paws. He ran a few meters away from her then. Giving himself some space from her.

"One more blow and then we'll go," Cheena said not giving him time to rest. She charged him again. Just like she had learned about going for a kill bite she aimed for his throat again.

Having a bit of space between them gave Eli a second more to evaluate the charge. She had long legs and in combination with the twisting of his body hurting his ribs, he decided to trip her up again. So just as she was about to reach him, he dove under her paws wiping out her step and then leaped into the air from under her. Thus causing her back end to become higher than her front end. She fell, sliding in the snow on her face with her butt in the air and her tail over her head. When she came to a stop, her butt plopped down. She lay there for a second before getting up. Shaking the snow off she turned around giggling.

"That was fairly sublime.
You're a quick study and I'd teach you more if we had time.
Just think before you leap and you'll be fine.
Come on, let's go but put some speed into it this time."

Together they ran through the soft snow, which was piling up on top of the ice layer. Eli made an honest effort this time to catch up with the sergeant and the army.

He felt proud his tripping her up plan worked. Watching her slide on her face with her butt in the air made him snicker. He figured she deserved it, especially for that first surprise attack she laid on him. But he knew the dogs wouldn't be so easy to trip up.

For one they were bigger than Cheena and secondly they weighed more, probably a lot more. Also he knew for certain their mouths were a lot bigger than hers. She just managed to grab part of his neck in her fake bite. Back in the tent, where Rad and the other dog had bit him, his entire body fit into their mouths. It was not the same at all.

Eli tried not to think about that. It made him want to slow down. Instead he decided to think on what Cheena said about watching how they moved to anticipate where he should move. He could see her point that the dogs were not as flexible as they were and he would keep that in mind now that he was running back to face them again.

His mind wandered over to Scratch. He wondered where he was. Probably back in another tree. At least with the army on its way they could get him to safety now.

Up ahead they could hear the clashing sounds of dog growls and cat screeches in the forest. In spite of everything in Eli's body telling him to turn around and get out of there, he maintained his pace.

The closer they got to the fighting the more anxious Eli became. A few hours ago when Eli heard those conflicting noises he had no idea who was winning or who was losing. Now he was about to see for himself how all the fighting transpired and it occurred to him he didn't really want to know.

The first dog that came into view through the lightly blowing snow was fighting two soldiers. As the dog dove to bite at the cats they would duck, twist and turn kicking up snow as they leaped out of his reach. The dog spun around in circles snarling and snapping at them. It was with tremendous speed and agility that the soldiers avoided its bite.

Cheena ran by them without a glance back. Eli followed her. Up ahead among the trees were more dogs and cats engaged in battle. Cheena ran around each one of them. Making sure to give them lots of space. Soon there were dogs and cats fighting everywhere in the forest and passing them by became tricky.

Eli could see the cats swiping at the dogs with their metalized claws. The dogs would swing their jaws around with such speed Eli was amazed the cats could avoid the bites. But they did. With planned jumps and leaps, forward and backward, over the dogs and under, the cats and dogs were a blur of motion.

Running past them all Cheena led Eli through the trees until they came to a very small meadow. Cats and dog were fighting everywhere. Spotting the sergeant here Cheena trotted over to him. He was engaged in a dogfight as well. Along with two other soldiers he attacked a large black dog.

When he saw Cheena and Eli, he snarled, "What took you? I told you to stick with me like glue, we have other things here to do!"

With dogs and cats fighting everywhere Eli didn't know what to do with himself. So he stood next to Cheena who took up a defensive position with fur raised under her coat, legs apart, and back slightly arched. Eli did the same.

"I'm tiring of this Rigger," the sergeant said to one of the soldiers. "Let's put an end to his vigor."

The soldier named Rigger nodded. He jumped away from the dog out of reach and swung his backpack off in one fluid motion. The sergeant and the other soldier continued their assault on the dog by swiping at it from every location except its face.

Eli backed out of the way as a tan coloured dog ran past them with its tail tucked between its back legs. Two of the three soldiers it had been fighting pursued him while one let them go. Eli watched him go help another set of soldiers that looked to be in need of assistance with their opponent.

Rigger had a rope out and waited until the sergeant was ready. The rope had a loop at one end. The sergeant got into position on the far side of the dog. With a quick visual exchange and nod of his head Rigger leaped over the dog's neck dragging the end of the rope with the loop with him. Before his paws hit the ground on the other side, the sergeant leaped onto the dog's shoulders with claws extended. Instead of snapping at Rigger who landed beside his chest, the dog spun his jaws around to bite the sergeant who flipped off him just as fast as he had jumped onto him.

Rigger in the mean time darted under the dog's chin grabbing the rope hanging over the other side of dog's neck and pulled it through the loop. Rigger then leaped out of reach of the dog's snapping jaws while pulling on the rope. It tightened around the dog's neck forming a collar and leash. The dog seeing he was leashed lunged at Rigger snarling out threats against him. Rigger aimed straight for the closest tree. He put the rope in his mouth to allow himself the dexterity of using all four paws then he dashed up the tree.

Both the sergeant and the soldier attacked the dog's back end to distract him from Rigger. The dog slowed just enough to realize what they were doing then continued after Rigger. This gave Rigger enough time to reach the first limb out of the dogs range and wrapped the loose end of the rope around it. Rigger pulled the rope tight leaving the dog barely enough room to stand. Securing the end Rigger jumped down and out of reach of the dogs snarling, snapping jaws.

The dog was furious ushering out threats to shred them to pieces. But the more the dog pulled on the rope the tighter it became around his neck. The dog quickly realized he had to keep some slack in the rope in order to breathe.

A rumble high above them indicated there may be lightning in the clouds. Eli looked up at the darkened sky. The large snowflakes that were falling increased.

The sergeant and the soldiers scanned the area for the next dog to fight. Spotting four dogs working together in an attack on two cats.

The sergeant turned to Cheena and Eli saying, "First we'll do some work here. So stay close, don't disappear."

Then he and his troops jumped in to assist. Cheena and Eli followed but Cheena first quickly led Eli to a nearby tree.

"Get in that tree but not too high in case we flee!" she shouted pointing to the tree then joined the sergeant in combat.

Eli climbed the tree taking a branch he figured was high enough from the dogs but not so high he couldn't easily jump down. Once he was positioned Eli looked around. There were all sorts of various paw-to-paw combats going on.

Eli watched the soldiers' use their metal claws in an onslaught of attacks. They used their claws by digging them into the dogs' bodies and swinging their own in and round the dog in every available direction.

They also used whatever was available to them to assist in their attacks. He saw them kick snow in the dog's faces to temporarily blind them, jump onto their backs from the trees, dash around the trees to avoid bites but most of all they used their flexible bodies to jump and twist to avoid the dogs snarling jaws.

Cheena was just as well trained as any of the other soldiers. Watching her swipe at the dogs in an onrush of attacks gave Eli some confidence in her ability to keep him safe.

The sergeant, however, was by far more skilled than Cheena and the other soldiers he was with. He clearly executed his attacks with precision and with confidence. His muscled body leaped easily around the dogs and his lightning-fast reflexes never missed. It didn't take long for a dog's jacket to become shreds.

Turning his attention to the dogs Eli noticed the dogs did not just use their mouths to fight; they used their paws as well. Just not in the same manner as the cats. The dogs consistently tried grabbing hold of the soldiers, or knocking them down to gain access with their sharp teeth. Often they would unbalance a soldier in midleap or stride but rarely did it give them much of an advantage because the tripped up soldier usually was able to roll, bend, or twist out of reach.

Together with the other soldiers the sergeant and his comrades slowly managed to get the upper paw on them. After numerous attacks on the dog's backs and under bellies the dogs began to put their behinds together, taking up a defensive position to protect their hindquarters.

All around him Eli saw many of the soldiers succeeding in capturing dogs. But not every dog and catfight went well. Every time a soldier got bitten they would screech out in pain. Or if a claw scraped too deeply along a dog's body the dog would shriek out a yelp. Cat screeches and dog yelps could be heard throughout the forest near and far. Each was a very recognizable cry of pain.

One thing Eli saw right away was that the cats, although they were cutting the dogs bodies with their razor sharp claws, were not actually trying to kill the dogs. Eli couldn't say that for all the dogs. Some of them were so angry at being swiped at they truly were trying to kill their assailants.

One particular cry of a cat in pain grabbed Eli's attention. Through the falling snow and bare branches Eli saw a soldier take a bite to its back leg. The dog did not let go and the soldier swung from its mandible as the dog violently shook its head back and forth. The instant the other fighting soldier heard the cry it leaped onto the dogs face. The dog reared up pushing on the attacker with his paws while spinning. He shook his head tossing the soldier in its mouth out of reach. When the soldier clinging to his face saw his teammate was clear; he leaped off the dog's face and rolled under the dog slicing the soft underbelly with his razor-sharp claws. The dog screamed, jumping and spinning around to bite at the soldier. The soldier fled in the opposite direction of his teammate, leading the dog away from the injured soldier.

The dog dashed after the cat but quickly changed its mind. While the dog was distracted the injured soldier crawled out of sight under an evergreen's heavily snow and ice-laden branches. The dog stopped, looking around he saw the injured soldier's trail in the snow. But instead of pursuing the injured cat the dog scanned the area, regarding the various battles going on around him. He then sat down to lick his wounds.

He must have been cut deeply because with his head down and

his tail tucked between his back legs he slowly walked back toward the dog camp ignoring everyone around.

Eli knew by the way the dog had shook its head violently that soldier was badly wounded. Once it was safe, Eli noticed his teammate go check on the injured soldier.

Eli realized then the cats worked in teams. Not one soldier that he could see fought a dog on its own or at least not for long. If one of the soldiers became injured enough to withdraw from the battle; their fellow soldiers would protect them by either distracting the dog in an onslaught of attacks or by leading the dog away in a bating 'catch-me-if-you-can' chase.

Eli went back to watching the sergeant's team in action. Eli could hear the sergeant suggesting to the dogs to submit and surrender. They didn't have to worry about being a defender. Promising them as soon as it was over, he'd show them where they could relax in some clover. The sergeant's voice was as smooth as he could manage given the whirl of motion they were in. The sergeant never ceased his verbal reassurances they were better off to give in. Eli began to understand why he was a leader. Other conversations could be heard between the cats and dogs but none as conflict resolving as the sergeant's.

Suddenly out of the blue a high-pitched whistle was blown far off in the west. The whistle was blown long and several times. It echoed through the cloud-covered mountains. Every one still engaged in paw-to-paw battle slowed their fighting, both the cats and the dogs.

Then the cat soldiers unexpectedly turned and ran toward the whistle. Some chose to climb the nearest tree but most ran off to the west, where the sound came from. The soldiers that chose to climb into the trees hid themselves in the branches blending in so as not to be seen.

Eli didn't know why most of the soldiers were leaving but he did see they weren't necessarily running as fast as they could have been. And many of the troops would check over their shoulders to see if the dogs were following.

Another crack of thunder sounded just above them. Nearly everyone flinched or jumped at the deafening crack. The wind blew hard in short burst with the increased snowfall. Rain suddenly was added to the mix of snowfall. Now it was just a matter of time before the forest became a skating rink again.

The sergeant and his soldiers let the dogs they had surrounded go. The sergeant and his two soldiers climbed nearby trees. Cheena quickly joined Eli in his tree. The other two soldiers who had originally been fighting the four dogs ran off to the west, toward the sound of the whistle.

The dogs just stood there dumbfounded. Not knowing what to make of the sudden change.

Eli was puzzled too. The sergeant almost had the dogs completely surrendered. Eli could tell by their defensive and tiring mannerism that they would have surrendered soon. But at the whistle the sergeant consented to the retreat.

Eli watched Cheena pick a spot among the branches that hid her body from the ground. She even laid her tail flat against the bough as to hide it from view from the ground up. She made an "shhh" sound with her paw to her mouth to keep Eli from asking questions.

The dogs were puzzled but in a matter of minutes, the dogs began celebrating the retreat with hoots and howls. Some of the dogs exhausted from fighting collapsed in a heap, grateful to be able to catch their breath and lick their wounds. Many of the dogs sniffed the air and looked in the trees to see what their attackers were doing in there. However upon seeing the majority of the soldiers' run away, almost instantly began to feel the excitement of victory.

Dogs with ranks soon began rallying everyone together. They barked out orders but found they were not united in deciding what they should do next. Eli heard some order to "regroup to recoup," then "let Ruby burn the trees and finish off these fleas." But others ordered to 'pursue the enemy brew because victory was due.'

The pursue order quickly became popular among the dogs' subordinates. A frenzy of barking erupted among them. Within minutes dogs from all over gave into the chase command. Encouraged by one another they banded together and bolted through the forest in pursuit of the fleeing cats.

Eli and Cheena remained in the tree, watching dogs run into view from the east, racing out of view to the west.

Even the black dog the sergeant had been fighting earlier raced by under Eli's tree. The rope around its neck flopped loosely as he ran. The edges were frayed from where the dog had evidently chewed through it to free himself.

After several minutes of dogs racing by, only the dogs who did not want to follow the pursue command remained. Eli saw most of them were either seriously hurt with deep cuts, or were exhausted from using up their energy in combat. Some also appeared to be very leery of the whistle.

From a distance Eli saw a couple of ranking dogs walking around recruiting the remaining dogs into order.

"Do *not* pursue! It may be a trap to ambush you! Regroup to recoup! Regroup to recoup!" They howled out.

The remaining dogs slowly began making their way toward the ranking officers.

Not waiting for the dogs to regroup to recoup the sergeant cried, "Disallow now!" and leaped down out of his hiding spot. At his call all of the remaining soldiers who were still well enough to fight jumped into view and into action. The sergeant and many of the soldiers raced toward the ranking dogs.

"Stay here but within ear!" Cheena said to Eli as she leaped down to join the sergeant.

The sergeant never bothered with the injured dogs that were making their way over to the officers. He simply darted past them. Many startled by the sudden reappearance of the cats tucked in their tails and got out of the way not wanting to be engaged in another paw-to-paw battle.

Others dogs spurred by cats racing by them barked out in objection and pursued them. When the sergeant and soldiers reached the ranking dogs instead of attacking them, they spread out around them allowing the pursuing dogs to take up positions along side of the dogs giving orders.

Already having the experience of fighting the soldiers the dogs decided not to charge them directly. They knew it would only bring on more deep cuts to their bodies and evasive maneuvers which ultimately just tired them out even more. Instead they grouped together protecting their backsides. With their rumps together it was difficult for the soldiers to attack them.

The soldiers who did not follow the sergeant drew their ropes and began rounding up the injured, the exhausted, and all the dogs still tied to various trees. Finding little resistance left in these dogs, the soldiers began forming groups of surrendered and tied up dogs.

A dog fresh on the scene trotted into view. Seeing what was going on with the ranking dogs, he charged Cheena who was closest to him and holding a position in the encirclement. Some of the other Soldiers warned Cheena of the new dog because her back was turned to it. She saw the dog just as it was charging her. Instantly she charged back. As they were about to collide she faked turning left then actually jumped to her right. The dog turned to her left to get her, but her split-second jump to the right put her out of line of his charge and his snapping mouth. The dog whizzed passed her running straight into the surrounded group. Cheena closed up the circle by taking up her spot again. The dog was stuck in the middle along with the other encircled dogs.

The sergeant decided it was time for these dogs to surrender whether they wanted to or not. Ropes were pulled from backpacks. After a few moments of conversation between the sergeant and the dogs the sergeant made a round motion with his paw above his head.

The soldiers surrounding the dogs spread out opening up more space between them. The soldiers nearest to the sergeant got in close to him forming a line of about 8 or 9 cats. It was difficult for Eli to see clearly as the falling snow and rain mixture increased.

Some of the soldiers got ready with ropes. All at once, the soldiers beside the sergeant attacked the two ranking dogs who were standing side by side facing the sergeant. While the dogs' cheeks and necks were being attacked two of the soldiers with ropes leaped onto the backs of the dogs' heads. Each spinning around to face the dogs' noses, they simultaneously threw their ropes around the dogs' muzzles. This attack happened so fast the dogs didn't know how to defend themselves. All they could do was rear up and try biting at the cats on them.

A few soldiers remained beside the sergeant. They waited only a moment before they rushed in lassoing the two dogs' front paws, which were both waving in the air. The soldiers on the back of their heads instantly swung off causing the ropes to tighten on their way down.

Others dogs in the surrounded group did not come to the aid of their leaders because every time one went to do so, they were attacked from one of the soldiers surrounding them.

The ranking dogs fell into the snow as their paws were lassoed and tied together. They could not escape or fight back while their jaws were muzzled shut. After this the others dogs submitted.

The sergeant stepped back from the captured dogs and let his troops take over in tying them together.

The sergeant assessed the captured dogs and selected a few of the dogs in the group to be muzzled too. Eli guessed it was because they demonstrated aggressive behaviour toward the soldiers and this way they would be less trouble.

When all the captured dogs in the vicinity were subdued with ropes, the sergeant waved at Eli to come join him.

Eli watched a wave of snow and rain fall in a gust of wind before he jumped down. Warily he made his way over to the sergeant. Cheena and the two soldiers, who never seemed to be far from the sergeant, also joined the sergeant. Together they followed the sergeant around as he gave out various orders to certain soldiers. Once he was satisfied everything was under control, the sergeant commanded they take the prisoners away. Without him saying so, Eli knew he meant up the mountainside to where the others were being held.

Turning to Eli, the sergeant said,
"Well we've gained control of one leg.
Now it's time to pull out a major peg.
Let's go, Eli.
Take me to that egg."

Chapter 21

Above the camp the clouds circulated over Dead Mouse Mountain Bypass in a low-lying ominous fashion. The westward wind flowing through Elliot's fur seem to be feeding the darkened clouds. It looked like Winter and Spring were still pulling together to hit the area again with another fierce storm.

Looking up Elliot got the sense it was storming high up on the mountaintops. Snow continued to fall but probably not like it was up there. Suddenly a creature appeared briefly in the clouds then disappeared again. It happened so fast Elliot couldn't be sure of what he saw. He blinked and it was gone. He scanned the clouds but he didn't see it again. He wondered if that was the creature everyone was worried about.

"Jack I saw something in the cloud.
It was there and then it was shroud."

Elliot approached Jack from behind. Jack turned around to face Elliot he had been adding kindling to the fire. Before Jack could ask, Elliot said, "I can't be sure. Such a quick glimpse is obscure."

"Well if it's the creature we want to shun
and it comes here, nothing can be done.
But I'll let the officers know.
Although, not much can prepare for that kind of woe," Jack answered solemnly.

Elliot went back to wandering around the sleighs. He was filled with anxiety. Not so far off in the forest there was a battle going on with the Monarch's army and the trespassing dogs. Elliot was glad not to be part of it, but that was likely going to change soon. He was filled with mixed emotions.

Eli was out there, somewhere. And so he was very drawn to the idea of going to go find him. But if only those dogs weren't so big and ferocious. Short of climbing a tree, Elliot didn't know what he was suppose do if he encountered one of those. And what about that flying creature, it had everyone stumped.

Elliot checked his sleigh again. Everything was ready to go. But for now they were told to sit tight, not to move until the time was right.

Elliot glanced at the captured dogs again. They had settled right down, curled up sleeping in fact. After Chill and the officers had come to some sort of plan Chill had vanished. In a gust of wind he had disappeared right out of sight. It was after Chill had left the dogs begun to relax. Evidently they were only worried about Chill and not too worried about the battle raging in the forest.

Now only some of the army cats remained in camp. All of the harness crews, a couple of the officers and just a fraction of the army troops were left behind to defend the camp. Two of the three sleighs were packed and ready to go into battle. One would remain here while two would follow the troops when they were ready for them. And that was only if things went according to plan.

Only the medical supplies and basic necessities were left here for use. Such as the Major Cat's big tent and tables. Major Cat himself had marched off with the troops falling in behind all of them. The cat named Striker had accompanied him.

It hadn't taken long for the troops to move out. As soon as each soldier had finished eating they immediately began packing up their things. Every one of their tents was taken down and anything the soldiers didn't want to bring along was loaded into the one sleigh that was staying here, such as the thick warm blankets they had used.

Elliot had watched the troops prepare for battle as he helped clean things up. Elliot was impressed with how compact their supplies could be. Each soldier carried their most basic needs such as dried meat, a metal cup, some matches, a thin waterproof blanket folded into a very small compact size, a few bandages, a special claw sharpener for their metalized claws, and an ample supply of thin (specially woven for strength) ropes.

Given the excessive amount of ropes they had Elliot figured they must have been planning to tie up every last dog they came across. It was the thin ropes that took up most of the room in their packs.

When it was time to move out. Some soldiers loaded the few small toboggans that had been brought along with additional ropes, chains and collars. Including the toboggan Elliot had used for gathering firewood. Now the remaining soldiers would have to carry firewood with their paws.

Since they were not relocating the camp, the fire was to be kept lit so pots of water were available as needed. No one knew what would happen within the next few hours. Everyone except the dogs was tense.

As Elliot paced around the sleighs, he noticed some of the soldiers stop what they were doing and look to the north of camp. Then Elliot saw a soldier sign that someone was coming. They made another sign Elliot didn't recognize. Whoever it was, they were coming from the north.

Elliot listened. He could hear a faint swishing and banging sound similar to the sounds his sleigh had made when they travelled. The wind blowing from the west was interfering with the sound so he walked over to stand on a small hill he thought might give him a better view.

After a moment of scanning through the burned trees, Elliot saw soldiers trotting toward them. They were using the same trail his troops had come in on. There seemed to be quite a number of them. Behind the troops were two sleighs. As the soldiers came closer they appeared tired to Elliot but not in too bad a shape.

Suddenly the dogs got up and started barking toward the north. In case anyone had missed the signal that soldiers were coming; they now were alerted. Elliot was glad he had heard them coming before the dogs had. It gave him the impression he had better hearing than they did. That could be to his advantage and given their size he'd take what he could get.

Elliot was ordered to fetch some tea from the supplies as more hot water was boiled for the approaching soldiers. When Elliot delivered the tea, Jack told him the soldiers were reinforcements, with plenty of food, medical supplies and the sight of them had his endorsement.

A number of the little white pop tents were put up for the new arrivals to rest in. As the soldiers came into camp Elliot guessed them to be about forty extra soldiers. The sleighs packed full of supplies were pulled toward his. That was when Elliot spotted her. She was dressed with the same white camouflaged coats the soldiers were wearing not a green one like his.

Samantha was with them! Elliot couldn't believe it. He was overjoyed at seeing her. Dropping the tea by the hot water Elliot dashed over to embrace his sister.

"Samantha, you came too! I can't tell you how happy I am to see you!" he called out while he was still running.

Samantha upon seeing Elliot turned her head away from him.

She knew he would be here and she was still angry with him. She wasn't about to accept his enthusiastic greeting.

That didn't stop Elliot though; he crashed into her with a huge hug, knocking them both down to the snow. He attempted to engage her in some playful roughhousing but her lack or response and the expression on her face made him stop. Rolling off her he could see she was still pretty mad at him. He knew why.

"Don't be mad," he said helping her up.
"I'm sorry I left without a word.
But the sight of you makes me so glad.
I won't do it again, rest assured.
Aren't you happy to see me, just a tad?"

Not waiting for her response, Elliot hugged her again grinning.

Samantha unable to fight the relief of seeing him and his enthusiasm at seeing her instantly forgave him and hugged him back.

But she couldn't let him off the hook that easy so she pushed him away saying sternly, "You left without so much as a good-bye. Who do you think you are? Mom would be furious don't even try to deny."

Her scolding appeared to hit home. Elliot let go of her at the mention of their mother. She would be mad at him for leaving without a word. He missed his parents. He hadn't realized how much until Samantha said that. Then Elliot felt the gravity of their situation.

He apologized saying, "You're right.
I'm sorry I gave you a fright.
But what are you doing here?
You definitely shouldn't be at this fight."

"Neither should you.
But here we are, so let's make do.
I am to assist the medics and prepare the food," Samantha answered tilting her chin up in the same manner he had seen his mother do when she had made her mind up about something. No point in arguing with her.

"I brake the sleigh, and run errands; I do whatever they say," Elliot informed her.

Looking around Samantha spotted the dog prisoners. Her

eyes grew wide. "It was a dog we saw," she said to Elliot. "Wow they're huge and look at the size of their jaw."

Elliot followed her gaze to the dogs. The dogs were watching them and the other new arrivals. That's when he saw the harness teams were harnessing up just as Samantha's was unharnessing.

"Whatever you do, don't show them any fear.
It's what the soldiers do when they go near.
The soldiers deliberately express dominance,
and it's something the dogs seem to revere.
At least that's how it does appear," Elliot told her.

"Why is my sleigh about to be drawn?" Elliot asked himself out loud. Then to Samantha he said, "Come on."

As they walked over to his sleigh a loud ear-piercing whistle was blown from within the forest. Coming from the direction of where Elliot knew the fighting was taking place. It was blown several times, echoing throughout the valley.

The soldiers immediately jumped into action. His harness team got into position while the medic soldiers starting pulling out medical supplies from the newly arrived sleighs.

"Elliot time to go," Jack called to him. "It's time to face our foe."

With all the harness cats in place Elliot turned to say goodbye to Samantha. Thunder cracked over the valley and echoed passed them to the west. The wind picked up and it felt like the temperature warmed a degree or two.

"I just got here and now you're going. Where are you off to, I hate not knowing?" She asked before he could say anything.

"We're off to war, I guess.
You better snag some rest.
Our return might bring a mess.
Pray Cat Above keeps us blessed."

Elliot left her then running over to join his team who were already pulling away.

As the falling snow changed to a rain snow mixture, Samantha watched the sleighs along with their accompaniment of soldiers disappear into the forest. Again she was left behind but it was okay this time. Not because he said "good-bye," technically he hadn't, but because she had started her training.

Chapter 22

Ruby soared high above the clouds, storing all the heat she could from the sun. The air was thin and ice-cold at this altitude but it was ice-cold below as well. Fortunately, her body was designed to store the heat the sun generated for weeks on end. Provided of course, she didn't over extend her energy levels. It was how her kind survived living on mountaintops.

Usually she would enjoy this time of soaking in the heat but not today. Today she was about as distressed as she had ever been in her eighty years. She could still feel the fear her unborn felt as the dogs put a crack in his shell. Unable to speak yet but well aware of his surroundings her son cried out to her in the unspoken connection he and she shared. Oh how she wanted to set them all a flame. But she could not without harming her one and only offspring.

The conversation with the captain still played in her head,
"And you didn't notice?
The cat escaped,
because it wasn't your focus?
I find this hard to believe, Ruby,
for one of my pack yes, but you?
You're not a newbie."

The captain was interrupted then.

At first Ruby was relieved his attention was taken away from her son. He was so angry when it came to light the cat had escaped. He had sent out a search party but when the report all his prisoners had been freed came in . . . and that little cat was responsible . . . the captain went ballistic!

In a fit of rage he had grabbed a hammer and cracked her baby's shell. She knew then she would never confess to letting the cat go and the captain would pay for his actions with his life.

She really had no idea that little cat would go back and free the other prisoners. She truly thought it would just high tail it out of there, thus saving its own skin. That's what any other prisoner would have done.

If her son hadn't taken a liking to the little thing, she would have stopped its escape. She didn't really care what happened to the cat. But for some reason, her one and only liked the creature and it was the first time he liked anything since he'd matured enough to be aware of his surroundings.

When she thought about what Chopper had endured from the captain, or was still enduring . . . she almost felt sorry for Chopper. Almost. However, she had seen what that mutt was capable of doing to its own kind let alone different species. So, "What goes around, comes around," she figured.

Ordinarily she didn't agree with torture. She had no use for it. If she intended to kill her prey, she simply did so. It was cruel to do otherwise. Nonetheless, ever since these dogs took her unborn and held him hostage against her . . . she had begun to see a use for it.

Just a few more weeks, Ruby told herself, and then she'd rid herself of these dog freaks. Just a few more weeks was all her precious needed, and then things would change and those dogs would see who was truly heeded. After all, her baby would be hungry and the trees in this land were bare.

She was glad she had lied to the dogs. She had lied to them from the start. She told them the egg needed another year. They clearly didn't know anything about dragons nor what they fed on. Luckily for most of them she didn't like the flavour of dog. She preferred the greens from the trees but wouldn't necessarily turn down an annoying mutt when the opportunity arose. Nevertheless she kept her dog diet a secret from them, at least for now. They thought she was strictly vegetarian but failed to notice the trees were barren in this land. And more importantly, they failed to notice a missing dog here or there.

The captain had ordered hunting parties to go out in pursuit of the escapees.

"Hunt them! Track them! Burn them all!
Escape from me? Of all the gall!
Now they think they're free from brawl?
Don't come back, Ruby,
until you've scorched them all!" the captain bellowed out his orders. Packs of dogs were sent out and Ruby took to the sky.

As she ascended she could see through the storm that the forest was alive with movement but she didn't have time for that. For days now the thick clouds had caused her to use up most of her energy just to keep warm. She had no choice but search for the sun first. So from high above she eyed the storm that was circulating over the valley below.

There was something unusual about this storm. There was thunder and lightning along with snow. She had never seen that, or heard of it for that matter. As she had flown through the clouds they were unusually dense, extremely dark with sections of warm and cold air, which caused fierce turbulence and electrifying results. It was all she could do just to get through them unscathed.

It was extremely dangerous to be flying into any storm with lightning but never had Ruby experienced anything like those clouds below her. It was almost like they were alive and watching her.

As she absorbed as much heat as she could from the sun she looked for a way down into the valley that would let her enter without going through those storm clouds again. The storm stretched for miles in all directions and the more she studied the darkened clouds the more it felt like they were studying her too. She had a bad feeling about them. She was going to have to enter the valley from one of the far sides and do what she could to stay out of them. There was something definitely wrong about this storm.

Chapter 23

Eli felt the blood drain from his head. His paws felt heavy and frozen in place. Was that why the sergeant wanted him along? To show him where the egg was? Eli took a quick look around to see if there was a hole he could crawl into. There wasn't.

Thunder cracked again. Then came the rain. Not just the light snow rain mixture it was before but a heavy down pour consisting of large ice-cold droplets.

The freezing rain soaking Eli's head inspired him to make a decision. Everyone was staring at him; getting wet and waiting for him to lead the way. Eli stared at the two soldiers who were never far from the sergeant.

"This is Rigger and Comet, by the way," Cheena said quickly introducing them, irritation clear in her voice. "Now you have no reason to delay so if you don't mind, let's get under way."

Growling under his breath and ears flat, he walked past the sergeant toward the dog camp. Suddenly he stopped, spun toward the sergeant. "You're insane! If we die, you're to blame!" he snapped. Then turning back around he loped off taking them to the egg.

The sergeant was a little surprised by the outburst. It had been a long time since anyone had spoken to him like that. But then Eli wasn't a soldier and reluctance was written all over in his body language. Which was why he hadn't told him his plans.

Catching up with Eli he calmly stated, "Death is always a possibility. And if we die, I bare full responsibility."

Eli was miserable. Everything was miserable, the weather, the dogs, everything. In typical feline fashion he didn't acknowledge the sergeant but maintained his pace. He had said he would help and so he would, even if it killed him. Which he feared it might.

Darting under the evergreens as much as possible to keep out of the freezing rain, the five of them moved toward the dog camp. Eli really hoped the sergeant had a plan because he didn't. But he did know how the camp was laid out. He remembered what it looked like from above when the flying dog had captured him, before everything went black.

Now that he thought about it he realized the best way in was also the way Notso had led them out. There were fewer tents in that area and they were wider apart. Also, the forest edge was closest in that area to the center of camp.

The soft snow that had fallen was quickly changed to ice from the rain but the warmer temperature kept the snow from freezing all the way through. Their paws were wet and very cold. Every other step in the snow had them falling through the thin ice layer. Ice pellets also fell among the raindrops and whenever the wind blew, it felt like tiny stones were hitting them. To add to the difficulty the tree branches heavily laden with ice and snow started to break, falling to the ground unable to withstand the wind gusts. Now the group had to dodge falling tree branches as well.

It was like Winter and Spring were warring amongst themselves and didn't give two hoots about anyone else. Chill's warning that traveling would be hindered by Winter and Spring's storm, seemed an understatement to Eli. However there was nothing to be done about it so they kept moving.

As they neared the open valley of Dead Mouse Mountain Eli stopped under a large well-branched spruce tree.

"You know, they will still be there tomorrow.
Running through this storm is its own state of sorrow.
Why don't we hole up for a while,
dry off, before we face the hostile?" Eli asked the sergeant.

"I've received word that now is the time to strike.
Winter and Spring are hitting them hard with this storm,
which has yet to spike.
But they are on our side,
so rest assured there is a plan astride,
and one to which I will abide," the sergeant responded to Eli with certainty.

The storm hadn't spiked yet? Grrrr and brrr, thought Eli. But seeing the determination on the sergeant's face as well as in everyone else's, Eli realized there was no way they were going to stop, no matter how cold and wet they were or what he said. Eli turned around and continued leading them through the storm.

Quietly he led them along the forest edge, heading toward the East side of the valley. Eli kept them hidden in the forest deep enough in so that they would not be spotted as they moved along. Everyone kept a sharp eye out for dogs. Although they did not come across any of the intruders, not even one, their prints and scent were everywhere. Eli figured it must be because most of them had either run after the fleeing army or been captured.

As they neared the area where he, Scratch, and Notso had come out of the camp, Eli began to look for the tree he and Scratch had been trapped in. Spotting the toppled tree Eli ran over to it.

"Scratch! Are you here? Scratch! It's okay to appear!" Eli called out as loudly yet as quietly as he could, not wanting the dogs in camp to hear him.

In a flash, Cheena tackled him yet again.

"Eli, stop this at once! Don't be such a dunce," she scolded just above a whisper as she sat on him in the sloppy snow.

Eli struggled to get up from beneath her.

"Your hollering will announce us, and lose our surprise pounce thus!" She got off him, her eyes wide as she looked around for any sign in the forest that they had been heard. Eli got up, shook the wet snow off and gave Cheena an indignant scowl.

He couldn't believe she tackled him again! This was becoming a nasty habit of hers and one he was going to have to put a stop to.

The sergeant trotted over to Eli while Rigger and Comet took cover under a nearby evergreen.

The sergeant immediately apologized,
"I'm sorry, son,
I should have told you before we begun.
Scratch was our friend too.
But now his lives are all done.
I had sent out a scout,
so there is no doubt.
Scratch is no longer here.
He was one we all revere.
And his service was devout.
I served with him for many years . . ." As the sergeant was still speaking Eli saw a tuff of orange fur at the bottom of a tree a number of meters away. "He had so many peers."

Eli slowly walked closer to it, leaving the sergeant to talk to himself.

Just a tuff of orange fur was visible, frozen like a furry rock. He had never seen a cat like this before. He had been told about death from his parents but it was usually used as a warning to keep him and his siblings' from doing things that may harm them.

Without getting too close Eli sniffed the area. He didn't doubt it was Scratch lying there but he wanted to know if there was blood . . . if the dogs had crushed him with their massive jaws. There was some, but not much. Perhaps he had succumbed to his injuries. They were pretty severe. It didn't matter Eli decided. Either way he looked at it, the dogs were responsible.

"You know he's with Cat Above.
Happy, warm, and loved." Cheena stood beside him.

"I do know," Eli answered after a moment.
"Because of dogs, he lies in snow."

Looking around he saw the sergeant on the other side of him, staring at the orange tuff of fur. Ice was building up in the fur and the last of it would soon be covered over. His soldiers stood not far from him. The sergeant appeared lost in his own thoughts.

What if this was just the beginning, Eli thought to himself. After everything he had seen . . . these dogs could not start winning . . .

"Okay," Eli said, finally finding the courage to face these foes, "let's deliver your blow, for these dogs really have to go."

The sergeant met Eli's gaze. He nodded his agreement. With that confirmation, Eli charged toward the dog camp. Within a minute they were at the meadow's edge.

Standing by a large barren tree they surveyed the camp. Winter and Spring were doing a good job of keeping the camp buried under snow and ice. Flashes of lightning could be seen to the west, followed with rumblings of thunder. The falling snow and rain made it difficult to see more than three hundred meters but the flashes helped to lighten the area. Many of the tents had fallen down from the weight of ice build-up but instead of setting them up again; the dogs had just left them. The largest tents were just barely visible in the center of camp. But from what Eli could make out, the largest one still appeared to be standing strong.

"This is the way we came out.
Here, fewer dogs were about," Eli told them quietly.

"The egg is in the largest tent,

towards the back but don't be slack,
many guards are present.
  The tent has six rooms;
four to one side, two to the other,
you may move between their gloom
as all are open under."
  Eli's claws dug into the snowy ground as he remembered the fear he felt when they had put the collar on him. He couldn't let that happen again.
  Don't think about that, you're not a scaredy-cat, he silently reminded himself and shook off the thoughts along with plenty of wet snow.
  Looking across the valley it seemed odd to Eli, that in spite of the weather, none of the dogs could be seen in camp. There were no patrol dogs circling the camp. No guard dogs posted at any of the tents they could see. The camp appeared empty. Maybe all the dogs had been sent out to fight the Monarch's army.
  After a few minutes of watching the camp, a couple of trolls emerged from one of the tents several meters away. Eli and his party ducked down, so as not to be seen. The trolls walked around the tent with sticks wiping and poking at the accumulating snow on the roof in effort to knock it off. After knocking the majority of snow to the ground they hurried back into the tent, out of the blowing rain snow mixture.
  Eli and the sergeant's team stayed low for a while waiting to see if anyone else would emerge.
  Glancing at the big tent, Eli wondered what the sergeant intended to do with the egg. Then he thought about its mother, how she had been watching him, how she had allowed him to escape without raising the alarm. Considering it had been her who had captured him in the first place, he puzzled over why she would let him go.
  Remembering he last saw her when they were still on the mountainside, he whispered to the sergeant,
  "The flying dog doesn't have a clue we're here,
lucky for you 'cause she's a good seer.
I saw her back at the mountain,
into the clouds she disappear."

"Yes, I saw her too.
Only for a moments few,
then vanish in the clouds she flew," Cheena confirmed.

Searching the sky the sergeant said,
"We better keep an eye on the sky.
At the time of your escape, Eli,
you said, 'the flying dog let you go by'?" the sergeant asked Eli.

"Oh yes, she spotted me with her big eye.
I don't know why she never let out a cry.
And so I ripped a hole in the tent, just a small little vent,
then I left like a sly little spy."

"Well that may change if we take her egg.
Her temper may rage and we would lose our peg.
So let's keep an eye on the sky,
'cause I'd hate to have a dragon drop-by," the sergeant told them.

"That egg's too big to carry.
I don't think it will move,
and besides, with a baby inside,
it would be hairy," Eli told the sergeant.

He couldn't see how they could move it. It was huge and probably heavy as well. He knew they wouldn't want to harm the baby flying-dog.

"We will cross that bridge when we get to it.
For now we are on a ridge, so let's make the best of it," the sergeant answered him.

The sergeant cautiously stepped out into the open meadow of the valley. Heading toward the closest toppled tent. He kept his body low but high enough to move stealthily. Everyone followed suit.

His last words bothered Eli. They sounded uncertain, like the sergeant didn't know what they were going to do with the egg. Unable to contain himself Eli caught up to the sergeant whispering while they scurried over to the tent.

"You said you had a plan.
And that sounded like you don't have a plan.
But you do have a plan, right?
We're not here just to insight a fight."

"Shhhh, of course there is a plan.

But improvisation is what lets any plan stand."

"Silence now! Not one more meow!" the sergeant ordered sternly.

Quietly they snuck from tent to tent. Deliberately making a wide circle around to the eastside as they moved toward the center of camp. This increased the length of time it would take to get there. At first Eli didn't know exactly why the sergeant was leading them around like this but after he observed the sergeant regularly sniffing the air, he realized the sergeant was trying to keep the dogs upwind from them. He never would have thought of doing that it. It made him feel a little better knowing the sergeant had wise little tricks like this to help keep them safe.

A couple of times the sergeant would stop and sign something to them. Although Eli didn't know sign language he was able to pick up the gist of some of the signs. For instance, dogs up ahead, hide your head. And the five of them would duck behind a snowdrift or tent.

Whichever direction the dogs came from all headed toward the largest tent and usually at a brisk pace. It became pretty clear after seeing a few dogs run past in the storm that they were stressed. No one's tail was up. They moved with purpose through the camp not taking the time to check out their surroundings. Otherwise on several occasions the sergeant's party might have been discovered.

As they passed by some of the tents still standing they could hear parts of conversations from within. Eli could tell some of the voices he heard belonged to trolls by the way they spoke. There were similarities to the way Notso spoke with lots of complaining or bickering, mostly about the weather. The sergeant listened to some of the conversations but when he determined nothing of importance was being talked about he led on.

About three quarters of the way toward the center of camp, two trolls came out of a tent they had just past, the five of them quickly ducked behind a large snow covered rock for cover. The trolls knocked the snow off their tent then left it heading toward the biggest tent.

None of them worried too much about the trolls catching them because trolls were fairly slow; they had an extremely poor sense of smell, poor hearing, and poor eyesight during the day. As cave creatures they could see very well in the dark, just as well as a cat if not better, but they struggled with daylight. It was only if they managed to get their strong hands on them that a cat would be in trouble. Trolls were very strong.

The closer they got to the big tent the trickier it became. The majority of the activity came from within it. Dogs would emerge from the tent and quietly trot or lope off. They could not see where the dogs were headed when they left but it was possible they were heading back into the woods. West was the direction they all went.

Once they reached one of the larger tents, which were also set up near the biggest one. They hid themselves around the corner it by digging into the snow. There they created a small sheltered area to monitor the activity of the largest tent. It was still raining but not as much as it was earlier. It was already evening and they knew as the temperature dropped over night it would soon turn back into the icy snowfall it had been.

They could hear numerous voices coming from the large tent but no one particular conversation.

"The hole I made is more than halfway on this side." Eli pointed to the area as he and the sergeant peeked around the corner. "Never did I imagine I'd use it to get back inside."

"You may not need to.
Someone needs to keep watch.
It's best if it's you," the sergeant whispered with his voice so quiet it was barely audible.

"Do you know who is their commander?
Does he blend in or is he a little grander?" the sergeant whispered again.

"He's a big muscled dog with a black face and tanned body.
Of aggressiveness and fierceness, he is the embody," Eli whispered back trying to speak just as low and barely audible as the sergeant had. The sergeant gave a little nod in acknowledgment then indicated he wanted Rigger and Comet to come over.

Eli moved to the back giving the other cats the room they needed. He tried to follow their signing to one another but their paws moved so swiftly it was lost on him. One day he would learn it. It was obviously a good skill to have.

Eli carefully surveyed the east side of camp by peeking over the edge of the snow wall they had quickly made. This side of camp was very quiet. About half of the tents stood while the fallen tents just lay there gathering more snow and ice on them. He could see some of the tents had so much snow and ice on their roofs it was only a matter of time before they fell to the ground too. In fact, as Eli looked around he began to recognize which tents were occupied by the amount of snow on them. The ones with little accumulation were the ones being knocked off regularly.

Searching the clouds for the flying-dog he could tell Sun would be setting soon. He could hear thunder rumble in the west and the sky was darker in that area than here. Eli felt exhausted. He hadn't slept in . . . he wasn't sure, but it was catching up with him. He needed some rest. However it wasn't safe out here so he could not relax.

As they huddled together along the east side of the tent, Eli began to wonder what was in this particular tent. There were no voices within and for the moment this tent was standing strong. He looked up in effort to examine the amount of snow and ice on it but little could be determined this close. Looking down in the snow for the bottom of the tent Eli dug until he located it. Finding the stitching that held the wall and floor together he extended his special claw.

"Let me do it," Cheena murmured, "It's easier with these to make a slit."

Eli stepped out of her way. Cheena extended one of her metalized claws. The thread holding the two panels together snapped instantly. She didn't have to saw or pull the threads out. Those metal claws certainly had their advantages. Eli determined he would get those someday as well.

"You know there is a saying about curiosity killing the cat," Rigger spoke quietly for the first time. "And it's usually followed with some sort of atrocity that lays you out flat."

"There is no noise within and I'm tired. A short nap is all that's required," Eli whispered back.

"A little rest would be a good reprieve. We're waiting anyway for Sun to leave," the sergeant ended the conversation with a nod for Cheena to continue opening the tent. She had stopped when Rigger spoke.

She made a hole large enough for them to crawl through one at a time. Comet went first, then Rigger, then Eli, followed by Cheena and the sergeant.

Once Eli poked his head through the tent, he saw the base of a wooden wheel. Upon pulling himself through the opening, he saw it was attached to a massive cart. A quick scan of the area determined this tent held all sorts of equipment. Including saws like what cut down the tree he and Scratch had been in, there were also axes, and a wide assortment of tools he had never seen before.

In the center of the tent was a pole with two shorter poles set up on either side of it about the middle from the center to the walls. It looked like the shorter poles were set up temporarily to help support the weight of the accumulating snow and ice. Eli was relieved. He didn't want the roof to come down on him while he napped.

He jumped up the very tall cart to see what was inside. It was also filled with equipment but mostly it had bags that smelled of some type dirt, in it. He jumped down on to one that was stacked flat in the corner upon others. Nope it wasn't soft, Eli noted but it would do. He laid down on it grateful to have his paws out of the wet icy snow. He closed his eyes to rest for a bit. He was so tired.

"Well this confirms the building plans our intelligence provided," he heard the sergeant quietly say from outside the cart. "Too bad they are so misguided. They won't be happy to drag all this away once all the fighting has subsided."

"Eli get up!" Cheena stood in front of him whispering, "We need you to set up."

"Set up what?" he asked squinting his eyes at her confused. "My eyes just shut."

"You've had an hour. That's more than enough, so don't look so sour," she said frowning at him. "You're our eyes and ears on the outside. To protect our hides should a threat come in stride."

The tent walls violently blew inward from a blast of wind. Thunder reverberated through the mountains. The whole tent shook with the wind gusts. Cheena jumped out of the cart then. Eli quickly got up and followed her out of the tent hole.

"I can't believe it's storming even worse. These powerful winds really are a curse," Eli exclaimed forgetting to be quiet. With his night vision on he looked around at the devastation the wind was doing to the camp. Many more tents had fallen while he slept.

It was only he and Cheena at the corner of the tent. He peered around the corner. He could see the sergeant and his soldiers had already moved to the side of the largest tent. They were looking for the hole Eli had told them about.

Cheena quickly leaped out from beside him and dashed over to join them. Seeing the coast was clear Eli did the same. Once he reached the sergeant he realized they still hadn't found his hole. Looking along the tent he could see they were nearly in the right place but not quite. He jumped in front of the sergeant and located the seam holding two of the outer wall panels together. He knew it also held an inside wall panel but you couldn't tell that from the outside. He dug down deep into the icy snow to reach the very bottom that held the floor panel attached. There he found his little hole.

Comet and Rigger quickly worked at making another little barrier of snow around the area so Eli could stay outside but be protected from the storm and hidden from eyesight. The sergeant extended his claw and made the hole big enough for them to fit through.

Then with a quick glance at each of them he poked his head in. Everyone was silent, listening to the sounds coming from within the tent.

There were plenty of voices to be heard. Numerous conversations were taking place making it difficult to listen to just one. Then the sergeant disappeared inside. Rigger was next to poke his head in.

He stayed like that for a few moments just as the sergeant had done, then he too disappeared inside. Next was Comet. Cheena stepped closer to Eli putting her paws on either side of her mouth she whispered directly into his ear.

"Don't follow us in. Stay here.
Only if you see the dragon appear,
are you to attempt at coming in.
And even then . . . imagine;
what would happen,
should we be exposed to those within?

So keep your head down.
If a dog catches your scent,
lead them out of town.
But should the dragon appear,
use sign not sound.
Like this to be clear."

Cheena put her paws down and moved back a little so he could see her plainly. Then she put her paws to her mouth and wiggled her digits as she moved her paws forward straight out in front of her mouth. She showed him the sign for dragon a couple of times.

"Do you understand?
This is your part in the plan," she whispered searching his face.

"Of course I understand.
Be a lookout and a decoy is your command," Eli answered her a little annoyed that she thought him too stupid to understand her directions.

Cheena left him then, poking her head into the tent. In an instant she was gone, leaving him alone.

What happened to protecting me? Eli wondered to himself... all that "I'll guard him with my life" decree?

Eli crouched down to keep out of the wind. He listened to some of the conversations going on inside. It sounded like the trolls really didn't like the storm. While he listened he scratched at some of the snow and ice that had entered through the holes in his jacket and had made a permanent home in his fur. He had gotten use to the feel of it but with nothing else to do he might as well attempt to remove some of it. He actually had enough dry fur between his skin and the little ice balls to protect him from their coldness. What bothered him the most was those little ice balls pulled on his skin when he moved.

"I telled you, Dicey," Eli heard one voice speak up louder than the others,
"I'm done with all this icy.
I go back to Big Ear Cave.
There I no worry about crazy ice grave."

There were some cheers and some objections to this comment among the other conversations. Eli carefully lifted a little of the tent wall to peer inside. Many trolls were in the largest room, some sat on the floor but most stood around talking. There were dogs in the room as well. Peering in between trolls legs, Eli could see the dogs were positioned in front of the door and along the hallway more than in the room with the trolls.

Two trolls stood facing each other standing along the center wall curtain close to Eli.

"We all agreed this is better," said one to the other.
"If you so cold, put on sweater.
Winter and Spring, they lose strength.
This storm already have too much length.
Just wait, you see. By morning you agree."
"No! The cats attack!" The other troll objected.
"This not just set back.
Winter be angry with us.
That why all this weather fuss.
I go home now.
You stay, keep your vow.
I no need your allow." He turned to leave.
"Sooty troll! You no stroll!" the other troll bellowed.
"I already said no!
Maybe you join Notso," he threatened.

The troll he called Sooty spun on his heel, "HOW DARE...!" he hollered just before he lunged at the troll.

The other troll didn't wait for the hit; he jumped high above Sooty coming down with fists on his head. The troll Sooty fell to the ground. Within seconds trolls were fighting one another in the open area.

Eli gaped at them unable to take his eyes off the fighting. Then remembering why he was here he quickly searched the sky. Seeing nothing but clouds, he took the opportunity to peek into the other room where he knew the egg and treasures were.

The sergeant and Comet were standing on the table examining the egg while Cheena and Rigger were keeping watch.

Along the curtain wall somewhat out of sight were the two guard dogs he had seen when he had been in there but they were lying on their sides with their paws tied together and their muzzles tied shut.

Eli watched the sergeant and Comet jump down. Cheena and

Rigger had their ropes out. Then the four of them disappeared under a curtain that made up one of the four rooms along the far wall.

Someone hit a center pole that had been placed there after Eli had left. The tent shook with the impact. The pole was located where the big red flying-dog had held up the tent with her head.

"STOP!" someone shouted. Eli recognized the voice. It belonged to the captain. He peeked back into the other room again.

"As much as I enjoy watching you flops,
swapping hits in the chops.
I fear it's my tent's prop
you're about to pop."

Eli could not see him directly. Too many trolls stood in the way.

"Now need I remind you?" He continued speaking from the hallway.
"Your clan leaders thought this through.
The decision has been made.
Your cards have been played.
You don't get to change your view.
This deal's been made."

The captain's voice was just as smooth as Eli remembered it.

"So from here on out,
And let there be no doubt.
If anyone leaves for any reason,
I will consider it an act of treason.
You will be hunted down by our mightiest snout."

"Ha, ha, ha, you think we afraid of you?" Sooty interrupted the captain, sneering he said,

"I say we through. I say I done with you."

"Oh dear." The captain's voice sounded worried,
"Sooty Blackspear,
you've interrupted my good cheer."

The captain moved a little closer to Sooty coming into Eli's view. The look on his face did not match his voice.

"I can see you're not afraid of being beaten," he said looking around at all the trolls. "That is why anyone who wishes to leave will be eaten."

The captain gave two large dogs a nod. Both dogs snarled and leaped at Sooty. Sooty put his arms up just in time to grab one dog. The dog yelped as Sooty threw it to the ground but the other dog reached his throat before he could bring his arms back up to defend himself. Sooty fell backward with the dog attached to his throat.

The other trolls jumped out of the way giving Sooty and his attacker room. A couple of trolls were about to step in to help Sooty but Dicey stopped them. Motioning to everyone not to interfere.

Eli pulled his head back out of the tent. He couldn't watch this.

After the grunting and growling subsided he heard the captain say, "That was most unfortunate.
As far as strong trolls go, he was a portrait.
Now let's get something clear.
And spread the word to all of clan Blackspear
You are here for the duration.
No one leaves without my authorization.
All departures will be dealt with most severe."

No one spoke in response to the captain. It was quiet in there.

Eli looked over the edge of the snow wall. The rain had changed back to ice-pellets inter mixed with regular sized snowflakes. Winter and Spring continued their gusting wind.

Slowly low toned grumbling started up amongst the trolls.

The big tent Eli had slept in, which was just southeast of him, sagged along its north side but did manage to remain standing. Eli turned around to look north along the side of the tent. That was the way he had run last time. He wasn't sure if it would be the best way to go this time. It didn't lead out of camp and there was a creek not too far in that direction that ran through the middle of the valley. Crossing it could be dangerous. Besides water wasn't his thing so he didn't want to go that way. No the best way out might be the same way they came in. But the fastest way he decided as he turned around again was straight south to the trees.

"What is this!" Eli heard the captain exclaim loudly from the room with the egg. "Must everything go amiss!"

Eli didn't have to peek inside to know the tied up dogs had been discovered.

Chapter 24

The Monarch's sleighs travelled through the forest at an impressive rate. In spite of the rain now falling on them, Elliot jumped in and out of his like a seasoned professional. Not erring even once. The snow had completely changed to rain causing the snowy ground to become slushy ice. The further they went the heavier it rained. After a while of running in this they started to hear the snarling, hissing and yelping of many fighting cats and dogs through the trees. As they neared the fighting area the sounds increased along with the rain and so did their anxiety levels.

They broke into a clearing where ropes that had been tied together circled a field. In fact the fence looked more like a net then a fence and it ran along the entire edge of the forest. It was open at one end and closed off at the other where a rock wall that spanned about fifteen meters in the air was. They sagged and dripped in the pouring rain. The sleighs pulled up alongside of the soaking fence and the harnessed cats began unharnessing themselves.

Inside the netted fence hundreds of soldiers and dogs fought each other in the downpour with skill beyond Elliot's imagination. Elliot was mesmerized by the speed and agility of both the dogs and cats. As they fought, numerous dogs were getting roped, muzzled and hog-tied. The dogs who were able to evade the ropes found themselves in an onslaught of attacks from various cats coming at them from any which direction. It looked to Elliot that nearly every platoon in the Monarch's army was here. The field was wild with activity.

When the wind blew the rain fell in waves blinding anyone looking directly into it. Elliot saw many paws slipping on the ground as they struggled for traction. The cats had an advantage because of their metalized claws however even they slipped here and there.

Groups of dogs were putting their backsides together for protection. This appeared to be the most effective way to avoid the attacks. The Soldiers had a harder time attacking them like that and simply resorted to roping them. However lassoing them this way proved to be difficult with the wind and rain, and also because the dogs could easily dodge the ropes aimed at their heads. Difficult but not impossible as Elliot saw a lassoed dog pulled out of a group and get taken down with more ropes.

Scattered across the slushy snow covered ground were not only the dogs who had been successfully muzzled and hog-tied but some very unfortunate soldiers as well. Elliot wasn't sure if these cats were alive or not but clearly they were in dire need of medical assistance. Elliot saw a soldier try to help another fallen soldier but in doing so a dog nearby attacked him. It looked to be dangerous to help those fallen soldiers.

Elliot's harness team as well as the other harness cats started pulling medical supplies from the sleighs and started examining the injured soldiers on this side of the fence. Several of the harness cats ran out onto the field to bring those fallen soldiers to safety. They ran as a team of six but only a two lifted the injured. The rest protected them from the dogs as they moved together as a unit back to the fence.

Elliot jumped into his sleigh to helped make room as some of the injured soldiers on this side of the fence were immediately put into it. He jumped out again as soon as he could to give the medical team the room they needed to tend the wounded.

Thunder rumbled overhead.

Scanning the area, Elliot noticed dispersed along the outside of the makeshift fence were soldiers. Some of the soldiers were attacking the dogs in a tag team method. One would run onto the field and attack then retreat to catch his or her breath while the other would run onto the field to take their partner's place in the attack. Many ran back and forth like this. Others had crawled off the field because they were injured. But Elliot saw that if their injuries weren't too serious they joined back in. Although everyone was soaking wet, no one let the weather stop him or her from doing whatever needed to be done.

Lightning flashed across the sky. Elliot looked up to see a big red bird like creature diving through the air right in the area where the lightning had been. It looked to be falling. Then with powerful strokes from its wings it regained its balance. The creature lifted itself up circling above the clearing then disappeared into the clouds.

Elliot looked around to see who else had noticed the huge flying beast. Everyone was busy doing something. He looked for Jack, but Jack was busy helping the wounded. Elliot spotted Officer Hiss across the field but he was engaged in a fight. Striker was in the field too but at least he was closer to this side of the field.

Searching the sky again, Elliot saw the huge creature reappear from the clouds. It circled the battlefield eyeing the occupants. Looking for someone to report this to Elliot spotted the Major Cat who was standing near the opened part of the fence yelling orders onto the field. Elliot raced over to him.

Interrupting him he shouted,
"Major Cat! Look up, sir!
The flying beast soars above that great fir!"

Elliot pointed as the creature arched overhead just above a very large fir tree.

The major looked up at where Elliot pointed. The flying beast sucked in a large volume of air but just as it was about to exhale, lightning struck again. It hit the top of the fir tree Elliot had just pointed to. There was a blinding light, and a deafening crack as the tree split in half.

The flying beast rolled in the sky spraying fire harmlessly across the sky. It was falling again until it managed to right itself with its huge wings. The tree sizzled on fire from the lightning. But that was the least of everyone's concern. They watched the creature suck more air into its lungs as it swung itself around to hit them this time with its fiery blast.

That's when they witnessed the might of Winter and Spring's power. Along the east side of the clearing a torrent of rain and wind came down like a wave from the sky. In a wall of grey it hit the trees with a force they wouldn't have believed if they hadn't seen it. The wall of wind snapped trees in half just like an invisible paw had reached out and flattened the forest in one swipe.

The force from the turbulence created from the blast knocked both cats and dogs to the ground. The sound reverberating through their bodies, echoing across the valley and up into the mountains. Trees fell on each other like dominos, one falling on another falling on another and so on.

No one moved. Everyone was stunned.

When the wind and debris settled down no one could believe their eyes. Tree lay upon tree stretching across the forest for nearly a mile.

The big flying creature was nowhere to be seen.

Miraculously, only the rope fence still stood in that section of the field. The cats and dogs that had been knocked down slowly got to their paws. In the field everyone was wide-eyed but the dogs looked especially frightened, some to near hysteria. No one wanted to fight anymore. Tails were tucked between legs and wide-eyed faces exchanged glances.

The Major Cat quietly said to Elliot,
"We'll trust Winter and Spring to battle the skies.
But let me know if that creature still flies."

Suddenly some dogs bolted for the opened part of the fence. The soldiers at that end quickly pressed together to block them. The major bolted to join them in stopping the dogs from leaving.

Then another group of dogs decided to make a break for it running straight for the trees next to the toppled ones where the forest still stood. It looked like they were going to jump the fence but the soldiers on that side cut them off stopping them in their tracks.

The dogs knew they were surrounded. They had been surrounded since they first ran into this trap. Only now they were coming to the realization there was no way out.

Thunder rumbled again and more icy-rain gushed down in a wind wave that made it difficult to see. Everyone braced for another powerful gust but none came. Elliot searched the sky for the big red dragon but it wasn't there.

"Trespassing dogs you are under arrest," the major hollered over the sound of the rain. "Surrender yourselves and cease your quest.
With the authority of the Monarch I will attest,
that your wounds will be dressed and your stomachs blessed.
What says you? End this now or will you contest?"

Everyone stood still. Steam rose off their wet bodies and their breath was visible with every puff. Some of the dogs in close proximity of one another started to mutter quietly to each another.

While the soldiers stood there, standing their ground, some cats emerged from the far side of the toppled forest. Everyone turned to watch them jump from fallen tree to fallen tree as they made their way across the newly felled area.

The major turned his attention back to the dogs again.

"In case you haven't noticed,
it should become your focus.
Mother Earth is on our side,
and she and her monarch have rules for you to abide.
So again, I ask you, *are* you through?
Because we've got food once you've subdued," the Major Cat hollered again coaxing them to surrender.

It started by the open area where the soldiers were in a standoff with the dogs. First one dog lay down. Then another. And another. Soon all the dogs lay down even those who had formed a group with their backsides together.

The soldiers wasted no time. They immediately began tying up the surrendered dogs. Swiftly moving from one dog to another. They rounded them up in a similar fashion to the way Elliot had seen them bring the first group of dogs into camp.

Suddenly it stopped raining. There were some cheers by the injured soldiers over by the sleighs. Elliot smiled and although only a few soldiers cheered, he could see everyone's mood was instantly improved.

The soldiers who had been working their way across the fallen trees made it across and went directly to the Major Cat. Elliot watched them give the major a report. Some of the soldiers standing within earshot stirred anxiously at whatever the news was they were telling him. The major mumbled something in response then turned around heading toward the sleighs. The soldiers who had just arrived also turned but in the opposite direction. They ran back into the forest heading northeast this time.

The major trotted past Elliot going directly to the lead harness cat on his crew. The next thing Elliot knew the injured soldiers in his sleigh were being moved to the other sleighs. When there was no more room, they were laid back down onto the ground.

Elliot headed over to find out was going on. As he walked there he watched the other two sleighs, fully loaded now with injured, pull out and head back to camp. His harness team got back into position in front of their sleigh. The lead harness cat signaled to Elliot to get ready. Elliot looked around for Jack, and found

him still assisting the injured. It didn't look like Jack was coming.
    Seeing Striker nearby he asked, "Where are we going?
Isn't this sleigh needed for injured stowing?"
    Sighing he answered, "It would be, indeed it would be.
If it weren't for a captured dragon's egg that needs freeing.
That's where we are about to be fleeing."
    Striker looked Elliot over then asked,
"Are you ready Elliot the brake cat?
Because we're headed for some more combat."

Chapter 25

Ruby pushed herself up, removing a tree from her chest to do so. The torrent of wind and rain carried her over the forest for at least a mile. She finally came to a stop when the wind makers had released their hold on her. She tumbled and rolled through the branches of numerous trees finally coming to a stop against one that had not broken.

"Who are you?" she asked in fear for her life.

"And why do you come at me from out of the blue?"

Never had she encountered anyone or anything other than another dragon who could toss her out of the sky. Who or what was this?

She had chosen to approach the valley from the far west side. The clouds in that area were less dense and not so formidable. She was right, there was less weather there as well. As she flew just below the clouds she saw a camp of cats on the ground ahead of her. Not wanting to alert anyone of her presence she hid herself by flying into the clouds only peeking out sporadically to make her assessment of the occupants below.

There were plenty of cats to be seen in the camp but it looked like many more had been there shortly before. Or at least she came to that conclusion based on the number of prints she could make out in the snow. She circled around the cat camp to be sure. In fact she would say there had been quite a substantial amount of cats there before. And oh, those little kitties have been busy, she thought as she eyed the captured dogs they had chained to a tree. Ah, they can stay there in their misery. She wasn't about to free them.

Noticing a heavily used trail going east toward the dog camp she decided to follow it. It occurred to her as she followed the prints that other than the odd bird, she hadn't actually seen anyone in this land other than cats and the trolls, of course, who had brought them here. All these cats might explain the lack of birds.

She followed their trail to a clearing that had been, as far as she could tell, set up as a trap. The cats had created a fence that v'd in a small meadow. At the end of the fence was a cliff wall spanning up along a mountainside. Having had her curiosity sparked she landed on the mountain's ledge to watch them.

In part, she was grateful to land as flying in storms took a lot of energy. The wind and air pockets took a lot of skill to maneuver through let alone strength. Fortunately she had just gotten revitalized when she had soaked in the heat from the sun. But that didn't mean she wanted to spend it all flying around in this crazy never-ending storm.

She watched the cats work diligently at putting together the fence and once it was completed they blew a whistle. Most of the cats dropped to the ground covering their ears when the whistle blew. It appeared to hurt them but it did not stop them from doing it. The whistle was loud but it didn't hurt her ears. But then again dragons weren't known for their hearing. Once they were finished with the whistle they disappeared into the forest.

Well, they thought they disappeared. She could still see them. Even with their funny camouflaged jackets on. Although, she had to admit, if they didn't move she could miss seeing them too. As a hunter, this hiding tactic fascinated her.

She noticed that they only outlined the edge of the forest as close to their fence as possible. She waited with them to see if this was the ambush for the dogs she suspected it was.

Not long after the whistle was blown did more cats appear. They raced into the clearing and only stopped once they reached the cliff wall. As the number of cats running into the clearing increased so did the number of cats along the wall. It made the little creatures look like they were the ones trapped. But she knew they weren't. That silly fence they made would never contain cats nor dogs for that matter.

She could hear the dogs coming. Barking their fool heads off as they ran through the woods.

Foolish mutts, she thought to herself. They give themselves away because their mouth never shuts. Running straight into a trap. Serves them right, the idiot little yaps.

She had no sympathy for the dogs whatsoever.

"And now what?" she asked herself.
Was she expected to save their hairy little butt?

Probably, although her orders were to "burn them all,"
and flame makes no distinction between species at all. But first she'd see which mutt would lose their gut, and then she would take the initiative to light them up.

She got herself comfortable; shielding herself with her wings from the wind and rain, and watched the dogs run directly into the cats' trap.

The ambush was predictable. The dogs followed the cats into the fence. Cats from the south side by the open part of the fence jumped out of the forest to close them in. The cats who appeared trapped along the wall revealed the truth when they ran out the sides. The dogs would have followed them out if it hadn't been for the other cats hiding in the forest along the sides jumping in and attacking them.

She watched them fighting noting to herself, the dogs were at a disadvantage. They were tired from a long run and now had fresh cats assaulting them. And those little cats clearly had more energy.

She watched the cat and dog show for as long as she could but when it became pretty clear the dogs were losing, she took to the air. She had to . . . for her son. If the captain learned of the dogs getting ambushed and she didn't do anything . . . there wasn't any doubt. He would break her egg.

That was when the clouds came alive.

"Stay out of this do you hear? Fly away, Ruby. Don't go near." A low voice rumbled above her head sounding like thunder.

Did she hear that right? She flew around searching for someone, maybe another dragon? She found no one. She must have been imagining things. Clouds don't talk. Nonetheless she could tell there was something different about these storm clouds.

She shook her head and swooped around to give the crowd below a blast of her fiery spray. The next thing she knew a lightning bolt whizzed past her. She rolled to her right just missing it but she was soaking wet, and a perfect conductor for the electric bold. She received a partial jolt as she rolled out of the way. Fortunately she didn't get the full force of the shock but enough to cause her to lose control. She didn't fall far before regaining control.

"What just happened? Was that on purpose? Have my wits slackened or am I just nervous?" she wondered. That lightning bolt almost looked like it was thrown *at* her. She flew into the clouds but there was nothing that could be seen. These were just storm clouds and storm clouds are dangerous, everyone knew that.

Her intuition however told a different story. She could feel the electrons in the atmosphere were intense. And clearly the turbulence was horrific. The wind and air pockets made flying extremely difficult. But more importantly, it felt like someone or something was watching her. As she thought before there was something different and wrong with these clouds. She flew out right away.

Circling the battlefield she decided that she must have been imagining things. That must have been a coincidence. She was flying in a rainstorm. Of course there was lightning. She would however, watch out for more of it.

She sucked in another large volume of air. Just as she was about to ignite her sulfurous venom . . . BOOM! Another strike of lightning was thrown right at her! She saw it this time. A billowy arm of cloud threw the lightning bolt right at her! She rolled again narrowly missing it. A fir tree below received the full force of the strike. Her fiery breath was lost harmlessly as she fell out of control again. She just barely managed to regain her balance before it was too late.

What on Earth! These clouds are cursed!

"I said no. Fly away. Or I'll deliver my blow." The voice rumbled through the clouds again sounding so much like thunder they could easily be mistaken for the real thing.

"I can't," she answered back, thinking of her baby. "Too much is at stake. I won't recant." As quickly as she could she flew through the turbulent air back to the meadow.

When the wall of wind and rain hit her, it knocked the breath out of her lungs. Her sulfurous venom ignited but her breath was again lost in the clouds. Never in her life had she ever experienced not being able to breath.

As she was carried away, she experienced a different type of fear. She truly believed for the first time that *she* might actually perish. All her thoughts had always been on her son's survival, never on her own survival. What if she died? What would be his fate then? Would the dogs raise him? That can't happen, she desperately determined.

As she sat on the ground she spoke to the clouds.

"Who are you?" she asked in fear for her life.
"And why do you come at me from out of the blue?"

At first there was no answer. She watched the clouds roll around within their darkened state. Then the voice rumbled in answer.

"These dogs trespass on my sod. It won't be tolerated. Not any maraud. You helped bring them here. You will help return them, are we clear?"

She watched as a face appeared in the cloud and then slowly a body emerged. It floated down out of the clouds. It was a being and he was glowing.

He was a beautiful transparent creature wearing flowing white and blue robes. He had white hair on his head and chin. His eyes were a steely blue with a coldness to them but not a meanness. She knew meanness and it wasn't there. He stood the same height as her as they looked each other in the eyes.

"They have my offspring. Any act against them will cost me everything," she explained.

"My soldiers are already on the grounds. They'll rescue your baby from those hounds. All we need to do now is turn them around and send them homeward bound."

He didn't sound like thunder anymore when he spoke. Now he sounded like snapping tree branches in this icy land. She had to listen carefully to make out what he said.

"Okay. All right." She nodded her consent. "You save my baby and I'll join your fight."

He smiled at her just before fading into a gust of wind that turned into a whirlwind carrying him back into the clouds. Ruby watched the whirlwind merge into the cloud. Then the cloud he vanished into darkened even more and headed over the dog camp.

Above the meadow where the cat's ambush was, the sky lightened and she could see it had stopped raining.

Chapter 26

Notso stood at the cave opening. He looked out over the valley. He could tell his eyes were healing. Things were not as blurry as they had been. He watched the storm rage in a circular motion above the valley. Round and round it went dumping buckets full of precipitation as either rain or snow. The darkened sky made it easier to see too. However he had to take care to close his eyes with the flashes of lightning. They temporarily blinded him. Often in the bright sunlight he would miss seeing the most obvious things because of the glare. So being able to see fairly well during the middle of the day was unusual for him.

He couldn't help but think that Mother Nature was pretty angry. He had never seen nor heard of a storm like this one. Not that trolls really go outside much. They didn't. The only reason any of them were out of the mountains and staying with the dogs was because of their promises. He'd bet his life away though, that they were getting quite tired of those ridiculous flimsy tents. He was glad to have some solid walls around him again. Even if this little cavern didn't go anywhere. The whole time he had stayed in those flimsy tents he had hated it and he knew he wasn't the only one.

But still, this storm had been going on for a very long time, ever since Ruby first set fire to the forest chasing that cat. That was weeks ago now, then came the rain, freezing then thawing, freezing then thawing. Mother Nature was angry. It was very possible she had sent both Winter and Spring to create this storm. And from here, as he looked across the horizon, he'd say she was angry at the dogs. It was very dark right above their camp. And if she was that angry at the dogs what was the possibility she was angry with his clan too? He wondered if she knew his clan led them here.

"What that whistle mean?" he asked the nearest soldier in the cave.

"It sounds like something going on, some sort of scene."

Moments ago a whistle had been blown far off on the west side of the valley. Instantly, the cats jumped up and started exchanging looks. At first it looked like they wanted to go somewhere but after a moment or too they settled down. A few of them signed to one another but no one spoke about it.

The soldier Cadbury was closest to him. He just shrugged in

response to Notso not giving away any information.

Out of irritation Notso grunted. Cats were never very forthcoming; a trait that was very unbecoming and could make the mind start thumping.

"I think I go down and check," Notso said watching to see what kind of response he'd get. "I think that whistle some kind of beck."

"That isn't necessary," Scrapper answered him from across the cave. "The whistle was just temporary and by the time you get there, they'd already have found a remedy."

Notso humphed loudly, he knew that whistle was a beckoning call. They were warring down there. He just didn't know what the actual reason for it was.

"Lucky for you I don't want to go.
Keep your secrets, it's a journey I'll forego."

He didn't care what the cats were up to. Notso hobbled back inside the cave to get out of the breeze. He sat down in the same spot he had chosen before.

Except, he did care, he realized as he sat there. The cats were warring against the dogs and now he wanted them to succeed. It bothered him that his clan was responsible for bringing the dogs to this land. He just didn't know what to do about it.

The dogs were all lying down along back. Most were sleeping or trying to. Notso closed his eyes to go to sleep. He was tired and needed to rest some more as well.

"Notso, we have company.
You should get up, in case our visitors come reluctantly," Bluey said to him from the cave opening.

Notso woke up at the sound of his name. He wondered how long he had dozed off for. He stood up just before a large volume of dog prisoners were escorted into the cave. The majority of them had injuries from fighting with the cats. Many of them had their muzzles tied shut. The ones who didn't hung their heads and hid their tails as they entered the cavern. It almost looked to him like they dropped their heads even lower at the sight of the previously captured dogs. Most of the cats stayed at the cave entrance exchanging information silently.

The corporal dog stood at their approach. Even with his

mouth tied shut he stood with the authority of his position within the dog pack. His head and tail both held high. The dogs entering were afraid to get close to him, choosing rather to skirt around him and edge as close to the walls as their ropes would allow. This gave him plenty of room to look them over.

One or two of the newly captured dogs also had symbols on their coats and proudly eyed him right back in challenge. But seeing as they were all tied together they got pulled along with the others who skirted him.

"You just as tied up as they are," Notso said to the corporal. "Go lie down, you no squad star."

Notso knew that would infuriate the dog. And it did. The fur on his neck stood up as he growled again at Notso but surprisingly he did lie down, with his back toward Notso. Seeing many of the dogs follow suit and they didn't pose a threat, Notso hobbled over to the entrance.

The cats were busy signing to one another; careful not to speak less prying ears should hear them and give away all their secretive plans. Notso was growing tired of their signing and wished they would just speak plainly. At least with his clan they spoke their thoughts and plans for everyone to hear.

Notso stepped outside to look out over the valley again. He walked to the mountain edge passing by the silently chatting cats.

"Notso," Bluey softly called him after a bit. He and a couple of others came to stand beside him in the wind. Gesturing to one of the cats Bluey said, "Ripple here has explained we've delivered a good blow.
We have control on the south side down below.
But it might help the overthrow, if you talk to your clan leaders. Perhaps this deal they'll forgo, and help expel these land bleeders?"

"That how I got into this position.
That request was imposition.
And their answer's pretty clear in my condition," Notso answered. He rubbed his ribs as he thought of the beating he had received.

Even though he was beginning to feel better he still needed more time to heal. And those new bites he obtained didn't help. Fortunately, whatever had been in that green goo had really helped to quicken the healing process. Plus they had fed him, and that had helped too.

Trolls healed fairly quickly without the extra help but they healed even quicker with a full stomach.

"Although," he added thoughtfully, "I know some who want dogs to go; but Dicey, he be your biggest foe."

He offered them the information they would need if one of them wanted to go talk to his clan. As for him going . . . nope, the next time he saw Dicey there wouldn't be any talking.

"He really like what these dogs bestow.
Riches and authority all promised to overflow.
He mostly set up this dog show.
Change his mind and rest will help overthrow."

"So Dicey is the clan leader?" Ripple asked. "Convert him and the rest won't teeter?"

"Dicey leader? Ha!" Notso laughed.
"He wish! No he just speaker.
And big fat loud mouth beaker," he added.

"He a problem though," he said more seriously.
"He just let his own words flow.
He not talk to true leaders in long time,
he way past due, it almost crime.
But in past, clan leaders back him far too much.
Now no one question him, or cross him and such.
Another problem: he have a lot supporters.
They follow him anywhere, even to dog quarters.
I think now true leaders afraid.
Too many, has Dicey swayed.
But no one really know for sure;
leaders keep at bay.
Behind closed doors leaders always stay."

Bluey, Ripple and the other cats signed to one another discussing what Notso told them.

Then Ripple said to Notso, "If Dicey is just a speaker, we will pass him by, and go straight to your leader.
Where are these leaders of yours?
In which mountain will we find their closed doors?" he asked.

Notso looked down at the cats wondering how they would fare coming into his clan's mountain. There would be nowhere for them to run and hide within those cavern walls.

"In Jagged Tooth Rock within Big Ear Cave.
I sure hope you brave,
because without permission,
it be your grave," he warned them.

Suddenly, there was snarling in the cave and cat soldiers raced back inside. Just as Notso turned to see what the commotion was all about, the corporal leaped out the entrance over the heads of the cats blocking him. The rope that had held him dangled around his neck. Some jumped up swiping at his underside but he ignored them running and snarling straight at Notso. He leaped again aiming for Notso's throat.

Notso grabbed the big dog's chest just as the two of them fell backward down the mountainside. Together they slid head first along the top of the snow. The corporal was snarling and snapping for all he was worth trying to reach Notso's throat. Notso's arms were just long enough to prevent the corporal from reaching his jugular.

Notso twisted flipping them onto their sides. The corporal tried to regain his footing as they slid but Notso knew he couldn't allow that. He grabbed handfuls of coat, fur and skin on either side of the corporal's shoulders to keep him down. The corporal pushed on Notso's chest with his paws snapping and biting wildly at Notso's arms. Notso pushed him slightly over his head on the downside of the mountain using their sliding to his advantage. Then he pulled his knees up from under him never once letting go of his hold on the corporal. This maneuver slowed their sliding down.

Then in one swift motion Notso jumped up and pulled the corporal under him. With the corporal pinned down on his back Notso straddled him, and held him in place with his muscular legs. But no matter how much the corporal's bites hurt and made him bleed, Notso would not let go. Finally their sliding came to a stop.

Then Notso did something the corporal never expected. He let go of his hold on his shoulders and grabbed the corporal's jaws. With one hand on the upper jaw and one on the bottom jaw, Notso pulled the jaw wide open. Blood ran from Notso's hands and arms into the corporal's mouth and on to the snow around them. Notso didn't care. He used the pain to fuel his anger like he had done countless times in the past.

Notso saw the corporal's eyes widened in fear as he realized Notso was about to pull his mouth apart. The corporal had underestimated his strength and this would be a lesson he would never forget. The corporal's fighting changed from an enraged offensive attack into a panicked defensive flounder. He wiggled and writhed beneath Notso desperately trying to free himself from Notso's unbreakable grip.

Suddenly the big grey cat, Bluey, jumped onto Notso's back. Cats showed up surrounding them.

"Don't kill him, Notso. It's not the way this should go."

The cat wrapped his paws around Notso's neck slipping a paw from under his chin onto his cheek attempting to turn his face towards his. No claws were extended but the threat of extending them was there.

"There's a better way, trust me, I know.
Release him, Notso, before this woe grows!"

Notso ignored the cat's attempt to turn his head away from what he was doing.

"I'm no cat! And I'm done with taking bites from this gnat! Your rules are not mine! In second I'll end this swine!" Notso spat out in fury!

"They're yours today! Please release him, don't delay! For there is a war at stake and we have another way!" The grey cat reasoned with him to let go.

Notso was right on the verge of destroying this dog's life. With everything he and the other dogs had done to him before throwing him into a cage . . . he had no intentions of letting go.

Suddenly hearing they had another way penetrated his thoughts. Maybe the cats did have a use for this flea-ridden canine, one that might tip the scales in winning this war. But instead of letting the corporal go, he shut the corporal's mouth, wrapping his bloodied fingers around his muzzle he held it firmly shut.

"What other way?" he demanded. "It better be good because I can still slay this stray." Neither Notso nor the corporal moved while he waited for an answer.

Bluey climbed a little higher on Notso's shoulder to get a better

view of the corporal. Looking down at him, he asked,
"Do you submit?
We know you're in the position to,
you're pinned on your back, you know it's true.
Just admit, this is the requirement for your submit.
So give Notso your commit.
He's earned it from you.
And at your submit he will quit."

The corporal knew they had him. Anytime a victor showed mercy to a challenger by allowing him to live, especially before the defeated challenger submitted, the defeated came under the rule of the victor. All defeated challengers were under the rule of the victor but not to the same extent as one who was shown mercy before submission. This was one of the most prominent rules of his kind.

Notso had won this fight fair and square. The problem with this was by giving Notso authority over him, he was giving Notso authority over every dog under his own authority. He knew he would not challenge Notso again for Notso was clearly stronger. The corporal could see no other way out. He relaxed his body and averted his eyes in submission.

Notso was a little surprised. He expected more of a fight.

"How can I trust him?" Notso asked.
"He can attack me again on a whim."
"Oh, he won't.
You've bested him.
He's taken note.
It's not a lesson he'll want to learn twice.
In fact, now you'll see how he can be nice.
Corporal, isn't that right?
Notso's won this fight?
Now, Notso, you'll get to see,
just how loyal one can be,
one who nearly lost his bite."

Bluey sounded very confident that the corporal would cooperate from now on. Notso wasn't so sure but he had seen the look of fear in the corporal's eyes, and that did amount to something.

The corporal would have nodded his head in agreement

but he couldn't move within Notso's grip. "Um hm," was all he could manage. With that confirmation, Bluey jumped off Notso's shoulder.

Slowly Notso's expression softened from the hardened murderous glare to a simple distrust. He gradually released him and slid off.

The corporal rolled to his stomach but didn't get up. He lay there catching his breath. The troll was heavy; he hadn't been able to breathe properly. He licked his lips feeling the ache in his jaw joints from being stretched to almost beyond capacity. He didn't think he'd be able to bite anyone for quite a while.

"Dog, you need to swear your obedience," Bluey said pressing the corporal to make his oath.

"Now is the time for expedience, and together you will benefit from this allegiance."

"What's the hurry, cat?" the corporal asked Bluey
"My fealty is sworn to him not you, hairy rat."

"What you swearing to me? Is this some type of decree?" Notso asked.

The corporal turned to face Notso, lowering his head and averting his eyes in submission he said,

"Notso, I challenged you, whether or not you were aware.
And in spite of that, you have bested me fair and square.
So now to you only, do I submit fully.
Pledging my obedience to you wholly."

The corporal looked around at the cats when he said "to you only" to make a point.

"What this mean," Notso asked?
"I the boss of you?
If that true, I might be keen," he said liking the idea of having someone to boss around instead of being the one bossed around.

"You now have authority over him.
It's a rare opportunity for you, not done on a whim.
But take care not to abuse your authority, as in all things, it can turn grim," Bluey told Notso.

"Someone get the paramedic. Notso's arms are pathetic," Bluey said to the cats standing around. One of the cats ran up the mountain, while one other cat slipped his backpack off and took some gauze out.

Notso looked at the bites. The stitches in his hands from the corporal's other bites had ripped open. On his arms muscle was exposed and dangling. Blood was everywhere, again. He hoped it wouldn't interfere with his hand movement too much. The pain from the bites was increasing. He silently hoped they would give him some more of that yucky green goo. In spite of the tingling feeling it numbed the pain.

He glared at the corporal as the cat started carefully cleaning his wounds with clean snow and the gauze. The corporal kept his gaze away in submission. He was bested by a troll and surrounded by cats. He wasn't going anywhere.

"About our request, Notso," Ripple said stepping closer to Notso to get his attention.

"Without troll permission, success in our mission would be low. But with you as our guide, access to your clan leaders would flow. And now with your dog escort," he motioned to the corporal with his head, "it wouldn't be easy to give us the old heave-ho."

Ripple was obviously in a hurry to confront his clan leaders as he brought the conversation they had started back, before the corporal's escape interrupted them. It was typical behaviour for a cat in the magistrate's army; their own agenda always took top priority.

Notso sat in the snow starring at Ripple wondering if the clan back home had heard yet what Dicey had done to him. If it wasn't storming, he knew they would have for sure but it was possible no one in the dog camp had gone back to Jagged Tooth Rock and informed them. He tried not to think of Dicey, he was already angry enough.

"Your access still may not last. If they've heard of my outcast, we'll all feel their blast," he told Ripple.

Ripple smiled at him. "So it's a go. Thank you, Notso. Your assistance in this overthrow exceeds the status quo."

Notso knew he hadn't actually agreed but before the sergeant had asked for his help with the dogs he was planning on going home to confront them anyway. It might actually be a good idea if he had the cats with him in support. He wasn't sure about the dogs though.

He grunted in response not sure what to make of the gratitude. Those were words his clan never spoke.

"Hey, these cats don't rule you," the corporal said to Notso. "If you don't want to go, just tell them you're through. Tell them to be gone, tell them to shoo." He was trying to dissuade him.

"I still don't like you dog.
Shut it or you'll get another flog," Notso growled at him.

The corporal looked away from Notso, but announced, "Well, I'm not going. Rise up against my pack? No way, I'm not showing."

Notso looked at the corporal who was still averting his gaze. He thought over what it might mean for him and for the corporal if the corporal turned against his own pack. Notso hadn't been an outcast for long but he still had a pretty good idea what it was like to be on the outside.

"Am I the boss of you?" Notso asked him. The corporal stole a quick glance at him but when he didn't answer Notso said, "Then you do what I do. That mean you come too."

The medic cat arrived and started pulling out his equipment. When he had finished sewing the holes in Notso's hands and arms; he bandaged them. Then together they walked back up the mountain.

The corporal stayed beside Notso as they climbed, matching his slow pace. The rope around his neck trailed between his paws. After a bit of trudging most of the cats decided to run up ahead losing patience with Notso's speed. Notso didn't say anything but he wondered if the corporal staying beside him was part of his sworn loyalty to him.

"How you get free?" Notso asked the corporal as they climbed. "How your attack come to be?"

He still didn't trust him but he was curious as to how he managed to get the muzzle off. The dangling rope around his neck was self-explanatory.

"I pulled the muzzle off with my nail.
Not easy, but I hate to fail,
then I hid chewing the rope beneath my tail," he answered truthfully.

Once they reached the top, the cats who had escorted them

joined the others who were still silently chatting at the cave entrance. Suddenly they all stopped, one cat made a particular sign and bolted past Notso and the corporal running down the mountain. At his departure, they started their signing again.

The medic was waiting for Notso with some more of his green goo. He motioned for Notso to join him over by a section of the rock wall that was somewhat out of the wind. The corporal followed along. He offered the goo to Notso right away. Notso noticed it was much less than the amount he had been given before. But he accepted it readily knowing it would help ease his pain.

For some reason known only to the cats and perhaps the dogs, no one attempted to tie the corporal back up. Notso thought this was strange. There were looks exchanged between the corporal and the other captured dogs but no words were spoken. Some of the cats eyed him warily but most turned their back to him like he was no longer a threat. And the corporal just stayed by his side making no motion to do anything else.

Notso no sooner finished his goo when Ripple along with Bluey approached him again.

"We're ready to go, Notso," Ripple said. "We cannot delay in expelling our foe."

"Just a minute, Ripple, perhaps not everything is planned, Corporal, how many dogs are under your command?" Bluey asked the corporal.

"None of your business cat.
Why would I answer that?
If you had half a brain you still would scat." The corporal knew exactly where the cat was going with this but he wasn't about to cooperate.

Notso could feel the effects of the goo starting to work right away but it was nowhere near as powerful as it had been the last time. He glanced down at the corporal who was now holding his head high in a staring contest with the cats.

"You on cat land," Notso informed him. "So, how many dogs in your command?"

The corporal ignored Notso.

"I know how this goes.
You think you can control me through the troll.

But I won't disclose." The corporal never took his eyes off the cat.

Both cats stood their ground staring right back at him.

Then Bluey said thoughtfully, "Hmm, some of you wear the same symbol, so perhaps the answer is simple.

They have the same authority as you, which leaves the majority under you." Bluey kept his stare up, waiting for any reaction from the corporal.

After a moment of no one talking the corporal growled, "Beware hair-ball! I have sworn nothing to you at all."

"True that," Notso said in agreement to the corporal. "And it something to look at."

The corporal broke his stare off from the cats to look up at Notso. He knew Notso sided with the cats so he dreaded anything Notso had to say.

"Sometimes cats annoying and often it seems they just toying." Notso started off saying,
"But they always kind,
I never been confined,
and in spite of all their sign,
they try to keep good in mind.
So I am inclined,
to say with them I am aligned.
And I be the boss of you,
so I think we join their crew . . . all together . . . intertwined."

Notso intertwined his fingers as a visible example.

Notso could see victory on the cats' faces at his statement and resentment on the dogs. But he didn't say it for the cats, he still hated the dogs and he intended to use the corporal to help right the wrong his clan had done by bringing them here.

Bluey ran into the cavern and started selecting dogs he wanted to bring along into the mountain. Notso could tell from his instructions he was choosing the ones who appeared most cooperative with the least amount of injuries. The rest would remain here until further notice.

Then Bluey gathered his teammates: Cadbury, Rumpus, Preena, and a few others Notso hadn't bothered to learn the names of, to move out.

They did not untie the dogs they had chosen but did inform

them that there was a new alliance between them and the cats. Thanks to their corporal. And once, if their loyalty was proven, they would be set free. Some of them grumbled in objection, but at the sight of the corporal it subsided.

"I hope there is a shortcut," Ripple said to Notso as they were about to head out. He and his crew had been ready to go for a while. "A certain tunnel to shorten the outside strut?"

"Dank Tunnel nearby. It make journey fly by," Notso answered him then took the lead.

The corporal said nothing but walked along side of him, lost in his own thoughts. *Acts of cruelty are outrageous, but acts of kindness are contagious.* The words of the old cat played in the corporal's mind.

These cats saved him from the troll. But then they enslaved him to the troll. How was that kindness? It appeared a bit more mindless. The old cat could have caused some serious damage, but even without using his claws, the old cat managed. So why were they so inclined to force everyone to be kind? What was it the old cat was saying? Act nice or they would be paying? Paying what, and to whom?

Lightning flashed. The corporal looked out over the valley. The storm hung just above the camp. Looking across the sky he realized it was only storming over their camp, nowhere else.

Chapter 27

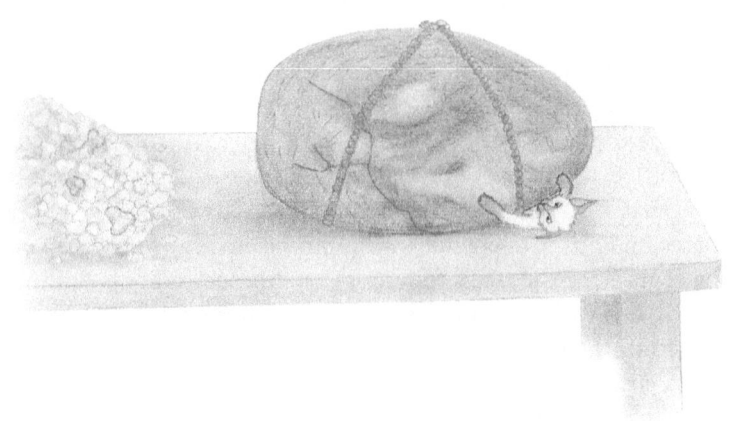

"Cats! I smell Cats! Find them! Find those hairy rats!" the captain bellowed. "Find them right now! Their organs I will disembowel!"

The tent came alive with talking, crashing, and barking inside.

Eli shrunk down low. What do I do? Stay? Run? I wish I knew! Once again panic threatened to overpower all his rational thought.

"I've got a trail! It's strong! I won't fail!" a voice howled out.

"So do I! There's at least three and that's no lie!" Barked another voice.

Eli could hear sniffing. A nose poked out of the hole and then pulled in again.

"They came from this same hole! And one's still there, the sneaky little mole!"

Eli bolted! He raced straight south. Dogs ran out of the tent heading for where he had been! But they spotted him running away through the snowstorm. Howling they alerted every one of his direction and charged after him. Eli heard Comet and Cheena's battle cries from inside the tent as he fled the area.

Eli raced straight for the forest. Once again heading to the exact same area he had left and returned in. He didn't know for how long he would be able to keep up this pace. His ribs were not completely healed yet and running at full speed was making the pain grow again.

Fallen tents covered in snow were everywhere but inside the ones that still stood, trolls emerged. Curious of the dog's barking they came out to see what was going on. Eli saw dogs step out of the tents with the trolls too but many limped or appeared injured in one form or another. They did not attempt to cut him off or pursue him. In fact no one attempted to stop him. To Eli's relief they just watched him race by.

Eli knew the dogs chasing him were gaining on him. He was beginning to think he wasn't going to reach the forest before they had him, when whoosh. A big gust of wind blew down from above and the claw of the huge flying-dog snatched him out of his run. Again he was airborne in the paw of the beast!

The flying-dog held him tight as it flew up in the blackened sky. Eli didn't struggle this time. He knew there was no point. He just let the flying-dog carry him away while he caught his breath.

The huge flying-dog headed east as it climbed upward. Eli looked down at the camp, where he had been. He was right; he wouldn't have made it to the forest before the dogs had reached him. He could see three dogs standing where he had been snatched; watching them fly away.

The big creature banked to her left, circling around to head west. Eli could see the huge tent through the gusting snow, just ahead of them.

"Not again, it will be worse this time," he thought to himself. "After what they did to that troll, they'll take my lives, all nine."

As they neared the tent, she did not descend. She maintained her altitude flying west. As she flew over the tent, Eli could hear the screeching and growling of a battle going on inside of it. Numerous dogs could be seen leaving the warmth of their tents to race toward the largest tent. Most of them were coming from the east side of camp. He feared the worst for Cheena and the others. They were already badly outnumbered; how would they withstand more dogs on the way?

Eli looked up at the huge flying-dog. She was not descending. Where was she taking him?

He looked around trying to figure out where they were going. Down below the camp appeared abandoned. He didn't see any dogs or trolls on this side of camp.

Then movement ahead of them among the tents along the camp's western edge caught Eli's eye. Cats! Army cats! There was a sleigh with a number of army cats traveling with it. Eli squinted his eyes to see further through the blowing snow. There was a fair amount of them maybe forty or so. Eli was delighted! What a welcome sight.

Movement on his right caught his attention. There were more cats on the north side of camp, along the forest edges. From what Eli could make out there was double or triple the amount of army cats over there. They were slowly sneaking into the dog's camp.

The huge flying beast started a descent picking an area open near the cats with the sleigh. As she came to a landing she pulled her leg up so as not to put any pressure on Eli. Eli saw the cats by the sleigh stop and ready themselves for battle. When she had stopped completely, she let Eli go.

"Fear not!" she said addressing the army.
"I've been instructed to join your little jaunt.
But let me be clear.
My truce is bound to the one I hold dear.
As long as no one harms my offspring,
I will help you defeat the wanna-be-king."

Some of the cats started signing to one another. As soon as Eli was released he trotted over to the group to stand with them. As soon as he reached them he turned to gape at the huge flying-dog along with them. After a moment he heard . . .

"Eli, is that you? Or do my eyes screw? This storm *is hard* to see through." The voice sounded just like Elliot's.

Everyone stopped signing. Looking between Eli and the one who addressed him, they opened up a path to the one who spoke.

"Elliot? Elliot smelly-pit!" Eli exclaimed recognizing the voice! He couldn't believe it! His brother was here but where was he? He didn't see him.

Joyfully Eli walked in to the opened path searching the faces of the soldiers for his brother. Eli stopped when he spotted someone standing on top of the sleigh who might be his brother.

Once Eli had spotted him, Elliot jumped down and cautiously started walking toward his brother. Part of him wanted to run but the other part didn't want to get close to the huge dragon.

The instant Eli recognized Elliot, he closed the gap by sprinting over and leaping at Elliot in a brotherly embrace.

Elliot welcomed Eli's tackle falling back into the snow easily when Eli collided into him. They rolled in the snow enjoying their reunion when a large grey tabby spoke up.

"We assume you've met one of the monarch," the grey tabby said to the massive flying-dog. "So they will hold you to that remark."

Eli and Elliot stopped their tussling. Eli's ribs ached but he didn't care. Elliot was here. With huge smiles they both got up and shook the snow off, Eli a little more gingerly. Everyone's attention was split between watching them and gaping at the dragon.

Striker stepped forward. "Eli! I'm very glad to see you're alive. And brought to us by a dragon is quite a surprise. But tell us what has derived . . . the last time I saw you . . . I wasn't sure you survived."

Eli gave Striker a broad smile. He bound over and gave Striker a hug. He had done it! Striker had outrun the dogs and reached the army. A weight, Eli hadn't realized was there, was lifted off his shoulders.

"It's good to see you too, Striker," he said. Then looking around at everyone, he told Striker, "But there's too much to decipher. Right now the sergeant is in trouble.
I know he's a fighter, but you better get there on the double."

Eli turned to view the dragon. She was covering her body with her wings to protect herself from the blowing wind and snow, but still stood where she had landed. There was no fear in her eyes as she waited on them. She knew she posed a threat to them and not the other way around. Eli scrutinized Ruby in an attempt to figure out her intentions.

"I don't know what to make of her.
I thought I'd be fed to the dogs, for sure," he told them.
"However, she just saved my life.
And I think that makes it twice,
so maybe she will help, and end all this strife."

"Actually, I saved your life three times.
If you're keeping count, accuracy is prime," Ruby spoke correcting Eli.

Three times? Eli was confused. What other time had she saved him?

"You don't mean the first time you swiped me?" he asked realizing that was the only other contact he had with her. "That doesn't count as three," he said challenging the large dragon's math.

Then feeling the need to explain himself, he spoke loudly so everyone could hear, "She delivered me straight to the captain, you see. He threw me in a cage and took away the key."

Eli turned back to face Ruby. "So it doesn't count as three."

"You had run straight into a hungry dog pack.
You would not have survived and that is a fact," Ruby spoke kindly to Eli in spite of her correcting him. She knew she was right. She stood proudly yet quietly waited for them to make their minds up

about her.

"Three times she saved me!" Eli said correcting himself, "I guess I will agree."

There was silence. No one spoke or signed. No one knew what to do with the dragon or what to make of Eli who gave no thought to challenging a massive dangerous fire-breathing beast.

"Eli, I am Major Cat." The large grey tabby broke the silence by introducing himself. "Can you explain where the sergeant is at?"

"Yes," Eli said addressing the major. "Sir, it's a mess. They are in a big tent in the middle of camp.
You can't see it from here, not without a ramp.
But they are outnumbered.
Not many remain this side of camp, so you won't be encumbered. Please, sir, you really need to race. If you don't pick up your pace, I fear there will be nothing left of them, not even a trace."

The major turned to one of the cats standing next to him. He signed something quickly. The soldier nodded and in a flash he, Striker, and about thirty others charged over a small hill toward the center of camp.

The major gave Eli his attention again. "Eli, do you know where her egg is?" he asked nodding his head toward the dragon. "Saving it would be our top biz."

"Yes and so does she," Eli glanced at Ruby. "In the largest tent where all the fighting would be."

"I can't help you save it," Ruby spoke up. Her voice filled with worry. "If the captain discovers my loyalty has split, my baby won't survive his fit. Understand, for this reason, I cannot fully commit."

"We'll get your egg, dragon. That's why we brought the wagon." The major reassured her. "If we're ready . . ."

"Sir, the army on the north side," Eli cut the major off. "Do they know where their efforts should be applied? And I didn't see a bridge, no hints of any crossing, not even a smidge."

"I'm glad to hear they are on the move,
but no one knew from where the egg would be removed;
so a tip in the right direction, might help with the correct tent detection," the major said looking at his remaining soldiers to decide which one to send.

"In this area I can deliver," Ruby offered, "and I can help

them cross the river." She leaped into the air beating her wings powerfully to gain height quickly.

Everyone watched her disappear into the snowy darkness; relieved she wasn't there to destroy them.

"She's going to scare the hair right off of them. They'll be frozen in terror and completely bare," Elliot said watching her fly away.

Most of the soldiers snickered at the comment. Eli grinned at his brother. He had forgotten that if a cat was frightened badly enough they could instantly lose a ton of hair in one big poof.

Now that Elliot mentioned it, he must have lost a ton of hair himself, in a variety of locations. It was just one of those things no one thought about or even talked about. He was glad Elliot was here. He had missed him and his humour.

"Well then, let's go," the major said. "We have some dogs to overthrow."

The major and his accompaniment broke into a slow lope; climbing the same small hill the soldiers had moments before them. Eli was about to ask Elliot why he was along when Elliot jumped into the sleigh on the downward side of the hill. Eli couldn't see what exactly he had done but the sleigh had a drag bar beneath it that was applied so the sleigh didn't gain too much speed. When the ground leveled out, the bar lifted up and Elliot jumped out of the sleigh and loped alongside again.

Elliot could see the question on Eli's face so he answered him before Eli could ask the question.

"I'm the brake cat. I get to apply that," he said pointing to the drag bar under the sleigh. As they headed toward the camp's center, Eli realized the sleigh (which was actually just a wagon on skies) set everyone's pace. The cats harnessed to it had to pace themselves because of its weight and everyone else just stayed beside them.

Aside from the slower pace, it took a bit longer to reach the center from this side of camp. The valley was longer then it was wider with rolling hills. Eli filled the major in with the tent's layout and what he knew of the sergeant's plans. The major wasn't concerned with the small hole they had been using; he had another idea. Although much of his plans were signed to his troops he did tell Eli and Elliot verbally what he expected from them, which was primarily to stay with the sleigh.

As they neared the big tents the sounds of fighting reached their ears. Cautiously the major led their party around to the north side of the tents. Lots of shouting could be heard from inside.

As the biggest tent came into view Eli saw strips of light coming from along the walls where there had not been light before. As they got closer rips in the tent walls revealed how the light could be seen. At first Eli wondered what had happened but his questions were answered the moment the major and half of the soldiers with him leaped through the rips into the tent.

The screeching and snarling was already very loud from battle but increased when the major and his troops joined the fight. They could see parts of the fighting through the rips as the wind blew the walls in and out. Eli along with the five remaining soldiers quickly led the sleigh around to the east side of the tent where no rips had yet been made into the tent walls.

Two of the five remaining soldiers quickly sliced the tent walls open with their razor sharp metalized claws while the harness cats made a U-turn with the sleigh pulling up along side of the tent for a quick getaway. Then three of the soldiers disappeared inside while two remained guarding the harnessed team.

Together they listened to the horrendous sounds coming from within the tent. Many angry conversations could be heard over the growls and snarls of battle. But after a bit of time, when the three soldiers did not return as planned, the remaining soldiers began signing with the harnessed soldiers.

"Eli, you are not here by random,
we need you to go in,
because the team we cannot abandon.
You know where the egg lies
and you know what's been devised.
Someone has to go in and check.
We need to get that egg on this deck," one of the soldiers said to Eli.

Eli felt déjà vu as everyone was looking at him, waiting for his response.

Oh dread, dread, dread, he thought. It should be one of them instead. But Eli knew they were right. It had to be him. Everyone else here had a job to do, except him.

"I'll go too. I'll go with you," Elliot volunteered to be supportive of his brother. He could see the fear on Eli's face. He was afraid too but they might do better if they went in together.

"No you already have a job to undertake," the soldier spoke up before Eli could. "Without you, the sleigh won't break."

Knowing the soldier was right, Eli and Elliot exchanged worried looks.

"I'll be fine," Eli attempted to reassure Elliot by sloughing-off the seriousness of the situation. "I do this all the time."

Elliot's blank expression revealed he wasn't convinced.

Eli hopped through the snow to one of the rips in the tent wall. He could see motion through it. Unlike the soldiers he did not just jump through into whatever was waiting for him on the other side. He cautiously poked his head into the room with all the treasure.

Cats and dogs were in a whirl of combat motion. There were far more dogs than cats and they were fighting with every ounce of strength they had. Some of the cat soldiers lay motionless on the floor. The other soldiers were leaping and swiping not able to stop and catch their breath. Eli didn't know for how long they would be able to keep that level of energy up. He hoped the soldiers to the north would arrive soon.

Many trolls had entered the room. They stood gathered along the dividing curtain and in the hallway with jaws hanging in disbelief at the manner in which the cats and dogs fought. None of the trolls fought alongside of the dogs, nor did they side with the cats.

Along the north side of the room many of the crates had been toppled over indicating someone had taken the battle on top of them. Someone was lying in between the crates. Eli didn't see Cheena, Comet, or the sergeant in this room but he thought it might be Rigger in among the crates. If it was him, he wasn't moving.

Eli watched the fighting for a moment. More dogs than cats had their backs to the table, which made Eli think they were defending it. The egg and all the other treasures still remained on the table, unmoved.

Seeing an opening to the table. Eli jumped through the ripped tent and darted in-between combating dogs and cats. He weaved his way around the fighting, darting under the table for shelter once he reached it.

Eli looked around to see if anyone had noticed him. The fighting wasn't confined to just this room. It appeared every room had its battles and from what Eli could make out every dog was preoccupied. So if any of them had noticed him they were too busy to do anything. A few trolls had seen him but they didn't look like they were going to interfere with him or anyone else. Carefully Eli searched for a way to get onto the table without drawing any more attention to himself.

Stealthy is the key. Think invisibility. Eli wished once again he could be invisible as he mentally encouraged himself.

There was less fighting along the north side of the table because the crates along the wall were in close proximity to the long table's edge. Only a couple of dog and cats fought there. Eli snuck along under the table then stepped out and jumped up on top of the table in one fluid motion.

The table still smelled delicious. The bones inter mixed with the gold under the warmth from the light, which hung above the egg, set off a wonderful aroma. Eli made himself ignore the smell and trotted as quickly as he could atop of the treasure to the emerald egg. Some of the golden stones fell to the floor from his stepping on them. Eli made no attempt to grab them. The emerald egg was his only focus.

Once reaching the egg he could see the baby within the shell. The baby appeared fine. There was a crack along the outside of the egg that had not been there the last time. However the egg seemed to be holding strong.

Ropes encircled the outside of the egg so it could be lowered to the ground safely. But the ends were loose and not fastened to anything. Eli looked around for something to fasten them to. Then the baby moved within the egg catching Eli's attention. Their eyes met for a second time. The baby had been watching the fighting but now it watched Eli.

A strange peaceful connection to this baby came over Eli as they looked one another in the eyes. It was odd and unexplainable to Eli, but the feeling was also undeniable.

"Don't worry, we'll get you out of here," Eli whispered. "And we'll keep you safe. You have nothing to fear." He put a paw on the egg reassuringly.

"You dare set your paws back in here?
And steal our dragon egg too, it would appear.
Your arrogance is pretty clear,
although it's at your brilliance, that I sneer!"

Eli spun around to face the voice of his accuser. Chopper stood peeking over the side of the table with his paws on the edge. He was much shorter than most of the other dogs and it was the only way he could see onto the table.

The memories of the last time he encountered Chopper flooded his mind. But Chopper didn't look quite the same. He had blood all over his face and part of his left ear had been bitten off. He smelled the same though, if not worse from the blood.

"Let us go, and you'll be spared, trust me I know." Eli didn't know what else to say. He was caught and surrounded by dogs. Even if they were distracted, he didn't want to draw any more attention to himself.

"Let you go? *Let you go!* Do you know what happened the last time *I let you go*?

Let me fill you in . . . I was hung by my paws in the place where you should have been!

I was bitten to pieces at the captain's command and when they let me go I couldn't stand.

You think I should *let you go*, well I think *no*! It was suppose to be you strung up receiving each blow!"

While Chopper was talking a dog fighting with one of the soldiers was stealing quick glances his way. Eli recognized him instantly. It was Rad!

Rad had obviously recovered from Notso's hit and had been fighting here the whole time. Chopper was oblivious to Rad drawing his battle closer to them at the table. The bandages were gone from his head and neck, and he was bleeding from the wounds Eli had previously given him as well as from new wounds. Eli's ribs ached at just the memory of Rad's teeth crushing his chest.

"What are you looking at?" Chopper asked turning around. Seeing Rad he said, "Rad, you got a cat! This one's mine, the little rat!"

"He was mine first. I'll switch you this one for that little curse," Rad said between dodging and snapping at the soldier he was combatting.

Without waiting for Chopper's agreement, Rad spun on his hind legs and leaped over Chopper's head onto the table. Eli jumped high in the air doing a side-flip to land on the other side of the egg. Rad slid across the table bumping into the egg. Gold and bones clanged noisily onto the floor. The egg rocked back toward Eli. Eli tried to steady it. The soldier Rad had been fighting with followed Rad onto the table sliding into Rad who then bumped the egg again. Rad spun around at his assailant bumping the egg yet again. They resumed their fighting. Gold and bones flew in every direction as they fought on top of the table.

At the third bump, Eli knew the egg was going over and he was too small to push it back into place. So he used his body as a cushion as the egg tipped over. Once the egg was down Eli was pinned under it. The egg was extremely heavy and Eli gasped for air. The weight of the egg was squishing his bruised ribs causing pain to sear through him. Eli struggled to breath as he squirmed trying to free himself. There was nothing within reach he could grab to help pull him out.

Eli could sense the babies fear when he got knocked over. As Eli looked around for something to grab onto, he saw Chopper's head bob in and out of sight as he attempted to jump onto the table. Fortunately for Eli, Chopper was too short to make the jump up. But his determination was evident as he continued to try.

"You're okay, baby," Eli gasped attempting to calm the baby within the egg. "You're still safe if not a bit weighty." Eli could see the baby wiggling through the shell it was beginning to panic.

Suddenly large tan paws were on the table and a smooth deep voice said, "Allow me, to get you free."

The captain bent down coming into Eli's field of vision. Using his mouth he grabbed Eli by his head, pulled him out from under the egg, and swung him across the room into the crowd of trolls. The egg bumped down at Eli's release.

As Eli flew across the room, he saw more soldiers were lying this way and that on the floor. Some dogs lay on the floor as well but so far the dogs were winning this battle. Eli hit the face of one of the trolls who caught Eli before he fell to the ground.

"You okay, tiny cat? I keep you here, so you no end up flat," the troll said holding Eli. He then began stroking Eli's head.

Eli let the troll pet him while he caught his breath. His ribs felt instant relief from being freed from under the egg but with each breath the ache returned.

Eli looked around weighing his options. He could feel his neck was a little strained from being flung across the room but other than that, and his ribs, he was fine.

Something stinky caught Eli's attention. It smelled like dogs breath. "Gross! Saliva dose," he muttered as he realized his head was covered with dog drool. And the troll was rubbing it into his fur.

Suddenly the roof on the south side of the tent was engulfed in flames. The dragon roared as she stormed into the tent.

Chapter 28

Trolls screamed and scattered, running for cover in whichever direction. The troll holding Eli screamed too; throwing him into the air as he ran to get away from the dragon.

Eli once again found himself flying through the air. He landed near the long table next to a large black and tan dog that had stopped fighting to stare at Ruby.

Most of the army cats ran for their lives, darting out of the tent's ripped walls. Everyone who had remained stopped fighting. Some stood and stared but most, including the dogs, looked for a way out as the roof by the entrance burned.

The captain stood by the egg staring at what Ruby had done. The ropes that had been tied around the egg dangled loosely in his paws. The huge flying-dog glared at the captain. He dropped the ropes onto the table.

"WHAT HAVE YOU DONE!" she bellowed. "Now you'll get what you begun the moment you took away my son!" She looked like she may blast him with a stream of fire.

In a flash, the captain jumped to the other side of the egg putting it between him and the huge dragon. He grabbed a large bone from the pile and held it up. Eli wasn't sure if he was going to use it against the flying-dog or if he was going to hit the egg with it.

Eli looked at the egg. It was still lying on its side. The small crack that been along the side had grown substantially and a fairly large piece of emerald shell had fallen out. The egg had a hole in it! Somehow he was able to feel the baby struggling within the egg.

"Now look here, Ruby, this crack was not from me.
If you need someone to blame, then search for the littlest cat.
He's the one who made this crack."

Eli was shocked! He had saved the egg from a hard knock down and quite possibly from rolling onto the floor.

Ruby curled her lips baring her fangs. She looked from the captain to Eli who still stood on the floor not far from the table. The big black and tan dog slinked away leaving Eli to stand alone.

Eli shook his head in denial but couldn't find his voice to say anything.

Elliot suddenly leaped to Eli's side. He had been watching through a hole made from one of the rips. The dragon was furious and he wasn't about to let Eli face her by himself.

She looked back at the captain but he ducked down behind her egg when he saw the fury on her face. Enraged Ruby sucked in a lung full of air. Raising her snout to the ceiling she expelled her anger in a fiery blast over all of their heads. The rest of the tent ceiling was instantly engulfed in flames. Right then more rips were made along the tent walls and a multitude of cats leaped in.

The few dogs that had remained to watch the scene unfold scattered leaping through the same ripped walls. The fresh soldiers on the scene grabbed fallen soldiers and pulled them out from the tent as it began to fall to the ground in fiery pieces.

Eli darted under the table for cover as the tent began to collapse. Elliot spun on his heels and raced back out the tent side but returned a moment later to the ripped wall when he realized Eli hadn't followed him.

"Eli, get out of there!" Elliot hollered at Eli. "The tents on fire! It'll burn all your hair!"

The table sagged above Eli's head and he saw the toes of the huge flying-dog curl around the edge of the table. Her back two feet and frayed tail remained on the ground behind him.

Eli could feel the baby flying-dog struggling to get out of the egg. He felt a powerful urge to help the baby. As if the baby was calling him to save him. "I have to save the baby! I've got to get him to safety!" Eli hollered back running under the length of the table to the same area he had jumped up before.

In a heartbeat, Eli was on the table. Pieces of burning fabric fell like rain. A piece of fiery fabric landed on his head. Eli shook it off unscathed; never realizing the drool on his head saved his fur from catching fire.

Above him the night sky opened up as the tent was consumed. The hissing sound from snow colliding with fire surrounded them.

The captain crouched down low, hiding beside the egg just out of Ruby's reach. He had put the bone down but kept it nearby. Ruby towered over him with her body protecting him and her egg from the burning tent. The captain was trapped there. There was nowhere he could go. If he jumped down she looked like she was going to bite him. For now her long neck curled around as she glared at him, unable to reach him from the protective angle she held.

The new soldiers on the scene darted in and out of the burning tent, pulling everyone they could find out to safety. Eli saw some of them jump out of the burning tent to stop, drop and roll when fire lingered too long on their bodies. He could hear them calling to him to get out.

Eli hopped over burning pieces of fabric lying on top of the gold and bones. He coughed a little from the smoke but trotted directly toward the captain and large egg. The captain's eyes narrowed as Eli approached but when Eli saw him cower back after glancing up at the huge flying-dog, Eli knew he could do it. He darted under the flying-dog's chin, and then leaped over the captain's head, under the narrow gap between the dragon's great belly and the egg, to land safely on the other side of the emerald egg.

"I'm here, baby. I'll help you reach safety," he said soothingly from the other side of the egg.

Eli could see the little flying-dog wiggling within the eggshell, struggling to break free. Eli could sense the baby's distress; calling to him to help somehow. Eli stood on his hind legs to examine the hole in the shell. He didn't know why the baby wasn't breaking it. He didn't know anything about dragons but he knew when baby birds hatched they pecked their way free.

Only the exterior had a hole in it. There was some type of membrane between the baby and the open air. He suddenly realized the baby was out of air and needed to breath! Baby birds made a hole from the inside out. This hole was made from the outside in but it hadn't broken the protective membrane.

"That's right," he heard Ruby say. Her big red head was just a few feet from him as she watched his and the captain's every move. "Rip that open and the rest will be his fight."

Eli extended his special claw and ripped the membrane open. The baby dragon stuck his nose in the area and took in his first breaths of air outside the shell. Eli felt the baby's distress dissipate as he filled his lungs.

"You're a dragon lover are you?" the captain growled at Eli.
"I never would have guessed it.
Not from any of your hairy brew.
Not that it will matter.
Not by the time Ruby's done with you."

The captain hadn't moved from where he crouched. Not even when Eli jumped over his head, to Eli's relief. His expression made Eli slink back to the other side of the egg.

"There's only one who's facing his end." Ruby's nose was dangerously close to the captain. "And it's not that cat I have penned."

Eli sensed the baby was gathering strength within the egg.

The captain sat up as he faced Ruby. Eli could no longer see his face but his hair stood on end and his voice sounded as smooth as ever when he spoke.

"Ruby, what is the meaning of this?" he asked.
"I'm not the one at whom you should be pissed.
I'm not the one who put a hole in his shell.
Look around you in case you've missed;
we've been attacked by cats and they brought hell;
we've been attacked by cats; it's them you should quell."
"See?" he said gesturing around them.
"Look around at all they have done!
Can't you see they are the ones?
They did this; they did this to your son!"

Ruby never moved. She barely blinked. The captain waited a moment for a response but when none came he continued.

"Look, Ruby, if it weren't for them your egg would be fine.
So stop blaming me the fault isn't mine!
And back away if you don't mind,
there's clearly no need to keep *me* confined."

The captain gestured with his paw for Ruby to back away and give him some space. But she remained.

Melted snow began dripping off Ruby as she stood covering them, glaring at the captain. Her lips curled exposing her fangs as a growl rumbled in her throat.

Eli looked around them as the captain had said to. The tent was no longer standing but was a burning rectangular shape all around them. All the walls had collapsed and now burned in a smoky sizzling fire. Most of the wooden crates had caught fire and burned along with the tent. The smell of burning dog food mixed in the air with the smoke.

All the fallen soldiers had been pulled out of the fire and now all around there were spectators watching through the flames and smoke from the safety of the other side. Eli could hear many hushed voices coming from the crowd. But the crackling and sizzling from the snow falling on the fire was the loudest.

The night sky was open above them now. The wind had stopped and the snow fell even heavier than before. It looked to Eli like Winter was diligently working at putting the fire out and it wouldn't be long before he succeeded.

The egg moved slightly as the baby dragon began pushing on his shell.

Ruby's voice rumbled when she finally spoke. Her anger was evident with each sentence.

"You are the one who stole my son.
You are the one with which this begun.
You were the one who held my egg hostage.
Threatening to eat him with ham and deer sausage."

The egg cracked some more.
"If it weren't for you, my son would be home,
basking in the sun, among the brome.
If it weren't for you the lands would not be pillaged.
You forced me to burn each and every village."

A piece of egg broke off as the baby dragon pushed his nose out the hole.

"You were the one who dragged us here.
I was your puppet, you my puppeteer.
You *are* to blame; the fault is *all* yours!
Because of you, I started wars."

Ruby took a breath as she remembered the past year. All the things she had put up with; everything they had done enraged her and now she could finally put an end to it.

"You've used my son to control me.
You used my son to torture me.
You risked his life, every time you started up strife,
you gave no thought, to whether or not, he'd bare injury."

The egg rocked as another piece broke off.
"Because of you my son hatches early.
Because of you this weather is burly.
Because of you the cats attack sternly.
Only you are the one with the conquering aim.

Only you are the one who plays these games.
Only you are the one who used my son, to state a land claim.
So you see dear captain, you *are* to blame."

The captain shook his head.

"You're losing it, Ruby, so pull it together, you just blamed me for the state of this weather," the captain said incredulously.

"Oh, the weather in this land is another thing; it packs a punch and carries a sting. And they don't want you here, so you will never be king."

A snarl escaped the captain's throat. More hair stood up on his shoulders and neck.

"They? Who is 'they'? You know cats are prey! Has your mind begun to fray?" he snarled back.

"There is a 'they' and you can be sure they'll make you pay. But don't worry about them, at least not for today," she threatened.

Her voice rumbled in a deep growl. Who exactly was the threat to the captain was being made clear with the tone of her voice.

Ruby stepped off the table to her left side, moving away from her protective cover. She lifted her right wing to maintain the shelter above her hatchling. The table straightened back into place as she moved off. The egg rocked again as another piece of shell broke off. The baby's toes came into view beside his snout as he worked at exiting his emerald egg.

Eli could sense the baby's excitement mounting to be free from his shell and his determination to complete the job.

Ruby moved several feet to her left so she could face the captain better. She appeared completely unconcerned if the fire touched her or not, as she stepped into several pieces of burning fabric. She never once broke eye contact with the captain, never moved her head or her right wing, only her body. Now she was in a position where she could strike the captain if she wished to.

From behind Eli saw the captain's ears flatten and his head and shoulders sink down a little. His hair remained raised.

"Up until now I put up with your demands," Ruby continued saying,

"Not risking his life as you conquered the lands.

Tell me, Captain dear,
did you give any thought,
of what food should be brought,
or in what manner he would be reared?"

The captain growled. The truth was he had given it a lot of thought. He already had the chains made. He wasn't sure on the baby's neck size so a few collars in various sizes lay in wait. That baby would never see freedom. But he wasn't foolish enough to tell Ruby that.

"That's why you're here, Ruby.
You are his mother,
raising him is your duty," he answered smoothly.

"Well for once we agree.
So let me tell you how it will be," Ruby said exerting her authority.

It was about time the captain felt *his* life threatened. He didn't know it yet but there was no way she was going to let him go free. As far as she was concerned, everything he had worked toward was already gone.

"My son will hatch hungry.
He will look for some food.
He'll crave vegetation, mostly prechewed,
of grasses and branches a mixture all-sundry;
all of which, are not in this country.

Shall we watch and see how he gets confound,
when he searches for food and none can be found?

What shall we feed him, oh, Captain, dear,
when he searches around and finds nothing here?"

The captain thought he might know where she was going with these questions and his anger increased. But at the same time he knew he had to be very careful of what he said.

"That's not my problem,
you are to search for the various blossom.
You are his mother and I'm sure you'll be awesome.
So stop asking me, on what will he feed;
I've left it to you, you are his breed," he answered her angrily.

"I am more than just his breed!" Ruby retorted.
"I am his mother!
You are right about that, there is no other!

But I am also a dragon so you better take heed.
My son requires more than just the odd reed!"

Ruby took a breath to calm herself. Inside she seethed with fury. This was what she had been waiting for. Finally she would be able to rid herself of the captain once and for all.

"Now the thing you seem to not understand;
is I've searched high and low across this land.
I have found nothing here but a bit of bog,
a pathetic resemblance of food amongst the log.

But have no fear, as dragons our menu expands,
and thanks to you we are in these lands.
That is why, as I flew through the fog,
I decided my son shall feast on dog."

The baby broke free of his shell. The captain jumped out of his way as the baby's green body slid across the table into the pile of gold and bones. Ruby snapped at the captain with her massive jaw but he dodged her and she missed.

"The hell he will!" the captain snarled back.

He leaped over the baby in a flash, keeping the baby between them. He scrambled close to the baby's head. Warily eyeing the baby, judging whether or not the little dragon even had teeth and was capable of biting him let alone eating him.

"Back off, Ruby, or his blood will spill," he threatened when he saw the baby had mostly gums with just the start of a few sharp teeth growing.

The baby fumbled on the table trying to learn his limbs movements. He was wet and slick from the amniotic fluid and he had an iridescent green shine. Steam rose from his body as the cold night air began cooling him. Gold and bones clanged off the table to the ground as he flopped about.

Ruby pulled her wing back to her side allowing the cold snow to fall on her precious hatchling as she moved again into a better striking position.

"I mean it! Back off this instant!" the captain warned her. There was fear in his voice. The smooth calmness was gone.

Ruby did not back off. She eyed him carefully, and then with surprising quickness she grabbed him with one fast swoop of her front foot. Lifting the captain high, she stood up on her back legs.

Eli

She quickly brought her other front foot up to hold him steady as she slowly lifted him to her snout. The captain wiggled and bit at her claws as he fought to free himself. He was a very large dog, almost too big for her to hold. She squeezed him tight struggling to keep him within her grasp.

Eli couldn't believe what he was seeing! She was about to eat him right before his eyes. Just like the dogs had done to that troll. It was wrong. It was evil. He couldn't stand it. All this fighting was because of them but it had to stop! Cat Above! Someone had to stop it! Eli looked around there was no one there but him.

"*Stop!* Stop stop stop Miss Flying-Dog!
You're right about him; he's not a nice dog."

Eli flew over the broken shells and leaped at Ruby's face, landing on her big red snout.

There were gasps among the crowd watching.

"But that's why you must stop,
in order to see through this moral smog."

Ruby shook her head to get Eli off her snout. He dug his claws into her nose to keep from falling. Ruby stopped shaking her head when she realized it was making him dig his claws further into her muzzle. If she weren't already holding the captain, she would have plucked him off with her claws. Lucky for the little cat her skin was thick. But she glared at Eli as she felt the pinch of his claws.

She couldn't believe the nerve of this tiny little morsel of a cat! Who was he to interrupt her long-awaited moment? She had deliberately dragged out eating the captain so he could feel just a little of the fear he had instilled in her and in thousands of others. It was her way of torturing him.

"If you swallow him whole or chew him up small;
you'll become the same, and these dogs won't learn at all!" Eli explained, releasing his claws when she stopped moving.

He had gotten her attention, now he had to get her to understand.

"Can't you see?
If they are to be better,
they must witness mercy,
right down to the letter.

You are right about him; for sure he's a tyrant.

But don't act like him; don't make him silent;
Especially not, because you became violent."

Eli jumped off her face back onto the table landing next to the baby flying-dog. The baby awkwardly turned to get a good look at Eli. Eli could feel the baby's affection for him and Eli moved to stand next to him. The baby sniffed at Eli rubbing him gently with his nose. He then turned to sniff a bone. Picking one up the baby began sucking and gnawing on it.

"That is the lesson that would be learned . . .
that you are just like him and cruelty is migrant;
that you are just like him, only the tables have turned.
No, you must be better.
You have to be better.
You're a dragon, don't you see?
You're a natural trendsetter."

Eli didn't know where this was coming from but he felt compelled to say it. It was like she didn't know and only he was available to tell her the truth.

Ruby looked from her son to Eli. She could feel her son's fondness for this little cat. The emotion baffled her and she wondered if it was healthy for him.

"Whatever you say, whatever you do.
We all watch, we admire you."

The little cat was flattering her but why? What did he have to gain by this? Was he trying to make a name for himself? Was he worried she would eat him too; that he'd be next on her menu? She puzzled over his motivation. She couldn't see how her sparing the captain would benefit the little cat at all. In fact, the captain would kill him in a heartbeat if given the chance, so it was actually to this cats benefit that she did snap him in half.

"So please stop, don't eat this dog.
We know he's no good and could use a good flog.
But if you choose to show mercy instead,
everyone will see and the news will spread.
We all know that he should be dead.
Especially after all he's done and said.
But you making a choice, right here, right now,
to be a leader in forgiveness and mercy, will wow."

Coming down on all fours. Ruby stepped on the captain just enough to hold him down without completely crushing him. Ruby couldn't believe what she was hearing. He actually wanted her to spare this dog's life.

Ruby scoffed the little cat,
"You think I should let him go?
After all he's done, after all his woe?
Are you out of your little kitty-cat mind?
He'll just do it again, are you so blind?
 Especially to you!
You escaped him once and that just won't do.
He won't hesitate to chew you in two.
 No, I'm doing you a favour.
I won't let him go.
In this I won't waiver." Ruby lifted the captain to her mouth.

"Oh no no! Don't let him go.
He will do it again, we all know," Eli readily agreed with her.
"Just stop for a minute and consider another blow."

Ruby stopped when her son nickered at her. With the bone still in his mouth, he nuzzled the little cat again. The cat responded with a little rub back but he never took his eyes off her.

Silently her son asked her to listen to his cat. *His* cat? Oh no, she thought, what has he done?

Lowering the captain from her muzzle she complied with her sons wishes and waited to hear the now annoying little cat out.

Eli didn't want her to let go of the captain. There was a good chance the captain would attack him or someone else if he were freed. He had already threatened the baby's life, what would stop him from carrying the threat out.

"No, he definitely should pay,
just not eaten alive, it's not the best way."

Ruby smiled with a devious grin, looking down at the captain under her foot she asked,
"Want me to scorch him first?
The flavour of burnt dog isn't the worst,
it's just that it creates such a thirst."

"Nooo," Eli shook his head, "you need to make your choices wise, choices respectable in everyone's eyes.

As a dragon, you have the power,
you can show love and forgiveness
or you can burn and devour.

Either way, everyone will watch and learn.
And that is why choosing right over wrong is such a concern.

When everyone sees you do what is right and good.
You'll inspire others to do as they should."

Eli hoped she understood him. He hoped she would use her power of influence to stop the violence.

Ruby considered the little cat's request. She placed the Captain back under her foot. Even her son was on the little furry rodent's side. After a moment she said,

"There is one thing you haven't done,
since your little moral speech begun.
And that is to bring up, the raising of my son.
You never used him in stating your case . . .
saying how his morals would be misplaced,
or how through my actions he could be disgraced.

And I have respect for that.
So I will consider extending grace."

Her voice changed to a low growl, as she looked down at the captain, stepping on him harder as she made her point.

"But I won't let him go.
He has met his end.
I want everyone to know,
he will never be leader again.
There will be nowhere he can go,
where he can ascend,
because he has been brought as low as he can go,
from this overthrow."

The captain grunted loudly as Ruby's weight pushed the air out of his lungs. If she pushed down any further he knew his ribs would crack in half. Ruby wanted him to be made the lowest in all the packs. She knew there was nothing worse for the leader of a pack to become the lowest.

Within a pack there was always the possibility of rising to the top again but it was difficult. And if all the packs in The Rest of the World accept this sentence they would keep him down no matter how many fights he won.

The Captain could not let this happen. He would rather die. There had to be a way out. Then he got an idea; there was a way to regain his stature, if she succeeded in taking it from him. He started planning his next course of action, and his revenge. Oh how he would make Ruby pay for this.

When Ruby released the pressure, both he and Eli sighed in relief.

"Thank you, Miss Flying-Dog," Eli said.
"Thank you for seeing through this moral fog.
I've heard making the right choice isn't so easy,
especially when dealing with one so sleazy.
But acts of violence really should be silenced.
They have always, and will always, only beget more violence.
I can see that it's true,
and I sure hope you can too."

Ruby looked around at the spectators. The fire was dying and creating a fair amount of smoke but they watched her and the little cat as a captivated audience.

Looking back at the little cat she remembered someone had called him Eli, when she had delivered him to the clowder of cats on the west end of camp. He was obviously young and had never encountered her kind before. Either that or he just wasn't very smart when it came to judging his own peril.

She could have blasted him with fire, all of them, anytime she wanted. Lucky for him she only killed what she intended to eat. Or maybe it was lucky for him her precious liked him as much as he did. Either way he was one lucky little cat and it was time he learned the truth about her.

"I'm not a dog that flies.
And I don't like what that implies," she told him, fed-up with being called a flying-dog. She found it insulting and he needed to stop it.

"You better call me Ruby.
I am a dragon truly.
So no longer be confused,
because you're no longer excused."

"May I call you Ruby too?
If you don't mind,
we'll take that dog from you," the major Cat said approaching Ruby cautiously through a wall of smoke.

Several large cats followed the major. They also had symbols on their coats. The fire was smoldering and nearly out. There was more smoke now than fire. Eli was glad Winter had stopped blowing the wind around because the smoke floated straight up instead of into their faces.

Through the smoke Eli saw the dogs had been packed together in sections. They had escaped the flames of the tent only to run into an army of waiting cats who had apparently wasted no time in rounding them up.

Eli spotted the sergeant over by Elliot's sleigh. He looked to be in rough shape but alive. The medics there were tending him. Elliot was standing nearby the sergeant but he was watching Eli instead of assisting the medics. The medics looked very busy attending the wounded, nevertheless Eli saw them steal glances his way whenever they could.

Without leaving the baby's side, Eli searched through the smoke for Cheena but he couldn't see her anywhere. He wondered where she was. He still feared the worst for her.

The baby dragon dropped his bone and nuzzled Eli again with his soft leathery nose. He shivered.

"Oh, baby, you're cold.
There's probably a blanket around we could unfold."

Eli stepped in closer to the baby's chest rubbing against it before sitting down. He tried to use his body heat to give the baby a bit of warmth. Eli looked where Elliot had been standing but now Elliot was gone. He didn't want to leave the baby's side to go find one but he would if he had to. First he'd try to get Elliot's attention and then ask Elliot to bring him one.

Looking around, Eli saw the major and the other large cats already had a muzzle on the captain, who was still under Ruby's foot. And they were in the process of putting a couple of chains around the captain's neck. Several of the soldiers had symbols on their coats similar to the major's. It was obvious they were high ranking officers.

Ruby was speaking with them but was also keeping an eye on her son.

Eli looked back where Elliot had been. Just then Elliot emerged through the smoke carrying a blanket. He trotted over and jumped up on to the table. Elliot's eyes were big as saucers as he looked over the baby dragon.

"I was on my way over when I saw him shiver, so I got one before he started to quiver," Elliot answered Eli's question before Eli could ask it.

Elliot was always good at doing that.

Eli quickly grabbed part of the blanket and the two of them covered the baby with it.

Elliot couldn't believe what Eli had done. He was astounded at his brother's bravery. After covering the baby he turned to Eli shaking his head in disbelief.

"Eli, you're insane," he said, gawking at the baby.
"So tell me, what's his name?"

"Hmmm, we haven't been properly introduced," Eli said realizing he didn't know it. "But then he did just pop his roost," he added excusing himself.

Stepping in front of the baby dragon on top of the gold and bones, Eli introduced his brother and himself,

"Hello, little guy. This is my brother Elliot and my name is Eli. It's nice to meet you. What name do you go by?"

The baby squawked then turned to his mother. Ruby stepped off the captain as several burly soldiers led him away. Ruby took a step closer to her baby, finally able to nuzzle him she bent her head down and the two of them took a moment for their own private greeting.

When she lifted her head, she held it high and proudly introduced her son to everyone within hearing distance.

"This is my son Emeraldson.
He is the first emerald male since the Jewel Dragon's begun.
He is fourth in the order of the Gem Stone Run.
And many believe that he will be the one.
The one who will rule our domain until the worthy one comes."

Chapter 29

Sun was just poking his head up over the tips of the mountains when Eli and Elliot left the dog's camp. Spring had officially taken over the throne of weather and throughout the night he had dissipated the storm clouds. It looked like it was going to be a nice warm spring day.

The troops were headed back to their encampment with the first load of injured for medical care. Two sleighs were required for the injured but only one sleigh was brought along. It had been a long night and Eli and Elliot were both exhausted, but Eli was even more so. He hadn't had a full nights rest in days. All he could think about was finding a warm spot to curl up in and go to sleep.

He could just barely see over the back of the sleigh from where he followed behind. The sleigh was filled to capacity with the severely injured and Emeraldson. Eli would have gladly stayed behind with the little dragon if it hadn't been for Elliot who insisted the baby be on the first sleigh ride back to their camp.

It didn't escape Eli's notice that Elliot only insisted after Eli said he would stay with the baby. Eli suspected Elliot didn't want to let him out of his sight again. Elliot had argued with one of the medics that the baby needed food. The dog's food had burned up and back at their camp there was plenty of food to be had.

Ruby was grateful for the care they offered and had permitted them to take Emeraldson without her. She would join them later. She had been asked to stay behind and help the magistrate with the trolls. Just in case they became unruly, which trolls were known to do. She had agreed but didn't want to be away from her baby for too long. Now that he had hatched she needed to find some of the right vegetation for him but what the cats offered to feed him would do for the time being.

After the captain had been captured, everything had calmed down fairly quickly. The dogs had been caught when they fled the burning tent. They never suspected that magistrate's army would be right outside their tent walls and they had run straight into a wall of soldiers.

Apparently, every available soldier had been given the order to descend on the camp and they came in from all sides. As they moved in, they had emptied the individual tents of their occupants. Gathering them together in an organized fashion.

Most of the dogs had already been captured outside the camp so the soldiers didn't have too much difficulty gathering the last of them up. The majority of these dogs were injured in one fashion or another and so they surrendered very easily.

While Eli had been inside the largest tent, one of the other big tents had been emptied out so the prisoners could be guarded in one location.

The trolls found in the small tents around camp were confronted too but not aggressively. It was pointed out to them that their cooperation was assumed, as they were Catland citizens living under the magistrate's law. They complied because they recognized the authority of the magistrate but most decided it was time to head home.

No one tried to stop the trolls from leaving because capturing the dogs was their top priority. Also because the magistrate's army did not have enough resources to capture both trolls and dogs. Trolls were much harder to capture due to their strength and size.

The trolls that fled the tent when Ruby set it on fire were also surprised to find the magistrate's army surrounded them. These trolls were stopped along with the fleeing dogs but to avoid a direct conflict with them the soldiers kept redirecting the trolls attention to the dragon, until it was sorted out which troll was in charge. Once they knew who was in charge, the soldiers nonchalantly surrounded him and his closet followers.

After the captain had been led away in chains, Dicey decided there wasn't any reason for him to stay. Everything he had hoped for was gone with the dogs. But when he announced to his henchmen it was time to leave, it was already too late. He was surrounded. Just as he was about to fight his way free, Winter descended from the clouds. It was only then that he realized just how much trouble he really was in.

Filled with fear, Dicey had turned to run away from Winter but the soldiers roped his feet together bringing him down with a crash. The instant he fell his henchmen gave up, complying with the army's orders. They were then brought to one of the other large tents, to discuss things over with Winter.

It was then that Major Cat asked Ruby if she would stay and help, just in case Dicey or one of his devoted friends changed their

Eli

minds about cooperating with them.

Eli was relieved Winter was here to deal with them. He knew everything would be taken care of now. He hoped he'd never have to cross paths with any of them ever again.

As they made their way through the forest, Eli watched the baby in the sleigh who was sleeping under a pile of warm blankets. There was no explanation he knew of that explained the connection he had with the baby. It was becoming more than just a sense of each other. Their connection was growing and a close friendship was forming.

As he watched the baby sleep he couldn't help but be envious of the lucky little dragon who was cozy, warm, and sleeping. Eli was so tired. He was sure there was room enough for him to fit in there too, somewhere. But that wasn't actually the issue. He was well enough to walk.

Next to Emeraldson laid Cheena. She was not so lucky. She also was curled up and sleeping. Well not so much sleeping but unconscious. She had lost at least one or two of her lives. She had been found in one of the little rooms in the tent and had gotten pulled out when Ruby set the tent on fire. She was severely injured and most likely would be scarred for the rest of her life. But Eli had been reassured that she would recover, given enough time.

Eli watched her for a bit too. Actually, maybe she still was lucky; he wondered if the same could be said about Rigger or Comet. They had both lost all their lives in the battle. He knew they were with Cat Above now and there was peace in knowing that. But was that considered a lucky thing, leaving this world to go to the next? He wasn't sure.

There was one thing he was beginning to believe, and that was Cat Above had helped him when he needed him most. He had courage and words when he was certain ordinarily he would not have had either. The more Eli thought about it the more he thought that Cat Above had taken him up on his offer of "going the distance" for Him. Otherwise, where had that courage and knowledge come from? Half of what Eli had said to Ruby he hadn't known himself prior to saying it. Of course he had no intentions of telling anyone that.

Rigger and Comet had fought brilliantly, saving the sergeant and Cheena several times most proficiently. Or so the sergeant told him when Eli had spotted the sergeant standing over their bodies. The sergeant was injured with a broken leg and several other wounds, but he seemed to have fared the best from the initial conflict.

Everyone who had not survived had been gathered together in one location, not far from Elliot's sleigh. They would stay there until arrangements could be made for their burials. Fortunately for Catland there were only a few who had lost all of their lives. The sergeant told Eli that Scratch would be brought over and included in the burials too.

Eli couldn't stop himself from mewing when he had seen Rigger and Comet. It hadn't been just about them that made him breakdown, but everything; Scratch, the terror of being captured, being chased, his life getting threatened over and over . . . everything. He cried uncontrollably for a while.

Elliot mourned along with him when he had heard about Scratch. But it wasn't until Emeraldson started wailing that Eli managed to gained control of himself.

Ruby had gotten quite perturbed when Emeraldson starting crying. Eli felt her glare on him the instant she poked her head out from the tent with the trolls in it. He hadn't realized the connection he had with the baby dragon could impact the baby's emotions like that. He felt it was something special they shared and he looked forward to hanging out with the baby. But to avoid a confrontation with Ruby, he stopped his mewing as quickly as he could.

Eli and Elliot spent the majority of the night talking and learning about each of their experiences. They were surprised to learn they both had known Scratch and Rigger.

Scratch had impacted both their lives by sacrificing himself. Putting others before oneself was part of the values of Catland, it was what made their society strong. Scratch died living out those values, and for a grumpy old cat, he was the embodiment of what Catland stood for.

As they talked, many of the soldiers came and went, paying their respects to those who had passed away. That was when Eli realized everyone had a tale to tell about each of the fallen soldiers.

He realized they were all interconnected in one way or another. And everyone in Catland would mourn these losses together.

It was midmorning when they stepped out of the forest into the little clearing where the encampment was. Spring was doing a good job of warming things up. Everyone was feeling pretty warm from the trek.

Samantha was there and came bounding over when she saw Elliot's sleigh. She was ecstatic to see Eli alive and Eli was thrilled to see her too. It didn't take her long to see that Eli was in desperate need of sleep. She offered both Elliot and Eli her tent to sleep in but was surprised when Eli told them he wanted to sleep with the baby dragon.

After seeing Emeraldson for herself, Samantha explained there wasn't a tent available that would fit Emeraldson's size. And because the medics needed to get in and out of the sleigh, he couldn't sleep in there either. So she proposed putting a tent up close to where the sleigh was parked. That way Eli would be close to Emeraldson while he slept. Eli was extremely grateful which continued to puzzle Samantha and Elliot.

The instant Eli crawled into the dome tent he couldn't stop himself from purring in delight. Within seconds of finally getting to take his ripped-up jacket off, he was fast asleep.

Elliot crawled in beside him and was about to say "good napping, no crapping" but stopped when he saw Eli was already sleeping. So Elliot curled up beside him, covered them both up with the blanket and went to sleep as well. He was grateful to have his brother back, his sister nearby and a warm cozy place to rest.

Several hours later . . .

"She's a dragon Eli! You could have easily gotten fried!" Samantha exclaimed.

Eli woke with a start opening his eyes to see Samantha's scowl inches from his face.

"You've been talking to Elliot," he said rolling over to go back to sleep. Mumbling he added sleepily, "Elliot smelly foot."

"Just wait until Mom hears," she said pushing on him with both front paws in effort to wake him.

"You're going to be grounded for years."

Ouch. Her pushing on his ribs certainly did wake him. Eli

rolled back to look at his sister and to stop her from pushing on him. It was just them in the little tent.

Eli heard many voices outside the dome tent in various conversations. It sounded to him like the makeshift camp was hustling and bustling with activity. He could hear Ruby out there too, and although he couldn't see Emeraldson, he knew the baby was close by the tent. Whatever Emeraldson was doing he was very content to do it. Eli suspected he was eating. Eli's own stomach grumbled.

"Yeah, but I didn't. I only got slightly dinted," he told her. The medics told him last night he had some cracked ribs with plenty of bruising. He had already figured out the bruising part but he was glad to hear he would recover fully in a short period of time.

"I'm really glad to see you," he said having a new appreciation for his family. "You won't believe what I've been through."

"I've heard about some. I heard about the dragon. Talk about dumb," Samantha scolded him, with her eyes wide in utter amazement at his foolishness.

"Ha! Ruby was the easy part.
It's those dogs that almost made me lose heart," Eli joked.

"And yet you saved the scoundrel,
and then gave a *dragon* counsel.
Elliot's right you are insane!" Samantha declared.

As if on cue Elliot came into the little tent carrying tea and hot boiled eggs. "You are so lucky you did not get maimed," she finished saying.

Eli sat up eagerly as his stomach rumbled again.

"Wow! Have I taken a hit to my brow?
Elliot's serving me breakfast!
I must have achieved more on this quest than I ever would have guessed!" Eli said grabbing an egg.

"Hardy ha ha! Don't get use to it. It's only because while you slept, you cried for ma," Elliot teased.

"I did not!" Eli sputtered with egg in his mouth. "Come closer so I can give you a swat!"

Eli swatted playfully at Elliot who leaned back dodging his swing.

"And it's not breakfast dim-wad." Elliot continued his banter smiling, "It's supper. Clearly your sense of time is flawed."

"Really?" Eli asked looking around to get a sense of where Sun was. "Oh. Well it's not that silly. I haven't slept in a week freely."

While he ate, Eli told them about his adventures, about meeting Chill and Winter, getting chased by the dogs, and out there somewhere under a rock was his backpack. It had their father's map in it, so he figured they probably should try to find it before going home. Although he silently wondered how he was going to get the baby dragon home, let alone explain Emeraldson to his parents. But he did have a dragon in his life now and he felt fairly certain it was going to stay that way.

While they talked, Eli ate and ate and ate. Elliot had to go out several times for more tea and eggs. Eli explained he wasn't fed anything while captured by the dogs. And then while he was with the sergeant he was only given small amounts of army rations. But that had been over a day or two ago, he wasn't actually sure because the lack of sleep made it seem like one long day that lasted a week. Elliot was right, he had lost track of time and his senses were far from prime.

But it wasn't until Samantha informed them, they were packing everything up and leaving for Whisker Creek first thing in the morning; that Eli's mood changed.

The dogs were already on their way back to the dog camp where they would finish packing up their belongings for their journey back to The Rest of the World. In fact all the dogs that had been captured around the valley of Dead Mouse Mountain were going there. Every available soldier was part of the escorting procession. Only the medics and injured were going to Whisker Creek and from there back to Purring City. That meant Samantha who had joined the medics and Elliot who was part of the sleigh's crew had to go to Whisker Creek and probably Purring City before they could go home.

Emeraldson overheard Samantha say they were leaving, and he and Eli suddenly felt a sense of panic. In the unspoken connection they shared, Eli knew the dragons were leaving too. But Emeraldson and Ruby were leaving for the land of Dragons. Eli knew Emeraldson didn't want to be separated from him anymore than he wanted to be separated from Emeraldson.

Eli didn't know what to do. This connection he had to Emeraldson, he liked it. And he really liked the little dragon too. This was special but what was he going to do, go with the dragons? Leaving Catland meant saying goodbye to his family and his home. But then it also meant hanging out with his new friend. And the two of them were sure to have a lot of adventures together. Eli was at crossroads.

"You look stressed, Eli. Like you are about to cry," Samantha said breaking into his thoughts.

"Yeah, it's about leaving and all that," Eli said not sure how to approach the subject.

"I don't think I'm going with you," he said carefully.
"I don't even know how to start this chat," he added struggling to find a way to explain the connection he had to Emeraldson.

He didn't even know if Ruby would let him go with them but he knew he wanted to stay with Emeraldson. It was weird. Even to Eli.

"You better think of a way, because you'll rue the day Mom learns you decided to stray," Samantha told him frowning. "And if she doesn't like what we have to say, she'll hunt you down to your dismay."

Elliot nodded his agreement. "Yep, you'll be sorry, once she hears of this story."

"I know; she's going to kill me," Eli said worriedly. Outside, Emeraldson bellowed.

"Not '*kill me*,' just be angry," he said turning his head in Emeraldson's direction to clarify himself.

Samantha and Elliot exchanged looks.

"Explain yourself, Eli. What is with you and the little fire-breathing guy?" Elliot asked.

"I don't know how to explain it.
We're connected, like an unspoken transmit.

It's so hard to explain,
like I know where he is,
as if we're linked with an invisible chain.
And I know right now he is being fed again.

And what's crazier yet;
is when I get upset, he gets upset.

But when he gets upset, Ruby gets upset.
And then I get met with her worried fret,
and believe me, that makes me want to wet.
    I know it's weird.
But at the same time I feel revered.
    It's like he's my best friend,
and hanging out with him is time I want to spend.
I don't know; it's hard to comprehend."

    "Eli, I can explain it to you,
Please come out here, and your siblings too," Ruby called him from outside.

    Eli, Elliot, and Samantha stepped out of the tent to find Ruby's big head over their tent. Her body stood next to the sleigh. Emeraldson was sitting near her side munching on a pile of prechewed greens. He was wearing a blue sweater and waiting for Eli to come out. When he saw Eli, he waddled over to nuzzle him.

    "Look at you, you're walking better, and it looks like someone made you a sweater," Eli said grinning as he looked over the baby dragon's sweater. It even had holes for his wings to fit through. Eli started purring as the baby nuzzled him. For some reason, he felt very proud of Emeraldson's ability to walk better.

    "You'd think he was the dad, the way he coos over that dragon lad," Elliot mumbled under his breath to Samantha. Both just stood there watching Eli and the baby interact.

    Ruby regarded them and her son for a moment.
    Then addressing Eli she said,
"Forgive me for overhearing your conversation,
but well, in a tent isn't a very private location.
    This connection Emeraldson and you share;
its one-way dragons communicate; it is a dragon's affair.
For Emeraldson to include you is fairly rare.
Not many species even know the ability is there.
    Why Emeraldson chose to connect with you?
I am unaware of the reason, and I wish I knew.
    However, you are right, Eli.
Emeraldson does want you to accompany him and I.
Back to our lands, over the mountains and across the big sky.
    And I get the sense that you should come along.

Not just because he wants you to,
or because you feel the same way too,
but because there is a greater purpose for you.
I think it's where you belong.
    This greater purpose, it's something I don't fully understand.
But I see the moral conviction you live by in this land,
and it gives you cats something pretty grand.
    I am beginning to truly believe;
with you along, Emeraldson will succeed.
I think your influence is exactly what he needs.
In a world filled with ignorance and selfish deeds;
he'll grow into the dragon he's destined to be.
    However bringing you to The Rest of the World was never planned.
So you should know, it's where evil takes a stand.
    That is why, if you choose to stay by his side,
acting as his moral guide,
Catland and I will become allied.
And for you I promise I will provide,
protect or return you, whatever, whenever you decide."

    Samantha and Elliot stood speechless. One look at Eli and they knew he was already gone. Neither of them looked forward to telling their parents about this.

    The next morning, Samantha and Elliot stood in the same spot, teary eyed. They watched the dragons and Eli preparing to leave. Jack and Gadget, two of Elliot's friends, had worked all night making Ruby a harness to hold Emeraldson and Eli while she flew.

    It came to light that she was going to have to fly home carrying him because Emeraldson wasn't big enough to fly yet. Even though he had hatched early, he was still too big for her to hold on to for any great length of time. It would be a dangerous journey over the mountains; that was why Ruby had questioned where the harnesses were made.

    In their lands she wouldn't have to fly far carrying Emeraldson because it was their home. And Emeraldson wouldn't have to worry about flying himself because there were plenty of dragons to watch over all the babies until they were big enough to learn.

"Eli, here's your jacket.
I mended it while you were sleeping,
And this is a spare medic's packet.
It's worth keeping."

Samantha handed Eli the jacket Chill had first given to him and the little medical packet. The ripped sides of his jacket were stitched together and looked suspiciously similar to the stitches Eli had seen on some of the injured soldiers. He put it on. Elliot took the packet from him and shoved it into a backpack he was holding.

"This is a spare backpack," he said admiring it.
"There's a few things in here I've seen soldiers pack.
Just a few things so you don't lack," he said shrugging.
"Like a spare jacket for when that one's too small on your back, and like when you get hungry, I packed you a snack." Elliot passed Eli the overstuffed backpack. Eli nearly dropped it.

"Just a few things you pack? I'd say there's a whack." He teased with a smile. Eli swung the backpack on causing himself to stumble around in the process. Then looking at his brother and sister he put on a brave face,

"You both look so sad.
Don't, I will come back.
And thank you for all this clad."

This parting was hard but Eli knew he had made the right choice. Emeraldson had nuzzled both Samantha and Elliot several times because the mixed emotions Eli was feeling. He was sad and excited at the same time.

Jack and Gadget had the harnesses in place. Ruby had thanked them many times as they had shown her how it worked. Her appreciation for their workmanship made them beam with pride and they began making nuisances of themselves searching for other ways to help her.

Emeraldson was in place under his mother's belly. Ruby's harness wrapped around her and attached to the back of Emeraldson's. She leaped into the air beating her wings only twice, testing the connection before landing on the ground again.

A thick fleece had been placed between Emeraldson's wings for Eli right beneath Ruby's belly. It looked to Eli like he would be travelling in comfort in that spot. Which was much better than in the iron grip of Ruby's claws. He was excited to get going. This was definitely going to be an adventure.

Eli jumped onto Emeraldson for the first time. Emeraldson was filled with joy to have his friend along and Eli could feel it. He radiated the feeling back to Emeraldson.

From his spot between Emeraldson's wings Eli looked down at his brother and sister.

Their sadness was written all over their posture as well as their faces. He would miss them too.

"I promise I will return,
so don't look so concern.
After all, there are not many places,
I can see your silly faces,
and for that, I will yearn," he said to them smiling.

Ruby leaped into the air beating her wings with strong powerful strokes as she carried them away. She swung around and headed east over the mountains. Home. Finally she would be able to bring her little prince back to where he belonged.

Elliot and Samantha sat side-by-side watching them fly away.

As they disappeared over the mountains Elliot mused,
"A dragon and a cat,
who could have imagined that?"

Epilogue

Notso looked down at the convoy, watching as they walked in to The Rest of the World from out of the side of Jagged Tooth Rock. He sat on a ledge of a mountain nearby on the border of Catland and The Rest of the World. The convoy was long with many dogs hitched to large wagons full of the stuff they had brought into Catland. No dragons were among them but a few trolls were. Dicey was. And some of his most devoted followers, although not all of them.

Served them right, Notso decided. Not that it mattered now. It didn't really matter to anyone anymore.

Nevertheless, the convoy was vulnerable like that, without the dragon to protect it; it was vulnerable to anyone who might choose to attack. And to make matters worse for them, the sky looked very dark over The Rest of the World. It was storming out there and the convoy was heading straight toward it.

The corporal sat beside him watching the procession. After what they had been through within the mountain, Notso knew they would be life-long friends. No one bossed the other around anymore. Something happened between them during that time within Jagged Tooth Rock and it had changed them, all of them. Notso would even say they were friends now, cats, dogs, and him.

The cats were true to their word and the dogs had been released. But the cats had released the dogs much sooner than Notso would have expected. He wasn't sure if it was a calculated move on their part or not, but it made for fast friends with the captured dogs.

His clan had heard about him getting cast out but that wasn't the only issue. He dared approach them without going through the proper channels, which was of course the speaker Dicey. The cats got to see firsthand what confronting angry trolls was like.

What had surprised Notso the most was, how well cats and dogs fought together when they were on the same side. It was amazing to see, even to his clan who were on the receiving end. Too bad it took his clan so long to get the message.

They got it now however. Now it wasn't just Notso or Dicey who was displaced, it was everyone.

If Notso had known what message Bluey and Ripple intended to deliver to his clan leaders, he would have refused taking them. Not even Notso would have done to his clan what Mother Nature did, or was about to. He had been right about Her though, she was angry.

Notso watched the convoy enter in The Rest of the World. Once they were all out of the mountain, it began to rumble as Mother Nature created an earthquake within the bowels of his home. Notso watched from the safety of his ledge on a nearby mountain, as Jagged Tooth Rock shook and crumbled in on itself. Everything his clan had made within that mountain was now gone, hundreds of years of tunneling, all for nothing, and all because of Dicey.

Notso look around at those who now looked to him to guide them, a mismatched clan of trolls and dogs. Notso still couldn't understand why they were following him. Most of his clan had left, heading north. There were some unclaimed mountains there that would hollow out nicely. But these ones had stayed with him. Notso looked at the group. Many of them were young unwed trolls, all starry-eyed as they watched him, with high hopes for the future. Ugh.

He had not been accepted back into his clan by his leaders when it came to light all that Dicey had done. Bluey had said something about shooting the messenger and avenger but Notso hadn't really been listening. He was too shocked.

Then for some reason, a few of his younger trollsmen had started following him. He had tried to tell them to go away but they wouldn't. And neither had the dogs. They were all free to go their own way, well the dogs were suppose to head back to The Rest of the World but they hadn't.

It figured anyhow. No one ever listened to him before, why start now. Notso got up. All eyes were on him.

Well, technically they were all on The Rest of the World side of the border but it wasn't an issue for him. He looked down at the Border Bush that spanned for miles in between the mountain valleys. He had absolutely no interest to go into there and he didn't need to.

"I like this mountain," he said. His words no longer flowed together smoothly. They never did on this side of the Border Bush. He struggled to find the right words.

"I going to call it Mount Canine.
And my first tunnel,
it be called Friendly Feline."

About the Author

Raised in Carman Manitoba Canada, Sherralee grew up an animal lover, particularly horses and considers herself fortunate to have been raised with many different types of animals. This privilege enabled her to study the anatomy of animals so she could work on improving her sketches of them.

She studied Graphic Design and Illustration at Capilano University in North Vancouver, B.C. and after graduating she successfully went to work developing her career in the advertising and print world.

Sherralee currently lives happily in the rural area of Edmonton Alberta with her husband, children, and has two horses, two dogs, four cats and a tank full of fish.

www.ingramcontent.com/pod-product-compliance
Lightning Source LLC
Chambersburg PA
CBHW030307080526
44584CB00012B/477